Reading Vampire Gothic Through Blood

The Palgrave Gothic Series

Series Editor: **Clive Bloom**
Editorial Advisory Board: **Dr Ian Conrich,** University of South Australia, **Barry Forshaw,** author/journalist, UK,
Professor Gregg Kucich, University of Notre Dame, USA, **Professor Gina Wisker,** University of Brighton, UK.

This series of gothic books is the first to treat the genre in its many inter-related, global and 'extended' cultural aspects to show how the taste for the medieval and the sublime gave rise to a perverse taste for terror and horror and how that taste became not only international (with a huge fan base in places such as South Korea and Japan) but also the sensibility of the modern age, changing our attitudes to such diverse areas as the nature of the artist, the meaning of drug abuse and the concept of the self. The series is accessible but scholarly, with referencing kept to a minimum and theory contextualised where possible. All the books are readable by an intelligent student or a knowledgeable general reader interested in the subject.

Barry Forshaw
BRITISH GOTHIC CINEMA

Margarita Georgieva
THE GOTHIC CHILD

David J. Jones
SEXUALITY AND THE GOTHIC MAGIC LANTERN
Desire, Eroticism and Literary Visibilities from Byron to Bram Stoker

Aspasia Stephanou
READING VAMPIRE GOTHIC THROUGH BLOOD
Bloodlines

Catherine Wynne
BRAM STOKER, DRACULA AND THE VICTORIAN GOTHIC STAGE

The Palgrave Gothic Series
Series Standing Order ISBN 978–1–137–27637–7 (hardback)
(*outside North America only*)

You can receive future titles in this series as they are published by placing a standing order. Please contact your bookseller or, in case of difficulty, write to us at the address below with your name and address, the title of the series and the ISBN quoted above.

Customer Services Department, Macmillan Distribution Ltd, Houndmills, Basingstoke, Hampshire RG21 6XS, England

Reading Vampire Gothic Through Blood

Bloodlines

Aspasia Stephanou

Independent Scholar, Cyprus

First published 2014 by
PALGRAVE MACMILLAN

Palgrave Macmillan in the UK is an imprint of Macmillan Publishers Limited,
registered in England, company number 785998, of Houndmills, Basingstoke,
Hampshire RG21 6XS.

Palgrave Macmillan in the US is a division of St Martin's Press LLC,
175 Fifth Avenue, New York, NY 10010.

Palgrave Macmillan is the global academic imprint of the above companies
and has companies and representatives throughout the world.

Palgrave® and Macmillan® are registered trademarks in the United States,
the United Kingdom, Europe and other countries.

ISBN 978–1–137–34922–4

This book is printed on paper suitable for recycling and made from fully
managed and sustained forest sources. Logging, pulping and manufacturing
processes are expected to conform to the environmental regulations of the
country of origin.

A catalogue record for this book is available from the British Library.

Library of Congress Cataloging-in-Publication Data
Stephanou, Aspasia.
    Reading vampire gothic through blood : bloodlines / Aspasia Stephanou,
    independent scholar, Cyprus.
        pages cm
    Summary: "Reading Vampire Gothic Through Blood examines the
    promiscuous circulations of blood in science and philosophy, vampire
    novels, films and vampire communities to draw a vascular map of the
    symbolic meanings of blood and its association with questions of identity
    and the body. Stephanou seeks to explain present-day biotechnologies,
    global neoliberal biopolitics, feminine disease and
    monstrosity, race, and vampirism by looking to the past and analysing
    how blood was constituted historically. By tracing the transformations
    of blood symbols and metaphors, as they bleed from early modernity into
    the complex arterial networks of global and corporate culture, it is
    possible to open new veins of signification in the otherwise exhausted
    and dry landscape of vampire scholarship" — Provided by publisher.
    ISBN 978–1–137–34922–4 (hardback)
    1. Vampires in mass media. 2. Blood—Symbolic aspects. 3. Blood—
    Social aspects. 4. Blood—Folklore. 5. Human body in mass media.
    6. Blood in literature. I. Title.
    PN56.V3S74 2014
    809'.93375—dc23   2014019301

To my parents,
Eftychios and Eftychia Christodoulou

Contents

Acknowledgements

I am eternally grateful to my parents for their support, sacrifices and their unwavering love. Their generosity is poorly reciprocated with this gift.

My heartfelt thanks go to my partner, Dr Andrew J. Sneddon, whose devotion, patience and constant encouragement have made possible the completion of this work. He has always been my first and most demanding reader. In many ways this book is also dedicated to him.

I would like to thank Professor Glennis Byron and Professor Fred Botting for their support and constructive comments.

Introduction

Blood Bank: A History of the Symbolics of Blood

> The blood had a will of its own, each strand moving blindly, instinctively upward, traversing the soil, hidden from the sun, seeking a host. This is the manner in which the blood worms were born. Within them they contained the remnant of the human blood, tinting their tissue, guiding them toward the scent of their potential host. But also within them they carried the will of their original flesh. The will of the arms, the wings, the throat...[1]

In the above quotation blood is a metaphor for vampirism, carrying within it both monstrosity and traces of its opposite, humanity. The scent of potential draws the protean blood worms from unformed darkness towards the solidity of flesh. On this journey blood as a symbol itself evolves. By shifting focus from a stringently vampire-based analysis to one that recognises the liquidity and transformation of symbols and metaphors, as they bleed from early modernity into the complex arterial networks of global and corporate culture, it is possible to open new veins of signification in the otherwise exhausted and dry landscape of vampire scholarship.

Dipping the pen into blood in order to write about the vampire is a two-fold task. First, an analysis based on the circulations of blood in different eras and mediums depends on tropes, metaphors and metonymies of blood to convey its rich meanings, transformations and transgressions. Carrying within it the potential both to pollute and to preserve, blood is subversive and conservative, maintaining the economy of the same, but also challenging it. In this vein it is both metonymy—the same; and metaphor—difference. It polices boundaries while attacking them with bloody fervour. As blood's symbolics

1

change through time, metaphors of blood dissolve into metonymies. Secondly, such an analysis is an attempt to write a genealogy, what Michel Foucault names as a 'history of the present.' The purpose of such a genealogy—a bloodline—is to diagnose, challenge and problematise current debates through recourse to the past by analysing how it was represented historically.

The rich metaphors of blood create, innovate and redesign the vampiric world. They establish new boundaries and transform reality. Similarly, scientific understandings are fictional, representing the world through claims to truth. Scientific explanations of vampires and blood are created in such a way as to be convincing and give the illusion that order is natural. Despite science's claims to the true nature of reality, vampire narratives reveal that science's authority is repeatedly threatened by the imagination, metaphor and monstrosity.[2] Empirical language is confounded by the presence of the vampire, the strange stirrings of the blood, and the occulted mysteries of the bite. Vampire gothic disturbs the transparency of scientific language. Metaphors of blood as life or as the container of one's selfhood threaten to eviscerate the unity of identity and science. At other times, scientific, medical and political knowledge threatens to realise metaphors of blood and vampirism, resulting in the monstrous dismemberment of reality and the horror of the death camp. At this extreme point, where modernity decomposes, the realisation of biological metaphors and the association of Jews with vampires and parasites becomes part of the political, the law and monstrous reality.

Moving away from the binary structures on which modernity is based and entering postmodernity's fragmented discourses, it becomes increasingly difficult to distinguish reality from artifice. Metaphors and vampires no longer reside exclusively in the realm of fiction, but spread virally into the world of simulations. With the monstrous potential of biotechnologies to enhance and alter humanity's biological capacities, it is impossible to separate the natural from the prosthetic, the useful from the useless. Genetically engineered vampires, vampire facelifts and blood-drinking are real and imagined cultural practices colouring our contemporary ether as the tremor of metaphor evaporates into the transparency of metonymy. The vampire has become a fashionable accessory and the vampiric is now associated with humanity's rapacious consumerist ethos. Today, therapeutic methods that improve one's genetic nature are indistinguishable from aesthetic interventions that enhance beauty and promise the restoration of youth. Therapeutic, aesthetic and economically profitable, biomedical technologies feed on the customers of neoliberal biopolitics managing, maximising and capitalising on their well-being. Vampirising the world around them, but also made vampiric by a brutal and repressive politics over life, the vampire individuals of neoliberal societies are no longer monstrous but the norm. With the appearance of vampire communities and 'real vampires', metaphor is literalised. The oxymoron 'real vampire' erases the limit between gothic and real, as well as the horror and intensity of both vampire and metaphor.

If metaphor used to be unpredictable, surprising, promising change and the possibility of a future, now the 'future collapses on a present that recycles and overwrites the past as it erases metaphor and monstrosity'.[3] If everything is literalised, haemorrhaging into endless imitations, then the magic of metaphor coagulates to a present that devours and restores vampires and metaphors indifferently. While commodities proliferate fast and vampires become more agile and flexible, learning new skills and moving speedily in the global networks of cyberspace, culture has become retrospective. The prevalence of anachronistic vampires and the pastiche of gothic figures in the twenty-first century are signs that time has stopped and that culture is dedicated to refurbishing the old.

This concern with the past is articulated, albeit in a different way, in the current attempts to write a history of the present, which is the same as 'writing a history of the past in terms of the present'.[4] For Foucault, a history of the present is a form of genealogy which has nothing to do with the search for origins or universal certainties, but seeks to challenge the way things are through revaluations of the past.[5] By returning to the past it is possible to identify the accidents, fragmented events, discontinuities, deviations and mistakes that gave birth to current events.[6] In this respect, *Bloodlines* provides the genealogy of an answer. It seeks to explain present-day vampiric biotechnologies, global neoliberal biopolitics and bio-genetic capitalism, women's metamorphoses, race, real vampire communities and blood consumption by looking to the past and analysing how blood was constituted historically. This book illuminates the multiple influences—economic, medical, scientific, technological, literary, cultural—that led up to the various meanings of blood and the vampire starting from premodern, and moving on to modern, postmodern and global times. The results do not seek to produce a unified theory or identity, but to disturb and dismantle those forms of historical and scientific knowledge that promote continuity and progress, while uncovering the accidents and buried knowledge that shed light on the present. An analysis of a symbolics of blood does not trace the uninterrupted continuity of blood from one century to another in order to produce a sterilised and unified history and affirm subjectivity. Instead, *Bloodlines* is concerned with blood's material and literary circulations in a particular time and place in order to unearth its degenerated movements and shameful deviations hidden behind lofty concerns. If the gothic and vampires challenge science's invented truths, so does genealogy by excavating and unmasking the inviolable certainties of science and dispelling its chimeras. In particular, the choice of blood as both filthy and vital matter, sacred and profane, low and high, contaminates the tidy categories of idealism and materialism. Similarly, against the tyranny of scientific authority, I have chosen 'lower' and more common forms of knowledge, from real vampires' documents to neglected historical events, popular texts and dubious medical theories, in order to construct alternative narratives that are no less honest or true.

The concept of genealogy is significantly entangled with the body and blood. Genealogy's task is to uncover a body imprinted by history and the process of its destruction by history.[7] It becomes clear that blood as a metonym of the body, but also as a metaphor for descent, is an apt symbol to trace the contagions and communications of self and other, as well as the emergence of bloody transgressions that colour our current views and beliefs about blood. Blood's messy, diverse, historically occulted circulations and eruptions through time unsettle continuity of being and break teleological movement, revealing that neither man nor his body is stable.

Bloodlines: Reading Vampire Gothic Through Blood examines the ways in which blood is represented through the discourses of science, continental, feminist and postmodern philosophy and in vampire novels, films and vampire communities. In particular, it follows the figure of the vampire and its metamorphoses in various texts and contexts from the mists of the nineteenth century and modernity's national boundaries to postmodernity's fragmented and multiple positions to the global networks of the neoliberal present. By addressing the symbolic meanings of blood and its association with questions of identity (including class, race, ethnicity, gender and sexuality) and the body (disease, death, epidemics, virus), the book seeks to create a vascular map of meanings that is concluded with a critique of simulations of vampirism, and blood's subsumption by the vampiric mouth of capital. In this respect, this study seeks to connect, through blood, symbolic representations of vampirism in literature and film to real-life simulations of vampirism in order to trace similarities, differences and discontinuities. These movements will be seen to parallel changing notions about embodiment and identity in culture. The general argument of the book is that an in-depth and extensive study of blood in literature and, in particular, vampire texts and communities, is absent. This gap manifests a failure by critics to engage with vampire texts and communities in ways that acknowledge the general advances in critical practice and cultural theory. In addition, when the symbolic meanings of blood are discussed in vampire literature, scholars either tend to privilege psychoanalytic readings or fail to acknowledge the historical context within which vampire texts were written. Consequently, they stress a limited spectrum of meanings of blood and use blood as a support for their specific discursive practices. While such readings enrich our understanding of vampire texts, they fail to appreciate the importance of blood as a vital fluid and, in particular, as matter and an object of scientific discourses circulating within a specific historical context. The study utilises psychoanalytic and historicist readings but also pays due attention to blood as material reality. The method adopted here is not strictly anthropocentric, and does not merely focus on the figure of the vampire. By focusing on blood, a wider range of meanings in such texts and communities is revealed. In this way, blood can be seen as the pulsing nexus of vital debates and anxieties about identity and the body. In particular, accounts that examine the manifestations of vampire communities usually celebrate vampirism and fail to place the phenomenon within the context of postmodern culture and simulations. In this way, as K.C. Hanson observes in regard to blood, 'Context is everything in determining its significance and emotive power.'[8]

A history of blood as symbol

The discursive dimensions of blood, its meaning and significance, its association with identity formation and power are not determined *a priori*, but are constantly transformed through the changing status of blood as matter, its materiality and its liminal position within and outside the body. In particular, the fluid's evocative powers rest upon its materiality, its vital role in sustaining life inside the body and its ability to flow outside of the boundaries of the body and cause death. This inherent physiological power of blood to give and take life has shaped and informed a symbolics of blood. In this section, I will first establish the traditional symbolic qualities of blood, beginning with ancient Greece and leading to medieval times and Christianity. Blood defines the boundaries of the embodied subject, but at the same time threatens and transgresses those boundaries.

Blood as a symbol of life is manifested in classical, biblical and medieval thought, and is intimately connected to the creation of community. Communion sacrifices can be traced in ancient Hellenic, Israelite and Nuer cultures.[9] Sharing blood to create a community can be witnessed in ancient Arabic oath rituals, and the idea of a symbolic communion with God is evident in late medieval Christian rituals. Real or symbolic, the sharing of blood gives birth to communities of life through premodern rituals that make blood pure or sacred. As René Girard notes, 'Most primitive peoples take the utmost care to avoid contact with blood. Spilt blood of any origin, unless it has been associated with a sacrificial act, is considered impure.'[10]

In pre-Socratic thought blood featured as life. The Pythagoreans believed that the soul was nourished by blood, while Diogenes of Apollonia imagined life as *pneuma* coursing through vessels. In *De Anima* Aristotle mentions that Critias was one of those 'who identified the *psyche* with blood: regarding sensation as the most typical characteristic of *psyche*, they believed that it was due to the nature of the blood'.[11] But it was also considered as the self or personality. In Empedoclean philosophy blood was the seat of perception. For Empedocles,[12] the warm blood enabled the body to nourish, digest, respire and think. In *Empédocle* (1965) Jean Bollack notes that 'blood is the main means by which the body adapts to and reflects the conditions of the universe around it through perceptions'.[13] A living self was a self that was able to think. In Empedoclean physiology blood was the physical basis of consciousness and thought. It contained the four material elements of fire, air, earth and water which governed the whole universe and, because of that, blood was the core of human existence and nature. Blood corresponded to a living consciousness, a living self and a living organism that connected man to the world around him. This humour had the power to sustain and nourish the body and also to enable the subject to understand and communicate. Blood established a sense of wholeness, a body that had a fixed self. Blood affirmed the existence of selfhood because it was thought to be synonymous to the psyche, soul and life.

The belief that blood is life is also manifested in the Hebrew Bible where the tribes of Israel are prohibited from eating blood: 'For the life of a creature is in the blood, and I have given it to you to make atonement for yourselves on the altar; it is the blood that makes atonement for one's life.'[14] The biblical scholar and rabbi Jacob Milgrom asserts that 'the identification of blood with life clarifies its function in the sacrificial system ... Impurity ... is the realm of death ... Only its antonym, life, can be its antidote. Blood, then, as life is what purges the sanctuary.'[15]

Here Milgrom points to blood as life and opposite to death, and William Gilders adds that blood comes from Yahweh and should be given back so as to purge his people. It is clear that Israelite sacrifice is based on the binary opposition between life and death and insists on the careful and sacred manipulation of blood by priests. In this sense, the powerful rhetorical language of blood gave voice to a political and religious play of power and facilitated in establishing a ritualistic community bounded by the blood of Yahweh.

In medieval devotional writing and thought blood is one of the most significant principles that produce the body and self. As Caroline Walker Bynum observes in *Wonderful Blood* (2007), 'a good deal of devotional and preaching language from the High Middle Ages implies that blood carries life or is the seat of life'.[16] Blood was identified with spirit, and the opposition body/blood pointed to the opposition body/soul.[17] Bynum cites a fourteenth-century German passage from the Sister-Books about a widow who wanted to become a virgin. In this passage the widow is taken to a wine press by angels where they press out of her body all the blood and replace it with virginal blood in order to change her condition. Bynum explains: 'It is as if the body is only a mold into which blood as animating force or soul or self is poured. To exchange the blood is almost (although not quite) to change the self.'[18] The obsession of medieval writers with blood was connected to the concept of blood carrying life and having the power to alter the subject and his/her identity. Body and self depended on blood, and blood here was related to the divine. There is an opposition between the divine pure blood and the blood of the widow who is guilty of her sins. Only the blood that the angels give her can purify her self, and clearly this reveals an underlying religious strategy of power and control through blood.

If blood as life plays a significant role in the construction of the individual subject, it also serves an equally important function for the group and is traditionally associated with the creation of community. In *Thicker than Water* (2005) Melissa Meyer observes: 'Attributing to blood the ability to transmit or reflect the essence of the family, clan, lineage, people, nation, race, or ethnic group stemmed logically from the widespread association of blood with life and fertility.'[19] By birth, marriage and the actual intermingling of blood, individuals created unity in a group. In Old Norse men 'gave birth' to male communities and called themselves 'blood brothers' or 'companions in blood'.[20] In her work on blood sacrifice Nancy Jay exposes the relationship between sacrifice and the maintenance of a patrilineal society. Men aspired to create patrilineal descent groups by participating in blood sacrifice and in this way realised what only women could naturally do: give birth.[21] Meyer observes how ancestor communities accomplished a 'ritualized symbolic immortality' and offered 'ways of organizing relations among the living'.[22] Here the creation of communities through blood was based on an exchange system of goods or power between men. Jaroslav Černý provides an example of this in his 'Reference to Blood Brotherhood Among Semites in an Egyptian Text of the Ramesside Period', illustrating how the Arabs used blood in their covenants. A man would cut the palms of the men's hands and then spread their blood on seven stones.[23] W. Robertson Smith adds that the specific blood covenant included blood-drinking.[24] Catholic scholar Dennis J. McCarthy points out that 'in these blood ceremonies a new member was being taken into the clan, of which the god was the first member and protector... Sharing blood (and other things) created kinship.'[25] Blood rituals sealed a compact between the participants and reaffirmed an individual's role among the community or in a group that shared the same identity—national, sexual or religious. However, these fictive kinship relationships were not mere social ties. Blood was used to establish and organise economic relations in communities that were based on a patriarchal structure.

In medieval Christianity blood formed Christian identity among the community of believers. Christ's body gives birth to a community that partakes in his blood. It spiritually nourishes Christians as a mother feeds her child with her milk. The religious discourse on Christ's blood and the powerful metaphors of Christ being a mother reinforced the belief in the power of divine blood. In addition, blood affirmed the body of believers and their identity as Christians through the performance of the Eucharist. The Fourth Lateran Council (1215) asserted:

> Christ is both priest and sacrifice. His body and blood are truly contained in the sacrament of the altar under the forms of bread and wine, the bread and wine having been changed in substance, by God's power, into his body and blood, so that in order to achieve this mystery of unity we receive from God what he received from us.[26]

The sacrament contains the body and blood of Christ and births a collective body that shares the sacrificial blood of Christ. But here identity is constructed according to Christian beliefs, and the actions of Christians are expected to conform to this divine truth. Such essentialist communities are characterised by communal fusion where symbolic blood forges common identity.

Blood creates kinship and collective identity, and this is related to the idea that blood symbolises life and thus produces and reinforces the role of an individual within a community. But blood in the Middle Ages was a complex symbol, and medieval devotion also calls into question this idea of blood signifying life. Blood is both *sanguis*/inside blood and *cruor*/bloodshed:

> *Sanguis* and *cruor*, blood was ambiguous because profoundly bipolar. Each term had both positive and negative connotations in the fifteenth century: the shedding of *cruor* could be heroic, health-bringing, criminal, or polluting; *sanguis* could be congested and unhealthy, or the very stuff of life itself...blood—all blood—signified life and death.[27]

Bynum analyses this paradoxical meaning of blood in medieval theological discourse and demonstrates how Christ's crucifixion and death give life. Blood, she writes, 'which is both life and death, expresses that which continues and separates. Unless his blood spills, separates from his divided body, Christ has nothing to give (to God or to humankind).'[28] But the power of blood to signify life and death in this strictly theological literature enforces the dominant medieval view of the body as an enclosed container where blood is situated inside or outside. In addition, it is Christ's blood that has the power to give life even in separation from his body, and thus this is not condemned but affirms the truth of his divine nature. This power of blood justifies the existence of a perfect divine being and provides a secure order through which the subject's identity is fixed. For medieval thinkers, identity was already ordained according to the divine law and the medieval individual had no agency in creating selfhood.

Medieval notions of self were formed around the dominant view of the individual as having a pre-determined destiny and adhering to the truth of a God that s/he should connect with. The blood of Christ in medieval discourse raises further issues concerned with identity. Bynum has argued that Christ's bleeding images suggest a feminine and maternal identity.[29] As noted, Christ's blood nourishes Christians like a mother's milk would nourish her child. Breast milk was considered to derive from menstrual blood,[30] and medieval physiological theories claimed that all body fluids were produced from blood.[31] Julia Kristeva argues that, like blood, milk 'mingles two identities and connotes the bond between the one and the other'.[32] Here blood and milk are associated with nourishment and the performance of maternal identity. Christ, like the mother figure, bleeds to give life to Christians. Bynum shows that in fourteenth-, fifteenth- and sixteenth-century paintings Christ's wound is associated with Mary's breast.[33] She argues that medieval artists and writers captured the figure of Christ as both male and female, being male but also resembling the female through his bleeding wound. Like Christ's body, every body was at the same time male and female,[34] revealing thus the fluidity of gender politics in medieval times.[35] This is also evident in medieval beliefs about all human body fluids; 'menstruation, sweating, lactation, emission of semen, etc.—were seen as bleedings; and all bleedings—lactation, menstruation, nosebleeds, hemorrhoidal bleeding, etc.—were taken to be analogous'.[36] Medieval thinkers insisted on the existence of an integral body. The tenacity with which medieval discourse stressed blood as formative of identity, and integrity of self, reveals what Lacan so enthusiastically explored: the return of fragmentation. Medieval Christianity is distinguished by the fixation with blood, bleeding hosts and fragments from Christ's living self. Such an obsession with blood and insistence on life over death, with life and body identified as such in fragments and eucharistic hosts, divulges a fear of splitting, of understanding the body as fragmented, and therefore attempting to secure it as unified and closed.

These premodern ideas about blood as a symbol of kinship and a vessel of identity, and more generally the ways in which the body is understood as a symbol of social organisation, have been theorised in the works of Mary Douglas and Michel Foucault. In particular, Douglas' *Purity and Danger* ([1966], 2002) and Foucault's first volume of *The History of Sexuality* ([1978], 1998) are significant here in order to elucidate the historical functions of blood within society. For the anthropologist Mary Douglas, the body and matter flowing from its orifices—'Spittle, blood, milk, urine, faeces or tears'[37]—have different symbolic meanings in different societies. The body, she argues, is a symbol of society: its organisation reflects the organisation of society. Bodily refuse is ascribed with dangers and powers, taboos and values, which symbolise social limits and transgressions. In this respect, she sees pollution as 'a symbolic system, based on the image of the body, whose primary concern is the ordering of a social hierarchy'.[38] Both she and Foucault see the body as a cultural construct. While I will return later to Douglas' emphasis on abject material through the work of Julia Kristeva's *Powers of Horror* (1982), it will suffice here to note that, unlike Foucault's, Douglas' understanding of the body as a mirror of social hierarchies does not account for the ways bodies are produced, controlled and disciplined through discourses of power. Because her work circumvents the ways social control is associated with power, I want to turn to Foucault and, particularly, his work on sexuality.

In the first volume of *The History of Sexuality*, Foucault sketches the transition that occurred in the nineteenth century from the premodern regime of a 'bloody' sovereign power to the modern regime of a 'bloodless' biopower. Premodern society was characterised by *a symbolics of blood*. In this society 'the mechanisms of sovereign power, its manifestations, and its rituals' were based on the spectacle of blood, its materiality and its highly symbolic functions.[39] This was a society of '"sanguinity"—where power spoke *through* blood'.[40] According to Foucault,

> The new procedures of power that were devised during the classical age and employed in the nineteenth century were what caused our societies to go from *a symbolics of blood* to *an analytics of sexuality*. Clearly, nothing was more on the side of the law, death, transgression, the symbolic, and sovereignty than blood.[41]

Unlike the modern regime of biopower based on sexuality and the management of life, this premodern regime of valued sanguinity was organised around the fear of death:

> the blood of torture and absolute power, the blood of the caste which was respected in itself and which nonetheless was made to flow in the major rituals of parricide and incest, the blood of the people, which was shed unreservedly since the sort that flowed in its veins was not even deserving of a name.[42]

The tortured body exhibited the power of blood to mark bodies, unveiling the mechanisms of sovereign power and a concern about blood, the law and transgression. In this respect, while blood was shed to protect the aristocracy from the contamination of its blood, on the other hand, the blood of the people was shed indiscriminately.

Blood was the fundamental value in a society characterised by 'systems of alliance, the political form of the sovereign, the differentiation into orders and castes, and the value of descent lines'.[43] Blood determined social class and facilitated or hindered alliances. For example, the blood of the aristocracy—the 'antiquity of its ancestry' and 'the value of its alliances'—distinguished it as a noble caste.[44] Alliances were created through marriage based on blood and status. In this way, the deployment of alliance permitted and guaranteed the 'development of kinship ties' and the 'transmission of names and possessions'[45] in order to reproduce the same social body and maintain the system of marriage and kinship ties.[46]

Blood was an important element due to 'its instrumental role (the ability to shed blood), to the way it functioned in the order of signs (to have a certain blood, to be of the same blood, to be prepared to risk one's blood), and also to its precariousness (easily spilled, subject to drying up, too readily mixed, capable of being quickly corrupted)'.[47] Blood was a reality—of famine, epidemics, violence, war and torture— with a symbolic function: to have, for example, noble blood and be connected to others of the same blood. Blood, then, reduced the body to the particularities of blood, to a mere vessel defined by the limited symbolic value of blood as a marker of social class and kinship ties. As will be discussed in Chapter 6, vampire communities' attempts to produce pseudo-genealogies based on blood demonstrate the postmodern individual's desire to appeal to this older symbolic law where blood is a symbol of status and kinship ties. In addition, nineteenth-century vampire narratives, examined in chapters 1, 2, 3 and 4, can be situated between this older system of a symbolics of blood and the modern regime of biopower, where fantasies of blood inject with life the new political power, and notions of heredity and racial purity become the preoccupation of the bourgeoisie. In some of these narratives disease and vampirism are manifested on the bodies of a dying aristocracy ('Carmilla'), while in others the corrupted blood of the racial other threatens to vampirise and pollute the pure family and nation (*Dracula; Nosferatu*). Vampire novels and stories are also examples of the competing meanings between an older understanding of blood as invisible and thus mysterious, and a new understanding of blood as a neutral medium that can be examined and manipulated within the laboratory. With the rise of new technologies and medical knowledge in the nineteenth century, blood enters the realm of science, no longer as a hidden property of the body, but as a visible matter that can be clinically analysed.

The nineteenth century saw the decline of the aristocracy and the rise of the bourgeoisie, the development and reshaping of medicine and the ways in which disease, the body and, in particular, blood, were understood. While the function of sovereign power was to kill, the role of biopower was to invest life.[48] The rise of biopower in the nineteenth century brings together two forms of power: the anatomo-politics and biopolitics which emerged in the seventeenth and the second half of the eighteenth century, respectively. While the first is a disciplinary technology which aims at controlling and disciplining the individual body, the second focuses on the biological body of the population, on 'the species body': its 'propagation, births and mortality, the level of health, life expectancy and longevity' and the production of wealth.[49] It is a 'technology of security' that seeks through regulations and controls to protect the population as a biological corpus.[50] While sovereign power has the right 'to *take* life or *let* live',[51] biopower 'exerts a positive influence on life, that endeavors to administer, optimize, and multiply it, subjecting it to precise controls and comprehensive regulations'.[52] Thus, it deals with living beings and not legal subjects.[53] The role of this new power was 'to *foster* life or *disallow* it to the point of death'.[54] Power establishes its domination over life and not over death; thus, it is only right to kill those that pose 'a kind of biological danger to others'.[55] As noted, the body of the vampire in many nineteenth-century narratives is imagined as polluted, degenerate and sick, something that needs to be disciplined or eliminated in order to secure the good health of the population. In particular, as will be argued in Chapter 3, the female body, under the patriarchal gaze, is seen as the embodiment of disease and threatening sexuality. For example, one of the ways to discipline and control the body within the modern regime of biopower is the institution of the clinic. Medical observations are imposed on sexed and passive bodies that seek to confine them within appropriate norms. Vampire narratives of the nineteenth century focus on the female vampire body as the site where anxieties about uncontrolled, weakening bodies, devouring appetites and consumption of blood proliferate. These fears are linked to the degenerate or unhealthy status of woman and her impure blood.

In the nineteenth century sex becomes 'a crucial target of a power organized around the management of life rather than the menace of death'.[56] This is why blood is substituted by sex: 'the blue blood of the nobles' is converted into 'a sound organism and a healthy sexuality' by the bourgeoisie.[57] The reality of blood in the premodern spectacles of violence cannot express the new function of power to administer and invest life. Sex is a crucial political issue because it gives access 'both to the life of the body and the life of the species'.[58] It is situated 'at the pivot of the two axes' of power, between the disciplinary and biopolitical technologies, between disciplining the body of the individual and regulating the population.[59] Sexuality becomes the 'stamp of individuality' and 'the index of a society's strength, revealing of both its political energy and its biological vigor'.[60] While the aristocracy's blood asserted its nobility through its ancestry and alliances, the nineteenth-century 'bourgeoisie's "blood" was its sex'.[61] The concern with the sexual body is manifested by the bourgeois family's preoccupation with hereditary diseases and defects. In addition, according to Foucault, the bourgeoisie's concern with its body is related to its hegemony. The 'indefinite extension of strength, vigor, health, and life' of its body was significant because it represented 'politically, economically, and historically' the bourgeoisie's present and future.[62] But this was also a biological matter which, in the second half of the nineteenth century, is manifested in the appearance of a 'dynamic racism'.[63] In Chapter 3, for example, the female vampire's corrupted blood is associated with heredity and the degenerate or vampiric appetites of the mother ('Aurelia'). But the inferior race of female vampires in Chapter 4 (*The Blood of the Vampire*) is also connected to their bodies as material entities and with blood as a polluting corporeal substance. As noted, Douglas linked bodily fluids with pollution and social hierarchies, and Kristeva connects these dangerous bodily fluids with the abject and the maternal body: what needs to be abjected in order for the subject to enter language and the symbolic order. The feminine and the maternal represent fears of impurity that need to be controlled and repressed. In vampire narratives racial impurity, and consuming appetites for food and sex, define the identity of the female vampire. As Elizabeth Grosz explains in *Volatile Bodies* (1994),

> [the] representation of female sexuality as an uncontainable flow, as seepage associated with what is unclean, coupled with the idea of female sexuality as a vessel, a container, a home empty or lacking in itself but fillable from the outside, has enabled men to associate women with infection, with disease, with the idea of festering putrefaction, no longer contained simply in female genitals but at any or all points of the female body.[64]

In these narratives medical knowledge and practices subordinate woman according to the status of her blood, the colour of her skin and her uncontrollable desire for consumption of semen/blood/food. Through discourses of race and sexuality the female vampire is pathologised and marginalised, subjugated and finally eliminated in order to protect the security, the purity of blood and well-being of the bourgeois family.

The dynamic racism[65] that appears in the nineteenth century transforms the premodern bloody slaughters and wars between two different social groups into a war for the survival of the population. According to Foucault, racism is

> a way of introducing a break into the domain of life that is under power's control: the break between what must live and what must die. The appearance within the biological continuum of the human race of races, the distinction among races, the hierarchy of races, the fact that certain races are described as good and that others, in contrast, are described as inferior.[66]

Unlike the previous notion of race war waged in a society separated into two different races, in the nineteenth century racism is introduced within a society which is seen as a single race: a population threatened from within. Racism creates 'caesuras within the biological continuum addressed by biopower'[67] so that the population is divided into races, healthy and sick, worthy of living and degenerate. The second function of racism is to facilitate a 'biological-type' relationship between one's life and the death of another.[68] The inferior race needs to be eliminated in order that 'I—as species rather than individual—can live' and 'proliferate'.[69] In this respect, 'the death of the bad race, of the inferior race (or the degenerate, or the abnormal) is something that will make life in general healthier: healthier and purer'.[70] Racism provides the ideology in order to identify and exclude or even eliminate the others so that the life of the population improves. According to Foucault, it is at this point where racism is born: 'when the theme of racial purity replaces that of race struggle'[71] that existed before the nineteenth century. Racism, in its current biological meaning, was nurtured by the 'mythical concern with protecting the purity of the blood and ensuring the triumph of the race'.[72] The preoccupation with blood and the law here is reminiscent of the old regime of sovereign power. Nazism, for example, calls upon fantasies of blood and combines them with disciplinary power: a 'eugenic ordering of society',[73] characterised by 'the oneiric exaltation of a superior blood' that 'implied both the systematic genocide of others and the risk of exposing oneself to total sacrifice'.[74] According to Foucault, racism underwent two transformations in the twentieth century: the State racism of Nazi Germany and the Soviet State racism, where those who did not agree with its ideology were deemed biologically dangerous, 'sick', 'deviant' or mad and removed from society.[75] Richard Matheson's *I Am Legend* (1954) offers a similar model of racism, where Neville, as the last human, is considered biologically dangerous to the new society of living vampires, and is eliminated. Maurizio Lazzarato argues that today, with neoliberal policies, internal (against immigrants) and external (against other civilisations) racism is 'one of the most powerful phenomena operating through disgust and animosity that contribute to the constitution and fixing of territories and "identities" and which "capital" lacks'.[76] Like capital, biopower secures and delimits territories and identities through racism by selecting who is included or excluded from the national community.

In more recent vampire novels, such as Guillermo del Toro and Chuck Hogan's *The Strain* (2009) and *The Fall* (2010), vampirism creates a society of biologically mutated and subservient beings, an inferior vampire race ruled by the superior and purer vampire race connected to the Master vampire. At the same time, both of these novels, as well as Octavia Butler's *Fledgling* (2005) and Justin Cronin's *The Passage* (2010), demonstrate the ways the notion of biopolitics has been transformed in the twenty-first century. Biopolitics, as Nikolas Rose argues, becomes 'a politics of "life itself" '.[77] The vital politics of the present 'is concerned with our growing capacities to control, manage, engineer, reshape, and modulate the very vital capacities of human beings as living creatures'.[78] Now, it is at the molecular level that life is understood and acted upon, reshaped, enhanced and changed. The body is no longer the integral body Foucault was referring to in his concept of biopolitics, but a body that is opened, dismantled and recombined. As Roberto Esposito notes, the genetically enhanced body of contemporary neoliberal eugenics should be understood within the history of twentieth-century immunising biopolitics, in particular Nazi thanatopolitics. If in neoliberal eugenics it is science and the marketplace that determine what is genetically normal or valuable, then in Nazism it is the state that makes such choice. Although different, both Nazism and contemporary neoliberal eugenics share a common biopolitical lexicon in relation to the transformation of one's body. In this way, the recurrent concern with blood and race, as well as the obsession with immortality and biological enhancement in vampire narratives, are themes haunted by Nazism's fantasies of blood. The promise of biotechnologies' investment in life and its perfectibility, in real life and in vampire fiction, is perhaps as dangerous as that of Nazi eugenics.

Blood, which from the 1990s has already been substituted 'symbolically and technically' by the genome,[79] is no longer understood as a whole substance but, as Catherine Waldby and Robert Mitchell point out, is 'fractioned into a number of components—plasma, red cells, white cells, and platelets—and rarely transfused as whole blood'.[80] In vampire novels genetic engineering and the vampire virus transform human life at the molecular level, while blood in vampire texts is dissected, manipulated and visualised in its smallest components. At the same time, as will be discussed in Chapter 5, blood has become increasingly commercialised and vampires have fashioned new ways of producing synthetic blood or farming humans for their consuming appetites. This, of course, reflects the growing market of tissues and blood and the ways biological materials have become commodified in an extremely prosperous bioeconomy. It is significant to mention here that while the symbolics of blood are no longer employed in scientific discourses, and blood is understood only as a vital scientific fluid, both for its biovalue and its importance in biomedicine, its symbolic qualities, in particular race, have not disappeared completely but haunt contemporary culture in its various manifestations. It is also worth noting that this brief cartography of the symbolics of blood and their association with the body and identity is intended as a general framework within which the examination of blood can be situated and is not limited by it. As Foucault noted, the transition from premodern to modern society 'did not come about...without overlappings, interactions, and echoes'.[81] Consequently, vampire texts with their obsession with blood are ideal for bringing to the fore and highlighting these various in-between meanings, not only as metaphors, but also as social, cultural and scientific realities.

Structure

The book consists of this introduction followed by six thematic chapters and a conclusion. The examination of vampire texts focuses on language, recurrent themes and tropes deployed, while the discussion of vampire communities centres upon imagery, practices and terminologies used by contemporary vampires in their material online or offline. Discussions of plot and narrative technique fall outside the scope of the methodology. Literature and films are both examined as texts, and I do not privilege one over the other. The analysis of vampire novels and films does not follow a specific order, but only attempts to enrich discussions by bringing into play both written and visual text so that anxieties, fears or obsessions about the status of blood come to the fore.

Chapter 1 attempts to write a genealogy of blood through vampire literature, film, biotechnology and nanotechnology in order to answer questions relating to current debates about blood, vampire life and uncanny technology. The growing understanding of blood as a medical fluid to be donated in blood transfusions, re-produced outside of one's body or artificially designed to improve the biological functions of real blood wipes out the rich symbolisms of blood. Blood no longer exudes the excess of metaphor, spilled in glorious effulgence or offered altruistically, but is put to work, used productively and profitably. Its associations with productivity and vitality extend the discussion toward the lifelikeness of technology, extension of life and neoliberal economics. If vampire gothic dramatises technologies of immortality, cryonics sells such fantasies as real.

In Chapter 2 I examine disease in relation to the concepts of biopolitics and immunisation. The body politic and life itself are immunised against the threat of invasion by infected others. In similar fashion, I trace the meanings of blood from the eighteenth to the twenty-first century through medical discourse and the trope of disease and contagion. The nineteenth century associated vampirism and blood with the epidemics of plague, the 1950s with communist threat and nuclear warfare, and the 1980s with AIDS. Vampire texts of the twenty-first century reveal fears about the invisible and identical threats of infectious disease and bioterrorism. By examining the language of disease, virus and infection in vampire texts, blood becomes the medium to express anxieties about the invasion of individual and collective bodies by the polluted blood of the other. What is at issue here is life itself and its subordination to politics.

Chapter 3 develops the previous chapter's connections of vampirism to disease. It investigates the associations of consumption with the disease of tuberculosis and vampirism, as well as its associations with eating others, cannibalism and sucking blood. In addition, it focuses on the metaphorical understanding of consumption as using up the bodies of others: incorporation, assimilation, colonial invasion and sexual appetite. In particular, by examining female consumption it is possible to trace the transformations of female identity and, more particularly, the ways it reinforces or subverts phallogocentric society and culture through the changing ideas about gender and sexuality. For this reason vampire texts are specifically chosen according to their representations of vampiric females and monstrous corporeality.

Chapter 4 acknowledges the resurgence of race in genomic research and seeks to understand its currency by examining historical understandings of race from nineteenth-century medicine and vampire texts to contemporary vampire narratives of genetic engineering. While race is not a scientific or biological reality, it remains a constant presence in these texts, foregrounding ideas about a stable body and identity that is endangered by difference and scientific experiments or enhanced through technology. The enterprising individual who takes responsibility for his or her own health through recourse to race-based genetics might do so within the context of treatment, but s/he nonetheless participates in a neoliberal politics that segregates minorities while promoting racial technologies that reinforce the biology of race.

In Chapter 5 I examine the associations of blood with money and the commodification of biological and synthetic blood in vampire texts from the nineteenth to the twenty-first century. Human individuals are reduced to things to be exploited for blood and money. Vampires' insatiable hunger for blood reflects their status as voracious consumers in a capitalist economy that invents and reinvents new methods of producing blood and satisfying the vampires' needs. Like contemporary society, vampiric order exalts the power of blood money as that which rules, produces and brutally consumes relations.

Chapter 6 examines blood in contemporary vampire communities and demonstrates how the symbolic meanings of blood analysed in previous chapters change upon entrance to the realm of hyperreality and simulations. In this chapter, I argue that the meaning of blood as a simulated or fantasised reality reflects the subjects' similar fictionalisation of identities within the specific context of postmodern culture. Postmodernity's fragmented knowledge and truth propels a search for origins, and this is evident in the real vampires' creation of vampire fraternities connected through mythological bloodlines. On the other hand, vampires' glorification of a self-sufficient vampiric identity, driven by a capitalist ethos, can be understood within the context of current neoliberal trends that lay emphasis on selfish and hedonic individualism.

This book ends by returning to the current debates about the politics of life itself and the anachronistic nature of a culture enamoured with monsters and populated by vampires. Blood animates a series of questions relating to contemporary biopolitics, race and the transformation of corporeal existence and vitality through new technologies. From investments in one's human capital to contemporary manifestations of real vampirism, and life-extension technologies, what is witnessed is the rise of a global petty bourgeoisie of selfish vampiric and rapacious individuals. But blood also points towards the dark side of a politics of death that is responsible for the exploitation and animalisation of disposable multitudes, bioterrorism and the mass production of corpses. In a world where blood is commodified and the vampire becomes the norm, defining the character of the neoliberal entrepreneur, community is dismantled. As metaphors travel from the occulted depths of early modernity to the sleek surfaces of global neoliberalism, they are bled dry. Exhausted, they turn into sterilised metonymies conserving the economy of the same.

1
A Matter of Life and Death: Transfusing Blood from a Supernatural Past to Scientific Modernity and Vampiric Technology

> The truly interesting and profoundly philosophical truth included in the expression, 'in the blood is the life thereof,' is admirably verified in the experiment of the 'transfusion of blood,' skilfully and successfully performed lately by Mr. Richard Ripley, of Whitby, and his able assistant. The last ebb of life had supervened, and the pulse ceased to beat, when reanimation took place by transfusion of blood from the veins of the sister and husband.[1]

In Mary Elizabeth Braddon's 'Good Lady Ducayne' (1896) a wealthy old woman is able to extend her life through the help of her personal physician who performs transfusions by secretly draining off the blood of her young and healthy companions. The short story is veiled with an atmosphere of occult mystery and gothic horror that arises from the bite marks and wounds left on the arm of Lady Ducayne's companion Bella, her unexplained loss of blood and deterioration of health. Science is vampiric, while those who employ it for personal gain and immortality are demonised as predatory and selfish monsters. With the mimicry of bloom upon her lifeless cheeks, Lady Ducayne sucks and drains people's blood to feed her putrid veins. She is described as 'a little old figure, wrapped from chin to feet in an ermine mantle; a withered, old face under a plumed bonnet—a face so wasted by age that it seemed only a pair of eyes and a peaked chin', with 'Claw-like fingers, flashing with jewels'.[2] An old woman of monstrous status and wealth, Lady Ducayne can pay 'her companion a hundred a year'[3] in exchange for strong and healthy blood. Her perverse desire to discover a treatment or elixir that can 'prolong human life'[4] describes not only the narcissism of an old woman, but anxieties about an uncannily undead life that transgresses the limits of the human. In the descriptions of Lady Ducayne's 'withered countenance' 'with its indescribable horror of death outlived, a face that should have been hidden under a coffin-lid years and years ago'[5] arises a fear about an unholy life that should not be living.[6] This kind of undead life is that of the vampire, but also of 'vampiric' technology that blurs the boundaries between organic and inorganic life. Behind the inert matter of technology and under the wrinkled flesh of Lady Ducayne undulates and writhes an uncanny and ghastly life, spilling out of the confines of natural life. Vampire gothic brings to the fore a play of surfaces and illusion, of mystical occulted depths and inner geographies where the external veils the darkness within. Like the mysterious blood that animates the body of the vampire or the horrifying life hidden within technology's apparent lifelessness, this uncanny doubling of life questions humanity's secure boundaries. The short story dramatises the vampiric exchange between science and the supernatural, while bringing to the fore issues and anxieties relating to the limits between living and nonliving, organic and inorganic, and animate and inanimate. It is concerned with conceptions of life itself and a vitalistic view of blood's nutritive power to reanimate and sustain life beyond death through the use of transfusion. It also questions the ethics of a technology used by those wealthy enough to afford it.

In this chapter I want to map the changing meanings of blood as it circulates from the eighteenth and nineteenth centuries to the present through transfusion and other technologies. First, a historical analysis of blood in vampire literature, film, biotechnology and nanotechnology will reveal the growing understanding of blood as a medical fluid to be donated in blood transfusions and re-produced outside of one's body to be used in the bodies of others, as well as artificially designed to improve the biological functions of real blood. One of the main arguments here is that science and the supernatural are a constant preoccupation in vampire texts evident through the competing meanings of blood as a symbolic or supernatural fluid and, on the other hand, as an empirical material. The intention is to draw connections between medical technologies and vampirism in order to establish the different ways bodies and identities are constituted and affected by the dangerous circulation of blood. Fears about the alteration of one's body or loss of identity are not evoked through the dangerous exchange between the vampire and his/her victim, but through blood as a living or polluting agent transgressing the boundaries of bodies. With the development of medical biotechnologies, blood's symbolics are diluted. Reformulated and divided into its components to be transfused in multiple bodies as fractions, blood cannot be associated with ideas about the gift, generosity, altruism and mutuality. If these values once circulated within the warm body of society creating social relationships among citizens, they are now cancelled by the cold, fragmented and complex circulatory networks of technology and economy.

Secondly, I want to draw attention to vitality and the changing concept of life through analyses of blood, technology and the vampire. Blood is at the heart of questions relating to vitalism and life. Current debates about the status of life itself and the life-like quality of our emergent technologies demand a temporal analysis that takes us back to notions of vitality and the dangerous circulation of blood inside and outside bodies. Eighteenth- and nineteenth-century theories of vitality resurface today through current vitalist ideas of growth and production. On the one hand, there is an inhuman vitalism that embraces inorganic life and life beyond the death of the organised body. On the other hand, the active and energetic vitalism of capitalism seeks to inculcate a model of indefinite production beyond the limits of life. This vitalistic horizon of neoliberal economics coincides with biotechnology's productivity and innovation. The vampire figure becomes here an eloquent expression of the circulation of undead life within the gothic networks of uncanny technology whose promises of an afterlife feed the insatiate appetite of fanged subjects. Issues surrounding the extension of one's life and the individual's freedom to choose and alter his biological condition are exemplary of contemporary strategies of life in a neoliberal era where self-interested subjects can choose to invest their bodies in the future. If transfusion was considered in the nineteenth-century vampire gothic a technology of immortality, today cryonics offers a similarly seductive possibility for the extension of life.

By contextualising blood within a history of biomedicine, developing scientific views about blood and the body from the eighteenth and nineteenth centuries to the present are established. This blood history is then connected to vampire texts as manifestations of anxieties about identity that arise through the symbolic value of blood, but also through its increasing medicalisation. With the reproduction of blood outside the body and its circulation within the bodies of others, as well as the possibility of designing mechanical devices that optimise the function of real blood, not only does blood lose its symbolic power, but life itself is stretched beyond limits. These changing views on life, the body and blood, along with the possibilities offered by new technologies, have transformed the ways individuals imagine and shape their identities. As the status of blood changes, so our status as human beings is reshaped.

Blood and the politics of life

The politics of life in the eighteenth and nineteenth centuries was a politics of health, preoccupied with health and disease, epidemics, birth and death rates, and ways to cure the body itself.[7] Blood in this context was a material substance to facilitate the restoration of life. With its use in transfusion blood was a gift, creating and reasserting the bonds of a community. In Bram Stoker's *Dracula* (1897), for example, blood becomes the medium to explain and understand vampirism: blood transfusions invite an exchange between the primitive energies of a barbaric past and the technologies of modernity. Victorian scientific positivism and the supernatural were conflicting forces in a changing world that manifested its anxieties about modern science, and faith in the supernatural and religion, through the vampiric and scientific powers of blood. Earlier vampire stories posit mysticism at the centre of the narrative, proving that science is unable to fight the supernatural powers of blood (*Dracula*), or attribute to science diabolical powers ('Good Lady Ducayne'). Later, vampire narratives of the twentieth century conversely marginalise the supernatural in favour of science that can provide the truth about blood and vampirism. As John J. Jordan explains, 'The scientization of myth occurs when scientific discourse ascribes within the culture a proper mode of understanding for mystical objects, allowing them a public, yet regulated and marginalized existence.'[8] Scientific discourse then dominates non-scientific discourse in order to discipline and ascribe to it a 'proper' and logical meaning. Blood, being inside the body, was believed to carry identity and the individual's temperament. Without the interference of scientific tools and knowledge, it was invested with magical and occult meanings as a vital rejuvenating fluid. In short, blood was a synecdoche of the body and of the embodied self. However, such meanings were contested by the development of medical discourse and technologies which offered a more rational understanding of blood as a neutral fluid of medical and social significance.

In the first half of the twentieth century the politics of health was shaped by the idea of inherited biological characteristics, and concerns about the mixing of blood. However, the present politics of life is not concerned with disease or health, of understanding and curing diseases in the name of the future of the race, but is concerned with a politics of life itself[9] and our increasing ability to control, manage, reshape and engineer the biological capacities of human beings.[10] The new ontology of biopolitics that is emerging through the assimilation of cybernetic and molecular knowledge is a 'recombinant biopolitics',[11] 'delving deep into the structure of the *soma* itself' and 'reconstituting what it means to be "embodied"'.[12] It is possible now to understand and engineer human life at this molecular level. No longer veiled behind superstition and mysticism, everything about our vitality becomes clear, legible and open to intervention in order to correct or reshape individual bodies and identities and secure the future of generations to come. While vampire narratives enchant and animate an occulted world beyond the human, biology and biomedicine retain a mechanistic view of biological life, plunging deep into the depths of the body and making everything appear intelligible. What we lose is the magic of the forbidden and unknown. If medicine in the nineteenth century was characterised by the clinical gaze focused on the body itself, techno-medicine is now dependent, not on the diagnostic gaze of doctors, but on highly efficient diagnostic and therapeutic equipment. The clinical gaze has now been substituted by a molecular gaze, an understanding of life, not in terms of the visible body, but life at a molecular level.[13] While blood in the eighteenth and nineteenth centuries was a stable substance understood as a whole, a part of a bounded body, and invested with mystical meanings, now it is considered as a vital fluid without any mystical powers. From 1975 to the 1990s the status of blood changes drastically. It is used for acquiring DNA samples; it is gradually displaced technically and symbolically by the genome; and synthetic blood and auto-transfusions are seen as the ideal.[14] Open to technological interventions, blood is fractioned into a number of components (plasma, red cells, white cell and platelets) that are being manipulated and used for different purposes in biomedicine, and distributed to multiple recipients, at different times and in different places across the world.[15] At the same time, we are witnessing the emergence of biocapital and the new relations between pharmaceutical corporations and science. Life itself becomes part of economic relations: it can be traded, exchanged and valued. Biopolitics[16] then becomes interrelated with bioeconomics. Within this context, where the biological body can be engineered at the molecular level, and tissues—from blood to organs and any other living matter taken from the body—can be managed, cloned, multiplied, and commodified,[17] our understanding of ourselves as corporeal individuals is being reshaped. While body parts can be exploited and exchanged, and human life itself reified, at the same time, as Nikolas Rose argues, we have the choice to intervene and reshape our own biological selves in ways that fundamentally affect our identities. In an era when the biological can be optimised and penetrated by the technological, notions of what is biologically alive or human are reshaped and opened to contestation. In the 'postvital'[18] era of nanobiology, where the uncanny amalgamation of machinic and living matter points towards 'the afterlife of life',[19] life returns 'undead, as the absent origin of those very scientific practices—from molecular biology to genomics to artificial life—effecting its dislocation'.[20] What is at stake in the present politics where the limits of life are reorganised and extended is exactly this ambiguous zone of life. Life now reverberates through the cracks and between the broken boundaries of life and death.

From the vitality of blood to machinic life

Blood becomes the vital plexus of questions relating to vitalism and life, unsettling the poles of biology and technology, human and machine. Notions about the mystical vitality of blood survive from the late eighteenth century through to the middle of the nineteenth century and influence understandings of transfusion. They are associated with the eighteenth- and nineteenth-century belief in vitalism and the existence of forces or principles in living organisms that could not be explained by the mechanistic approach of physiology based on physical or organic-chemical techniques. It is significant to mention that the idea of life[21] was only defined at the end of the eighteenth century by the vitalist Xavier Bichat who wrote that 'life is the totality of those functions which resist death'.[22] Indeed, understandings of the vitality of blood are associated with, and depend on, the concept of life as 'a motive principle' that animates and enables living bodies to operate.[23] Equally, it is assumed that blood is permeated by a 'principle which enables it to effect the formative operations of the machine' and that 'we must allow the blood to be alive'.[24] Vitalism significantly influences the idea of blood as life, and John Hunter's vitalist definition of blood is referenced and celebrated in the *Lancet* and various early nineteenth-century medical journals. The principle of life in the blood Hunter calls *materia vitae diffusa*[25] and it is considered a material agent that through the fluidity of blood 'pervades every part of the animal machine, regulates its various functions, and repairs the waste occasioned by the operations of life. The phenomena of vital energy are only characteristic marks of the blood's vitality.'[26] But blood is also infused with spirituality and understood within a theological discourse reflected in John Murray's medico-religious truth in the epigram of this chapter. Similarly, for mid-nineteenth-century New Orleans physician Samuel Cartwright, blood is the 'fundamental type of life' and this can be most clearly understood through the Pentateuch's physiological doctrine, 'The life of the flesh is in the blood'.[27] For Cartwright, blood becomes the seat of all life, an extreme vitalism that seeks to overwrite that of Hunter: '[Hunter] never dreamed that life, in its broad, full and plain meaning, with all its attributes of sensation, motion, consciousness, will and intelligence, existed in the blood, and that the nerves, flesh and other solids possessed no life, but that which is in the blood thereof.'[28] While such vitalistic analyses might betray a naive belief in some mysterious principle and seek to impose upon life a transcendent model, they, however, undermine the rigid, sterile and reductive nature of physiology's mechanism.

In this vein, there is a line of thought that connects the eighteenth- and nineteenth-century vitalism with the new vitalism of theorists like Gilles Deleuze. These early vitalisms show, as Sarah Kember, Mariam Fraser and Celia Lury argue, how and why the idea 'that life cannot be explained by the principles of mechanism—matters now'.[29] Unlike the narrow vitalism of some of the theological vitalisms of the eighteenth and nineteenth centuries, with their focus on the closed organism and an occulted mysterious life force, the new vitalism of Deleuze is purged from all mysticism. It embraces death and inorganic life and, thus, expands life in order to include matter and other 'living' forms beyond the limits of the bounded organism. Similarly, Donna Haraway's 'dirty ontology' seeks to include the more-than-human worlds and address the 'mineral, vegetable, animal, and technological cosmoi heretofore colonized by the natural sciences'.[30] The thread that runs through these various vitalisms entices one 'to move beyond the conflation of life with the (life) sciences' and 'to conceive life as not confined to living organisms, but as movement, a radical becoming'.[31] Life then should be understood beyond the narrow boundaries of biology and in a nonanthropocentric way as nonhuman flow, a multiplicity and a network of vital forces; a 'machinic phylum'[32] whose constant variation of machinic components—of humans, organic and nonorganic life— produces different forms and combinations of life: microbes, epidemics, parasitism, packs, a-life.[33] Vampire narratives provide various examples of such life as multiplicity. Nosferatu is an embodiment of the plague as a collective form of life coursing through the different bodies of the vampire, rats and humans.

In this sense, while in the eighteenth and nineteenth centuries the vitalistic conception of blood veils in a mysterious and gothic aura blood's reanimating capacities, today the possibility of creating nanomedical devices that act as artificial red blood cells—not only able to reproduce some aspects of blood, but designed to be more biological than biological blood—transposes the biological beyond living. If James Blundell's experiments in the nineteenth century revealed blood's uncannily alive and therapeutic qualities, today emergent (nano)technologies appear themselves uncannily alive and lifelike. What produces fear and anxiety is the confusion between what is human and what is vampiric, or what Christopher Langton has named as 'life-as-we-know-it' and 'life-as-it-could-be';[34] biological life and the lifelikeness of machinic or artificial life.

Transfusing blood

Beginning from the late nineteenth century and moving on to the twentieth century, I want to trace the circulation of blood as topos in vampire texts. The discovery of the circulatory nature of the blood system by the seventeenth-century English physician William Harvey, along with the publication of his book *De Motu Cordis* (1628), prompted experiments in blood transfusion. Jean-Baptiste Denis, with the help of C. Emmerez, performed the first blood transfusion to a human from an animal in June 1667 in France. A similar transfusion was performed in November of the same year in England by Lower and King.[35] Denis' blood transfusion from a lamb to a human ended in excessive bloodletting and the man's death, and led to a ban on blood transfusion by the Parisian Faculty of Medicine.[36] Charles Darwin's grandfather, Erasmus Darwin, proposed in 1794 that blood transfusion could possibly allay fevers and malnutrition, but there is no evidence of him performing it.[37] Writing in 1873 Gustave Lemattre explains how the transfusion of blood in the seventeenth century 'never acquired any true scientific importance' because it was imagined 'as a universal panacea, aiming at the mastery of life, and triumph over disease itself'.[38] It would be much later, at the end of the nineteenth century, that such 'extravagant pretensions' and aspirations about transfusion's ability 'to give universal, indefinite life' were superseded by 'facts in the seclusion of laboratories' and the understanding that transfusion is merely a 'scientific process'.[39] Because of the ban on blood transfusions, the first transfusion of human blood was not performed until 1818 by James Blundell at the United Hospitals of St Thomas and Guy in London.[40] Although the patient died, Blundell's experiments revitalised interest in transfusion and led to experiments with new technologies and methodologies.[41]

The development of this biotechnology was a mystery for the scientists themselves. Transfusion experiments revealed blood's vitality: 'No other fluid could be injected into the veins, which would restore animation, and prevent death, as blood had done.'[42] In 1836, referring to the transfusion of blood between two animals, Henri Milne Edwards emphasised how when the blood of a living animal is 'injected into the veins of the one to all appearance dead, we see with amazement this inanimate body return to life, gaining accessions of vitality with each new quantity of blood that is introduced, by-and-by beginning to breathe freely, moving with ease, and finally ... recovering completely.'[43] Blundell conceived blood in vitalistic terms, as a re-animating fluid, while his descriptions of transfused women, characterised by gothic romanticism,[44] evoke 'the ghastliness of the countenance' found in vampiric victims.[45] As the vampire is reanimated by blood, so transfusion stories and documents are fascinated with the reanimation and resuscitation of bodies through the nutritive and life-giving qualities of blood. In his analysis of the 'Management of the more Copious Floodings' Blundell describes how women after floodings 'sometimes die in a moment, but more frequently in a gradual manner; and over the victim death shakes his dart, and to you she stretches out her helpless hands for that assistance, which you cannot give, *unless by transfusion*'.[46] Blundell's eloquence transforms the transfusion of blood into a 'Romantic re-animation of the apparently dead'.[47] For him, while blood is alive, the technology and instruments of transfusion are inanimate. This leads him to the question 'whether the blood would remain fit for the animal functions after its passage through the instrument',[48] and to the construction of specific instruments that would retain blood's life-giving qualities. The Gravitator, for example, transmits 'the blood in a regulated stream from one individual to another, with as little exposure as may be to air, cold, and inanimate surface'.[49] While, for Kim Pelis, this demonstrates his understanding of blood as life, at the same time it reveals a concern with technology as lifeless and the preservation or circulation of blood-life outside the body through artificial apparatuses. This can be connected to a concern, shared by other physicians at the time, between notions of vitality and life, between what constitutes something as alive or dead.[50]

In the second half of the nineteenth century transfusions were becoming popular again, but were generally unsuccessful because of the lack of sterilisation procedures, knowledge of blood groups, and blood clotting in needles and tubes.[51] Until the 1880s, these medical practitioners were usually obstetricians 'who transfused the blood of "strong" male donors into depleted females'.[52] From Blundell's view of blood's reanimating capacity, via the mid-century view of blood's nutritive quality, we finally arrive at the late 1880s medicalisation of blood. No longer a 'privileged substance, but instead an analyzable fluid, blood could be replaced by saline and other solutions'.[53] The saline infusion's triumph over blood was celebrated in the 1894 edition of *The Lancet*.[54] By 1906, however, blood transfusion would return with the work of George Washington Crile, whose research in 1898 would reveal that saline solutions and blood were not exchangeable.[55] In 1901 Karl Landsteiner would discover the ABO blood grouping and agglutination reactions, which would win him the Nobel Prize years later in 1930. It was in the early twentieth century with George W. Crile's successful surgical transfusions, and later Alexis Carrel's experiments, that blood transfusion would become a 'dramatic spectacle' with several 'vivid reports of the dramatic and colorful story of moving blood between bodies' in American newspapers.[56] As Douglas Starr notes, by the end of the 1910s 'surgeons were performing some 20 transfusions a year at Mount Sinai Hospital in New York alone—with Crile's and other, related techniques—and charging a handsome $500 fee'.[57]

While blood transfusions became a profitable business, blood remained associated with symbolic meanings. Newspapers that documented blood transfusion stories stressed the power of kinship when families and relatives donated blood, or celebrated the concept of sacrifice as celebrities and ordinary people offered their vital fluids to save the lives of strangers.[58] In the public imagination the idea of transfusing blood between bodies emphasised blood as a gift creating community. But, as a carrier of one's vitality and identity, blood also drew attention to the danger of changing one's sense of selfhood with the blood of another. Following Marcel Mauss' anthropological examination of the gift in archaic societies, blood can be imagined as a gift creating social cohesion and relationships of obligation and indebtedness between individuals. Because it is '[i]nvested with life, often possessing individuality',[59] it 'is not inactive. Even when it has been abandoned by the giver, it still possesses something of him.'[60] Because the gift, and, in a similar way, blood, 'possesses a soul' and exerts 'a magical or religious hold' over the receiver, 'it follows that to make a gift of something to someone is to make a present of some part of oneself'.[61] Drawing on Mauss' system of gift exchange, Richard Titmuss conceives blood as a voluntary gift that circulates outside of economic networks as a part of one's self donated anonymously for the benefit of the community. In this sense, blood donation and transfusion are acts of responsibility towards the community that reinforce individual identity, social relations and communal bonds.

In Braddon's 'Good Lady Ducayne' as well as in Stoker's *Dracula*, science attempts to bring the supernatural under its control by equating vampirism and blood transfusion. However, by trying to explain vampirism through scientific advancements, such as blood transfusions, science becomes supernatural, while vampirism is rationalised. The narrative not only gothicises blood transfusions,[62] but draws attention to the reality of the transfusions themselves, and the conditions within which they are performed, the subjects involved and their motives, as well as nineteenth-century discourse on blood and transfusions. 'Good Lady Ducayne' raises anxieties about the unethical use of blood transfusions by physicians and the dangers for the donor's life. When the doctor—Bella's friend, Herbert Stafford—discovers the scars on Bella's arms, he reproaches her for letting 'that wretched Italian quack to bleed you. They killed the greatest man in modern Europe that way, remember. How very foolish of you.'[63] While blood transfusions are presented as dangerous, they also demonstrate the obsession and concerns about health and medical treatment characteristic of upper-class Victorians,[64] as well as the Victorian obsession with fluids.[65]

Lady Ducayne's donors are poor girls who are willing to work as companions, but are unaware that their blood is siphoned off by the old lady's physician. The young girls' deaths from blood transfusions are interpreted as 'young lives that have been sacrificed' to Lady Ducayne's 'love of life'.[66] Dr Parravicini's attempts to prolong the old woman's life through 'experimental surgery'[67] are not free. Lady Ducayne reminds him that 'I have paid you thousands to keep me alive. Every year of my life has swollen your hoards.'[68] Science is presented at the service of capital, while blood, and the bodies and lives it signifies, is sacrificed and exchanged for money to feed the wild dreams of an 'old female Croesus'.[69] In like manner it can be argued that 'Good Lady Ducayne' is exemplary of the ways blood and transfusions were beginning to enter a financial arena, and it prefigures the unethical and unequal exchanges present in biomedical practices today.

In the Victorian era blood remained metaphorical and symbolic; it was invested with the individual's temperament and race, while its social life remained bound to the older notions of blood ties and blood lines. In the narrative blood is placed between this older metaphorical meaning and a new scientific one, through the performance of blood transfusions. The short story reflects nineteenth-century ideas of the relation between the life of fluids inside and outside the body.[70] Such ideas are developed by George Henry Lewes[71] in *The Physiology of Common Life*[72] ([1859], 1860), where he considers the blood within the body as a dynamic fluid which carries the individual's temperament, and the blood in scientific experiments as a neutral medium. Blood, as a neutral medium, then, has no power, and does not carry the individual's character. It functions only as a mechanism to sustain the role of the organs it connects. Thus, for Lewes, blood transfusions cannot alter the personality of the recipient, are useless for curing any disease, and should only be employed in cases of dangerous blood loss.[73] As he explains, the ancients were wrong to believe 'that by infusing new blood into an old and failing organism, new life would be infused; and wild dreams of a sort of temporal immortality were entertained'.[74] As he writes, 'The tissue which is in an unhealthy condition cannot be made healthy by bringing to it a "purer" blood (were such obtainable); it can only be brought back to its healthy condition by the cessation of those causes which keep up the morbid action, and these are not in the blood.'[75]

These misconceptions are reproduced by Lady Ducayne's insistence on transfusing blood from young girls. She inquires whether Bella has 'good health', whether she is 'strong and active, able to eat well, sleep well, walk well, able to enjoy all that there is good in life'.[76] Bella's youth and vitality, evident in her 'fresh complexion' and 'rosy color',[77] are qualities contained in her blood, and thus she becomes a producer of commodified 'healthy' blood in a vain system of exchange. By the end of the narrative, Lady Ducayne realises that the transfusions of blood are unsuccessful and useless, and blood is nothing more than a neutral fluid with no inherent power.

On the other hand, in Stoker's *Dracula* Van Helsing's blood transfusions are not only equated with vampirism, but are also used to counteract the vampire bite. They inject the narrative with various symbolic meanings and anxieties about the transgressive nature of the circulation of blood between bodies. At the same time, their use is also criticised intermittently. Blood transfusions at the end of the nineteenth century remained experimental and very often resulted in casualties.[78] They were a 'ghastly operation', as Dr Seward observes,[79] which was painful for the donors and the patients. In *Dracula*, after the fourth transfusion, 'Lucy had got a terrible shock, and it told on her more than before, for though plenty of blood went into her veins, her body did not respond to the treatment as well as on the other occasions'.[80] However, Dr Seward's empirical observations are overshadowed by symbolic explanations of blood, and the use of folkloric elements such as garlic that substitute for the lack of scientific knowledge.

The four transfusions that take place in *Dracula* are the gifts of blood from Arthur Holmwood, John Seward, Van Helsing and Quincey Morris to Lucy. According to Van Helsing, the blood is chosen from strong and healthy men and not from women, as he fears 'to trust those women, even if they would have courage to submit'.[81] In addition, after the last transfusion, Morris fears Lucy's fragility, since she 'has had put into her veins... the blood of four strong men. Man alive, her whole body wouldn't hold it.'[82] The blood that is chosen for transfusion is gendered since male blood is preferred for its vigour and power. Nevertheless, masculine and 'muscular' blood, embodying the essence of man himself, can be too powerful for the 'weak' female body. *Dracula* remains focused on blood's vitalistic and reanimating capacities that resonate, as Pelis shows, with Blundell's ideas.[83] Specifically, Van Helsing chooses Arthur as the first brave man; unlike Van Helsing and Seward, he does not 'toil much in the world of thought. Our nerves are not so calm and our blood not so bright than yours!'[84] His blood then reflects social notions of a masculinity and identity, gendered with a healthy, strong male body and calm mind.

As with Lady Ducayne, so with Lucy: blood transfusions fail to inject life into the waning female body. However, in *Dracula* the representation of transfusions demonstrates a sceptical attitude towards science, which is not found in 'Good Lady Ducayne'. Yet, blood remains a potent symbol of vitality, and this symbolic quality is manifested in the fleeting change in Lucy's health following the transfusion: 'Her spirits even were good, and she was full of a happy vivacity',[85] and there was a 'return of colour to the ashy cheeks'.[86]

The three subsequent transfusions retain metaphorical meanings and introduce the element of sexual penetration. Blood is interpreted as a symbol of ties and family bonds, but it also becomes a substitute for semen.[87] For Van Helsing, 'No man knows till he experiences it, what it is to feel his own life-blood drawn away into the veins of the woman he loves,'[88] and, making the sexual implications of the act even clearer: 'Said he not that the transfusion of his blood to her veins had made her truly his bride?'[89] Seward's second transfusion is to be kept a secret from Lucy's fiancé because it will 'frighten him and enjealous him'.[90] Seward is not permitted to offer as much blood as Arthur, because he is not 'her lover, her fiancé'.[91] Lucy, the 'sweet maid', is described finally, as a 'polyandrist', and Van Helsing becomes a 'bigamist' by offering his own blood to Lucy. While his wife is dead, he remains wedded to her as 'one flesh' through the Church's law,[92] and the transfusion of blood marks a second union, a communion equated to a wedding and sexual penetration. For Christopher Craft, the transfusions are 'displaced marital (and martial) penetrations'[93] and reassert 'the conventionally masculine prerogative of penetration'.[94] Despite the presence of science, blood in *Dracula* remains a vitalistic and fetishised fluid.

In Tod Browning's 1931 film adaptation, *Dracula*, medical science and its technologies are relegated to mere symbols of authority and reason. Blood transfusions, and tools to analyse blood lend authority to Professor Van Helsing. The blood transfusion is staged in an anatomical theatre in front of medical students and scientists, all dressed in white uniforms and masks. The act of transfusion does not take place on screen, and the focus falls on the two bite marks on Lucy's neck. In this sequence, the mise-en-scène becomes the embodiment of science. Through the presence of medical paraphernalia, the white uniforms, the anatomical theatre, the sterilised and careful movements of Van Helsing, and the description of his findings through his strict and clinical voice, science is brought to life. But while science frames the scene and sets the atmosphere, the description of the bite marks, as well as the 'unnatural loss of blood' from Lucy's body, infiltrate the scene to produce a mysterious effect.

In another sequence, where Renfield's blood is analysed by Van Helsing in the company of Dr Seward and other men, the focus falls on Van Helsing the scientist and his use of scientific instruments to analyse blood. Van Helsing, dressed in a medical uniform, is shown to be an authority on blood, separated from the other characters, who are casually dressed and sitting around his desk. His analysis is justified by a short excerpt read from a Latin medical text, and he finally utters: 'Gentlemen, we are dealing with the undead.' He proceeds immediately to explain that 'the vampire attacks the throat. It leaves two little wounds.' From the blood analysis he can conclude that Renfield is obsessed 'with the idea that he must devour living things in order to sustain his own life'. While Dr Seward replies that 'modern medical science does not admit of such a creature', and the 'vampire is pure myth, superstition', Van Helsing confidently reassures him that 'the superstition of yesterday, can become the scientific reality of today'.[95] Van Helsing's anachronistic and supernatural explanations serve to marginalise his own scientific discourse and practices. The Latin medical text and other scientific tools are used merely as props to sustain Van Helsing's authority, and have no other function in the film. In this sense, the spectre of science perversely lends gravitas and reason to superstition.

Medical science and its technologies might frame these two scenes, but supernatural discourse defines them.

While the supernatural often dominates science and its technologies, Erle C. Kenton's Universal horror film *House of Dracula* (1945) presents a different relation between the two. *House of Dracula* closes an era of Universal films featuring gothic monsters, and is specifically significant since after 1945 science fiction becomes the dominant form of horror film, characterised by scientific monstrosities and Cold War paranoiac scenarios. The film's characteristic place between gothic and science fiction horror is also reflected in the treatment of its themes. The use of blood transfusion literally stages the exchange between the supernatural forces of a primitive past and the technologies of science. Dracula visits Dr Edelmann to help him treat his condition. In the laboratory blood tests show the existence of a peculiar parasite in Dracula's blood cells that leads Dr Edelmann to perform a series of procedures, in which the 'pure culture of a parasite when introduced into the parent bloodstream will destroy not only its own kind but themselves as well'. Unlike the previously discussed films and texts, this film relies on, and uses, scientific knowledge and practice without recourse to occult or primitive beliefs about blood. During the blood transfusions, both the supernatural body of the vampire and the natural body of the scientist are treated in the laboratory in a similar way, and they both receive and exchange vampire and human blood. Science is not subordinated to the gothic, supernatural mysteries of vampirism.[96] Rather, in an interesting inversion, Dracula, instead of contaminating the scientist with his vampiric bite, actually transfuses his vampiric blood to Dr Edelmann, thus using science instead of any supernatural ability. Nevertheless, after his contamination, the scientist succeeds in killing the vampire, not with technology, but with folklore, since he lets sunlight burn Dracula in his coffin. Neither the supernatural forces nor scientific practices dominate the other: both are utilised and successful.

Kathryn Bigelow's *Near Dark* (1987) celebrates the complete triumph of science over the supernatural through the use of blood transfusions that cure vampirism. The film reaffirms the traditional family values of 1980s America. Caleb's father, a veterinarian, manages to save his son from vampirism by simply transfusing his own human blood to his vampire child. Caleb's cured blood is then transfused into the female vampire Mae, who is also cured and introduced to her new human family as a substitute for the absent mother. While Caleb's initiation into the vampiric family is marked with the vampire kiss, his return to the human family is facilitated by the patriarch's transfusion of blood that reverses the vampire condition. Blood then is a carrier of identity, and the exchange of blood signals entrance to a family. On the one hand, blood transfusions are victorious and the supernatural is killed. On the other hand, scientific knowledge about blood and references to the AIDS epidemic are completely absent. The film remains conservative in its celebration of traditional blood ties, and anything that might spoil the Hollywood consumer's enjoyment, or 'infect its box-office offerings',[97] is silenced. However, the transfusion scene between the father and son should not be read as merely symbolic. In the film the father's blood is not alleged to be pure and powerful. The blood's power to reinscribe a paternal order is factual and not a mere argument or possibility.

While the nineteenth-century vampire texts 'Good Lady Ducayne' and *Dracula*, as well as the 1931 film *Tod Browning's Dracula*, present and play with supernatural and symbolic meanings of blood, *House of Dracula* departs significantly from supernatural explanations of blood. Its use of medical and technological instruments and scientific language defines blood as a neutral medium to be analysed and explained. Even when the scientist is unable to classify the strange parasite in Dracula's blood, the film does not regress to supernatural explanations, but introduces the idea of antibodies to fight the vampire parasite through blood transfusions. While in its denouement 'Good Lady Ducayne' treats blood as a neutral, non-occult fluid, such a realisation occurs only after the misuse of blood transfusions, and the misconception that 'pure' blood from young females will transfuse new life and vitality in her body. Unlike 'Good Lady Ducayne', *Dracula* and *Tod Browning's Dracula*, where blood is transfused into vain or helpless women, *House of Dracula* stages the exchange of blood between men, acting as both recipients and donors. Whereas the body of the vampire retains its supernatural powers, blood enters the laboratory to be treated rationally and scientifically. Finally, in the late twentieth century *Near Dark* celebrates the power of science to cure vampirism permanently. *Near Dark* not only celebrates the re-establishment of paternal authority, but demonstrates how biomedical procedures can discipline difference through technologies of control by regulating the vampire blood.

From vampires to vampiric reproductive technology and aporetic life

The scene is that of the operating table where the prone body of a woman is penetrated by the fangs of vampire bats controlled by Count Orlock from F.W. Murnau's 1922 silent film *Nosferatu*. The mad doctor

Nosferatu sits in a sterilised teleoperating cubicle where his claw-like fingers operate the joysticks that manipulate the bats' blood-drinking. A medical stand holds a transfusion bag that is attached to the woman and the bat. As the blood circulates from human, to animal, to machine and vampire, a strange ceremony takes place. This is the vampiric, infectious and illegitimate trafficking of vital substances and the dangerous circulation of blood and data across the different categories of gender, race, species and machines. Lynn Randolph's 1995 painting *Transfusions*, painted in interaction with Donna Haraway's chapter 'Universal Donors in a Vampire Culture: It's All in the Family, Biological Kinship Categories in the Twentieth-Century United States', interrogates the circulation of blood—and its symbolic associations with kinship—within biomedicine and information technology. While in *Modest Witness* (1997) the painting initiates Haraway's discussion about the biological categories of blood and race and their pollution by the figure of the vampire, here, however, I want to emphasise the painting's representation of the vital circulations of blood between human and machine, between the organic and the inorganic through the figure of the vampire. Such exchanges within contemporary biomedicine and, as I will argue, nanotechnology, can no longer evoke blood's symbolic associations. The status of blood, as well as that of technology, has changed, and with it the mythology and fantasies of purity and community, and the symbolisms of race, intimacy and connection. As *Transfusions* shows, the transfused blood is controlled and manipulated by a sterilised and cold vampire technology: there is nothing sacred here. As blood becomes detached from the organic body and one's identity through the intervention of science and technology, its symbolic and transgressive qualities are erased. Questions then arise about the symbolic meanings of transfusing blood in contemporary biomedicine where blood is rarely transfused as whole, and one-to-one donations are the exception.[98] Indeed, the processing, circulation and transfusion of blood have changed dramatically since Titmuss published *The Gift Relationship* in 1971.[99] For Ronald Bayer and Eric Feldman, 'As blood plasma is increasingly subject to transformation by pharmaceutical firms, it is difficult to sustain the symbolic attachments evoked by whole blood.'[100] In addition, with autologous transfusion the gift relationship between donor and recipient is transformed into the gift of self to self.[101] The AIDS contamination of blood during the 1980s, the unmanageable and potentially risky nature of donated blood, and the fact that transfusion can amplify infection are some of the dangers that have turned citizens towards autologous donations and transfusions. These anxieties about blood as a poisonous gift reveal the limitations of Richard Titmuss' gift of blood based on generosity and trust among citizens. Within this context, notions of altruism or sacrifice no longer hold.

Indeed, transfusion is no longer based on the circulation of blood from one body to another but on a licentious and interlaced plexus of global, commercial and manifold exchanges of blood between different bodies.[102] Since 1996 blood transfusions of whole blood have already diminished in the UK to less than 5 per cent of all transfusions.[103] With the technological procedure of blood component therapy or separation, blood is now separated into its components: red blood cells (erythrocytes), white cells (leucocytes), plasma and platelets, and transfused as fractions of blood to meet the needs of individual patients. In this respect, a single blood donation can be processed and fractioned into its components and transfused to several patients in different parts of the world. On the one hand, the prolific character of this technology has re-enchanted the concept of the gift. In North India donated blood has been imagined through a spiritual lens as a form of 'generative generosity' that produces kinship and familial relationships through its reproduction and circulation in the bodies of those who are 'saved'.[104] Within this context, the technology of blood component separation is a reproductive gift that generates new life, for example, 'in saving the life of someone yet to produce offspring'.[105] On the other hand, such productivity maximises profits. Technology is now utilised indistinguishably for both therapeutic and economic ends. The augmentation of the biological capacities of blood results in a 'surplus in vitro vitality' which 'may eventually be transformed into surplus commercial profits'.[106] It can be argued that the regenerative possibilities of blood component therapy create a vampiric economy of blood where one's blood circulates within the bodies of several others, like the blood that circulates within the vampire family of *Near Dark*. So, today, fractioned blood circulates within more than one body. From the supernatural powers of blood, we arrive at the 'uncanny' reproductive powers of donated blood and technology. If vampire gothic has fictionalised the exchanges between vampire and human blood, (un)death and life, through the resuscitating powers of blood transfusions, then now biotechnology has the capacity to amplify and augment biological processes so that blood becomes more useful and prolific.

The reproduction of blood and its regenerative possibilities manifests a concern with the productivity and enhancement of life itself. This contemporary normalising vitalism is obsessed with the organism and its fruitful productivity and can be related to the concept of life that came to be understood in the nineteenth century as a process of evolution, production and development.[107] From the extension of one's life through blood and the existence of one's blood beyond his/her biological death in the bodies of others, to biotechnology's augmentation of blood's capacities, blood is at the centre of notions relating to growth, life and the organism's biological capacities. What's more, this productivity extends beyond the biological to include the nonbiological and programmable matter. Robert Freitas Jr has proposed a nanomedical device called 'respirocyte' which will function as a mechanical artificial red cell on a long-term basis in order to augment the body's natural red blood cells and regulate such processes as oxygen transport in the blood. According to Freitas, 'The baseline respirocyte can deliver 236 times more oxygen to the tissues per unit volume than natural red cells, and enjoys a similar advantage in carbon dioxide transport.'[108] For Freitas, nanomedical devices have the potential to 'extend natural human capabilities'[109] and thus can have a variety of applications from therapeutic and critical care medicine, such as blood transfusion, anaemia, and cardiovascular procedures, to sports and battlefield applications.[110]

In particular, the advantages for blood transfusions will be the result of the respirocytes' artificial nature, their indefinite life, their availability and their ability to 'be used as the active oxygen-carrying component of a universally transfusable blood substitute that is free of disease vectors such as hepatitis, venereal disease, malarial parasites or AIDS'.[111] Mechanical red cells are shown to be safer and less dangerous than real biological blood and can operate indefinitely, beyond biological red cells' four-month lifespan. Because of their artificiality they have no symbolic value, are not infused with spirituality, and cannot conjure up notions of identity and life associated with whole living blood. In this respect, as Freitas argues, respirocytes, 'like other artificial blood substitutes, may permit treatment of devout Jehovah's Witness patients and others who refuse transfusion of natural blood products on religious grounds'.[112] The paradox here is that while the transfusion of biological blood is forbidden on the basis of the scriptural prohibition on consuming blood, and its sacred and symbolic associations with life, the transfusion of respirocytes may be accepted because they are artificial. What Freitas so readily ignores is the uncanny lifelikeness of these inorganic machines whose sole purpose is the sustenance and improvement of life. The respirocyte is understood as a technological response to the biological model of the red blood cell and thus is an example of our contemporary postvitalism where the biological can be engineered, blurring further the boundaries of the organic and the inorganic.

The prospect of producing technologically artificial red blood cells raises concerns related to the mixing of bodily and machinic components, and of what is human or nonhuman (or even posthuman). The possibilities opened by molecular nanotechnology and the creation of these artificial-mechanical devices that aim not only to mime red blood cells but to surpass their functions and integrate within the biological body and bloodstream transpose blood at the uncanny crossroads of the biological and the technological.[113] Nanotechnology returns to the body viewed at the atomic-molecular level, a return that Eugene Thacker recognises as 'an extreme mutation of the body, a "supernatural" body, a body more biological than the biological, technically enhanced through the instrumental use of biological structures and processes'.[114] Indeed this return to the biology of the body through the mechanical engineering, enhancement and augmentation of biological processes is a desire to make manifest the materiality of the biological and natural body.[115] The living body becomes more biological and productive through the mediation of inorganic matter in a phantasmatic, 'undead' space where living and dead materials coexist, no longer distinguishable from each other.

Like the mysterious blood that animates the vampire, so the ambivalent nature of the respirocytes circulating within the bloodstream raises questions about a vampiric, aporetic life. Respirocytes, like other programmable matter, are a *matter of life and death*. If vampires are 'figures of lifelike death', then similarly lifelike death is 'the ambivalent attitude towards a life that should not be living, an unholy life. This lifelike death is aporetic life: the dead that walk, the immortal being that is also the basest animals (bats, rats)' but also 'the domain of nanotechnology, the idea of inorganic life, programmable matter, an undiscovered "occult media" '.[116] Life now resides in this uncanny space where the organic is inhabited by the inorganic and the human by the nonhuman.

This uncanny vitality has always been a quintessential characteristic of the topology of the gothic. It resonates with Wilhelm Worringer's early twentieth-century definition of gothic architecture as imbued with nonorganic life. For him, the gothic ornament gives the uncanny expression of 'a life that seems to be independent of us'.[117] While it has 'no organic expression', 'it is of extreme liveliness' and 'super-organic expressiveness'.[118] The gothic's organic and inorganic characteristics are not the result 'of a harmonious comingling of two opposing tendencies, but of an unclear and, to a certain degree, uncanny amalgamation of them'.[119] Similarly, today, behind the polished and indifferent surfaces of our technologies lurks the uncanny vitality of vampiric machines and artificial matter: 'behind the lifelessness of things an uncanny ghastly life'.[120]

Real vampires, biological immortality, and neoliberal subjectivity

In its attempt to overcome the limits of death, technology becomes vampiric while life itself cracks open. In contemporary technoscience death is stretched, turned into vitality, infinite production and productive energy. No energy is lost to death and nothing escapes the circuit of production. Without an origin or death, there are only flows and optimised reproduction which reflect the 'indefinite production which is desired by capital', the 'indefinite and discontinuous process of production, where nothing gets lost or wasted, but everything becomes useful'.[121] Indeed, Dracula, as Franco Moretti argues, consumes as much blood as he needs without wasting a drop: 'His ultimate aim is not to destroy the lives of others according to whim, to waste them, but to *use* them.'[122] Parasitically feasting upon the lives of others and growing without limits, vampires embody the dream of infinite accumulation and growth beyond death.

This delirium of growth and wealth needs to be contextualised within the intertwined histories of biology and political economy. In her account of biotechnology and capitalism in neoliberalism, Melinda Cooper follows Michel Foucault's analysis in *The Order of Things* of the parallel development of classical political economy and the modern life sciences in order to emphasise their mutual insistence on biological life's creative forces.[123] In the concept of 'organic structure' modern biologists discover the principle that 'corresponds to labor in the economic sphere'.[124] Hence, reproduction and growth become characteristic of both political economy and biology's terrain: the 'organic becomes the living and the living is that which produces, grows and reproduces'.[125] In this sense, the realms of biological reproduction and capitalist accumulation are very closely interconnected. Indeed, what connects the productivity of markets, the productivity of technology and life sciences, and the productivity of the vampire is their endless reproduction and growth. Today it is almost impossible to consider the circulation of blood, biological tissues or biotechnologies without having recourse to the circulation of money. As will be examined in Chapter 5, they both converge and reinvigorate each other. The vampire then becomes a useful metaphor for both neoliberalism's insatiable desire for productivity beyond the limits of life and its medical sub-jectivity of private investment in the future through technologies of life extension. Such a vampiric subjectivity characterised by its insatiate appetite for growth and immortality finds expression in the beliefs of contemporary self-identified vampires.

Although vampire communities will be analysed in detail in the last chapter, here I focus on the Temple of the Vampire as a vampire religion that supports ideas and beliefs in immortality and physical extension of life. While in the past blood was, for the Temple, a symbol of vam-pire life and status, now such fantasies have been substituted by science and its promise of life. Their website offers links regarding molecular nanotechnology, transhumanism and life extension in order to sup-port their ideas scientifically and show awareness of advances in new technologies of immortality such as cryonics and life extension theo-ries based on the work of the English gerontologist Aubrey de Grey.[126] Through links described as 'future', 'present' and 'past', the Temple implies that immortality is not a distant utopian possibility, but achiev-able in the near future. Links such as futurist Ray Kurzweil's idea of the 'Law of Accelerating Returns' and the radical technological advances in changing human nature and extending human lifespan in the near future, evident in his books such as *The Age of Spiritual Machines* (1999) are exemplary of the Temple's transhumanist agenda. Transhumanism and its various currents, such as immortalism and cryonics, express the belief that human beings should desire and take advantage of new technologies to become more human: eliminate aging, and enhance human intellectual, physical and psychological capacities.[127] For the vampire Temple, such definitions serve their philosophy of Nietzschean self-actualisation and belief in technological advances to produce a technologically superior posthuman individual. However, these new technologies are envisioned as the privilege of a superior and select elite.

The problem here has been expressed by Francis Fukuyama in his cri-tique of the commercialisation of human enhancements and the value of being human in *Our Posthuman Future* (2002). While Fukuyama's critique is not interested in distinguishing between the terms 'posthu-manism' and 'transhumanism', there are differences between the two. Eugene Thacker separates posthumanism and techno-critics such as Donna Haraway and Katherine Hayles from transhumanists such as Richard Dawkins, Hans Moravec and Ray Kurzweil,[128] whose thought is characterised by the philosophical foundations of Enlightenment humanism and individualism, the obsession with human enhancement and perfectibility. Such a vision, according to Elaine L. Graham, is 'in many respects a cybernetic version of social Darwinism, anticipating a future meritocracy founded upon the survival of the fittest, represented by the intellectual and psychological superiority of postbiological humanity'.[129] This vision is shared by the evolutionary determinism of the Temple. Postbiological humanity is based on the promise of artificial and technological innovations which will guarantee the survival of a vampire elite of overhuman individuals.

Instead of entropy and death, transhumanists support the principles of extropy as a symbol of continued improvement and flourishing, of vitality and life-affirming practices that contribute to human growth and innovation.[130] Indeed, for the father of cryonics, Robert Ettinger, immortality 'is an opportunity for growth and development'[131] where the frozen would not only be resuscitated but 'enlarged and improved'.[132] Cryonics is imagined as 'a bridge to an anticipated Golden Age, when we shall be reanimated to become supermen with indefinite life spans'.[133] For the vampire religion, technologies of immortality like cryonics represent the scientific truth of vampirism and a possibility to rise above humanity's fragile nature.[134] At the same time, extension of life and immortalism are dressed as a vampire religion, a form of scientism, where scientific beliefs have become the ideology of the temple to sell to its privileged consumers.

If in nineteenth-century fiction the figure of the vampire problematises the relation between technology and the circulation of blood as life, similarly, contemporary self-identified 'real vampires' problematise the convergence of the life sciences and economy through their predatory neoliberal vampirism and desire to extend their life beyond the grave. While 'Good Lady Ducayne' presents the possibility of immortality and extension of life through the technology of transfusion, today technologies of immortality such as cryonics are possibilities open to subjects that desire the extension of life. The frozen corpse of the 'cryopatient' is a dead body in an undying state: an undead patient who awaits its own revival, as if death were a temporary state of disease. The cryonic subject exhibits a perverse desire to be present at his/her own death,[135] to control death, which is constantly kept at bay, resisted and annulled. Preserved in an artificial state or, as Ettinger puts it, in 'as nearly life-like a condition as possible',[136] the corpse is detached from the growth of putrefaction and the messy decay of flesh; death is now cleansed. As the frozen body remains aloof from death, so identity is frozen forever in the present. The cryopatient's identity is that of the 'endless rendering of the same—"me me me"'.[137] The cryonic project of personal immortality, as Richard Doyle notes, does not resonate with the promise of communal immortality but 'sounds the note of identity:

"me me me me" '.[138] The cool indifference of the cryonic subject is that of the self-interested subject of neoliberalism.

Carlos Novas and Nikolas Rose have introduced the notion of the somatic individual and the emergence of new modes of subjectivity that are related to the changing views and mutations of concepts of life, identity in advanced liberal societies, ethics of health and illness, and new genetic thought and techniques. Here genetic ideas about one's corporeal identity together with an ethics that stresses individual obligation to increase life and its future quality, intertwine with contemporary norms of selfhood characteristic of neoliberal practices of government that emphasise autonomy, self-actualization, personal responsibility, prudence and choice.[139] Similarly, Waldby and Mitchell discuss the emergence of a neoliberal medical subjectivity within the context of such practices as the private accounts of umbilical cord blood to treat future blood disorders.[140] Such strategies are oriented towards 'the entrepreneurial maximization of future health' enabled by the development of new medical technologies and their future possibilities.[141] Health now becomes associated with personal responsibility and is opposed to the forms of solidarity and collective participation generated by public donations and transfusions. The body in cryonics becomes a capital enterprise invested in future technological advances. It is a vampire enterprise nurtured by the blood of neoliberal ideals.

In *Dracula*, for example, blood transfusions are collective and engender relationships and solidarity among the men as a group and as members of a nation united against the foreign threat of Dracula. However, in the era of voodoo economics, *Near Dark*'s blood transfusions are a family affair and a private enterprise not corrupted by the blood of others. While the blood of the father cures the vampire son, the rest of the vampires are destroyed or killed. Given the fact that, as Nicola Nixon points out, a year before the film was released John Doolittle 'sponsored a Senate bill that "legalized the creation of designated-donor pools to keep donated blood *within families* so as to prevent transmission" ',[142] the film celebrates autonomy and responsibility instead of altruism and collective participation. Indeed, this kind of neoliberal strategy resembles the subjectivity that the Temple of the Vampire supports. As their website states, they value the individual instead of the group or nation, individual freedom and control over one's life 'through wealth, health, personal power, and unlimited life extension'.[143] More significantly, the idea that an individual can make of oneself anything one chooses is based on a capitalist vitalism which translates everything into the useful, the good, abundance and productivity. As they emphasise, they paradoxically embrace only those aspects of the vampire that 'include a love and respect for all life, physical immortality, individual elegance, proven wisdom, civilized behaviour, worldly success, and personal happiness' while rejecting those tendencies that are 'anti-life, anti-social, deathist, crude, gory, self-defeating, or criminal'.[144] This frenzy of self-interested growth and success culminates in the vampires' concern with life extension technologies. Real vampires' desire for immortality and self-actualisation is exemplary of the relationship between theories of biological immortality and the emergent possibilities of new technologies and life sciences, and neoliberal theories fixated on investments in the future, growth and accumulation. The *Homo vampiricus* is the emergent neoliberal entrepreneur of himself, his own producer that can profit from his own corporeal assets and tissues, investing in his own body and blood and in the future of technologies that promise life after death.

Conclusion

The blood-life that flows from the mists of eighteenth-century occult vitalism to the light of modernity's belief in scientific truths and contemporary biotechnology and nanotechnology's reproductive networks animates, produces and reshapes individual bodies and identities. Circulating from the realm of superstition to that of science and technology, blood's metaphors recede into metonymy. Blood no longer spills out to infuse our cultural universe with its symbolics, but is contained in sterilised categories in order to be technologically altered and separated into useful and profitable fractions. Its vitality is not occulted but unveiled and becomes productive in the service of biotechnology's regenerative practices. In this respect, transfusion and the *in vitro* productivity of blood demand an ethical handling that takes into consideration individual donors and also the good of the community.

If transfusion in nineteenth-century vampire narratives was occulted and imagined as a technology of immortality, today cryonics is literally a gothic technology that suspends the body in a state between death and the promise of rebirth. As technology promises the seductive triumph over permanent death through cryonics' uncanny deferral of death, so subjects themselves choose to reshape their future by submitting to neoliberal strategies of life that praise individual responsibility and choice. The subject of cryonics is literally and metaphorically a vampire. While real vampires believe in immortality and an afterlife, at the same time they exhibit those selfish and predatory characteristics of a neoliberal subject that would pursue its self-interest beyond the grave.

Indeed the investment in the future of cryonics and one's body is also an investment in 'the body of a capital yet to come'.[145] At the cold heart of cryonics lies the utopian belief in the afterlife of one's self and capital, a belief that is already present in Lady Ducayne's faith in blood's reanimating powers. Such a faith, however, remains anchored to the idea of life as essentially biological and submitted to the disciplinary control of science.

A historical analysis of blood and its technologies colours our views about animate and inanimate life and forces us to rethink life through a critique of anthropomorphic conceptions of life. From fictional vampires and gothic technologies of reanimation to real vampires and undead life, boundaries dissolve, while gothic symbols and vampiric life cross over into the side of the real, confusing further life and death. Today vitality can be imagined as a wound spouting little arcs of life and death, a slashed artery from which life splatters across the cultural horizon. In abandoning the concept of biological life, we need to approach the nonorganic and inanimate matter as germinal and nonhuman life. From programmable matter and the biological function of nanodevices such as the respirocytes to a-life and the gothic's vampiric entities, monstrosities and epidemics, we are also invited to think of life not as one thing—life force or code—but as multiplicity and networks of matter folding and unfolding, swirling and metamorphosing. Agency emerges from within these in-between spaces of material folds and reversals as that which is not the property of the rational human subject. Behind the seductive and alluring mask of the vampire lies fear and anxiety generated by matter's capacity of transformation: of blood spewing out, polluting, generating and reproducing. Blood not only remains the symbol of life as we know it, but also becomes that of an uncanny vitalism that promises life beyond the organism.

2
The Biopolitics of the Vampire Narrative: Vampire Epidemics, AIDS and Bioterrorism

> The general biological conception of the organism as a federation of organs and tissues, living in symbiosis, and yet fundamentally hostile, or "selfish", is helpful in the study of disease.[1]

> Nevertheless, where there is revolt and invasion and breakdown of established social barriers by disorderly elements, we cannot avoid seeing at least a strong superficial resemblance to cancerous processes.[2]

The association of politics and biology that I want to pursue in this chapter is captured in the British novelist Morley Roberts' analogies and connections between politics and biology, and between the organism of the body and that of the nation. In his 1938 *Bio-politics: An Essay in the Physiology, Pathology and Politics of the Social and Somatic Organism* he argues that the understanding of the state as a living organism and federation of cell-colonies affected by disorders and diseases can help defend it from outsiders and safeguard its continued life. Biopolitics, then, is responsible for detecting organic disorders that afflict the body politic and establishing those appropriate biological apparatuses to defend its health. Roberts' bacteriological imaginary describes life as invaded from within by disease that threatens order and law in the form of malignant growth and infection. In this respect, he echoes the organic language of Baron Jacob von Uexküll's *Staatsbiologie* (1920), where the German body is threatened by disease and parasites feeding off its vitality and, later, the epidemiological repertoire of Nazi propaganda portraying Jews as vampires and parasites. The threat to the body politic is also the threat to the collective body and life itself that needs to be immunised against the invasion by infected others. For Roberts, the 'alien racial intrusion' of immigrants, particularly Jews, results in the body politic's immune reactions analogous to anaphylactic shock.[3] Such perilous immigrations, understood as the 'peaceful penetration by members of a powerful alien social organism',[4] are comparable to disease and cancer in which 'the epithelial cells of the animal body, which are the active invasive element in cancer, are always endeavouring to invade the very tissues which provide them with nutriment'.[5] While in a healthy and balanced body these invaders are destroyed, the body is, on the other hand, in danger when they are not fed.[6] The mixing of political and biomedical languages reveals the precarious boundaries between metaphor and reality, and the dangerous possibility of the transformation of biological metaphors into political realities. Militaristic metaphors of invasion,[7] of vampiric and parasitical feeding off the body of the state and of disease spreading malignantly, penetrating and poisoning the very lifeblood of the nation, are characteristic not just of a deadly politics of life—of a biologisation of politics—but also of contemporary biopolitics. In an age where the previously hygienic boundaries are now porous, contagion becomes the central metaphor to describe the intensification of contemporary anxieties about global contamination and contact with the other that are countered by the demand for the construction of new prophylactic barriers.[8] From the political discourse of the nineteenth century to the contemporary discourse of the war on terror, the language used to describe the enemies equates them to parasites, degenerates and microbes that seek to 'infiltrate' and 'infect' the body of the nation. It is no coincidence that the vampire and blood as agents of contamination and contagion, transgression and migration, mingling and corruption, come to embody those fears of global contact and infection. The politics of vampire literature and of undead life, imagined as a 'life unworthy of life', bring to the fore a whole bestiary of enemies and a demonology of contagion that repeatedly poisons human contact and being in common by reducing the 'uncivilised' and 'savage' other to the nonhuman status of vermin and parasite.

Blood's fluidity and dangerous circulation symbolises today these fears of contagion and transgression of limits. In this respect, I want to link the 'bio' of biopolitics, understood in Foucauldian analyses as the life of the population, both in its biological and its national and political-economic spheres, to blood as the material and symbolic expression of biological and political meanings related to life and its human or nonhuman forms. Historically associated with infection and pollution,[9] blood is the poisonous fluid of the degenerate and infected vampire that threatens the health and lifeblood of the body politic. But the paroxysmal centrality of blood in vampire gothic fictions and films is also indicative of its symbolic connection to a primordial vitality and its status as the guardian of the nation's identity that needs to be immunised against disease and its contamination by the enemy's bacteria, parasites and viruses. In such biopolitical analyses as Morley Roberts' *Warfare in the Human Body* (1921) the emphasis on the blood's 'bactericidal qualities' and how 'the blood-plasm, when healthy, destroys or incapacitates invaders'[10] demonstrate its mythical place as a symbol of purity and guarantor of the health of the race. And in Nazi thanatopolitics, blood is the racial indicator that gives one the right to exist in the category of people: it is 'the ultimate criterion for defining the juridical status of a person'.[11] Subordinated to politics, (human) blood becomes the 'norm of life'[12] and thus the instrument to measure and normalise the life of the population. Vampire texts lay emphasis on the double power of blood as *pharmakon*, carrying within it both the possibility of the cure and the threat of the poison. In this respect, the contagious bad blood of the vampire race might bring the dissolution of the old organic body but also the possibility for a new formation. As René Girard points out, 'Blood serves to illustrate the point that the same substance can stain or cleanse, contaminate or purify, drive men to fury and murder or appease their anger and restore them to life.'[13] Beyond, however, understandings of blood as good or bad, polluting or cleansing, there is also the need to see blood as a neutral and fluid materialisation of life that circulates through, and animates, the bodies of humans and vampires while carrying within it other forms of life such as parasites, bacteria and viruses.

This chapter proposes a historical analysis of blood as a perilous matter polluting individual and collective bodies and spreading disease in vampire literature and film. The examination of the changing ideas about blood and disease reflect fears and anxieties about life itself and its subordination to politics. From the infection of the individual body, to that of nations and the body of the world, vampirism is transformed from being the threat of the plague, to that of biological warfare and bioterrorism. The threat of the individual is progressively imagined as the threat of the vampire multitude, while the visible threat of the diseased vampire and rats is transformed into the invisible and identical threats of infectious disease and bioterrorism that are transforming twenty-first-century neoliberal politics of life into a new politics of military security. What is at issue today is not the threat of losing individual identity or control of one's body, but the transformation of the human race into a monstrous and undifferentiated multitude by biological means.

Here older understandings of infection through blood have also undergone mutations. Today infectious disease is visualised and understood at the molecular level where the causative agent is genotyped. While quarantines, travel restrictions and the policing of space are still operative at the visible level of the body, on the other hand pharmaceutical companies and therapeutic research extend their actions at the molecular level where 'therapeutic agents are selected, manipulated, trialed, and developed, and in molecular terms that their modes of action are explained'.[14] What remains, however, constant is blood as a symbol of life and race and, consequently, the incestuous and lethal comingling of its biopolitical meanings.

The fear of infection that threatens the conflagration of the community mobilises new biopolitical mechanisms for the protection of life. Against the risks of vampiric disease, biopolitics seeks to defend the body of the community by immunising life and erecting new boundaries between self and other. The other—the foreign, the immigrant and the vampire—is the degenerate, the nonhuman, the already dead, whose blood is the breeding ground of contamination. These concerns can be elucidated by the paradigm of immunity that comes to define so eloquently our contemporary horizon. In *Bíos: Biopolitics and Philosophy* (2008), *Immunitas* (2011) and *Terms of the Political: Community, Immunity, Biopolitics* (2013), the Italian philosopher Roberto Esposito's diagnosis of contemporary existence centres around the 'coagulating point' of immunisation and its widespread proliferation to all strata of society: 'Everywhere we look, new walls, new blockades, and new dividing lines are erected against something that threatens, or at least seems to, our biological, social, and environmental identity...The risk of contamination immediately liquidates contact, relationality, and being in common.'[15] Immunisation—the vaccination of the political body with a part of the same pathogen from which it wants to defend itself—is a negative form of the preservation of life that reduces the power of the individual and collective body to develop and expand.[16] While immunisation to a certain degree protects life, when carried to extremes it ends up 'sacrificing every form of qualified life' and reducing life to its bare biological existence, *zoé*.[17] This immunitary logic that permeates the fibres of vampire narratives seeks to block vampiric transformation, difference and growth within a framework of prevention. More particularly, what is at stake in such immunitary procedures is the life of the population. If in order to safeguard life, life itself is vaccinated with the same thing that it wishes to avoid, then life itself is in danger of being crushed and obliterated.[18] In a similar way, the preventive war of contemporary biopolitics turns on the same body that activates it. The weaponised bodies of the vampires in *The Passage*, whose lives are immunised against death but also become the bringers of death, turned against the same community that created them, are fatalities of an obsessive immunisation that negates life itself. In this sense, by subordinating life to politics, the life of the community is destined to destruction and regression.

Vampire plagues

By looking at vampire texts and films which deal with epidemic disease and contagious infections from the nineteenth to the twentieth centuries, I want to show how disease is socially and biologically constructed. Through the analysis of both the medical and social-cultural aspects of disease and, in particular, the role of blood as a carrier of disease and a medium for its dissemination, I want to examine the ways individual and collective bodies and identities are defined and understood.

From the 1500s to the 1770s Europe suffered from various epidemics of the plague. Until the mid-seventeenth century, disease was thought to result from God, influences from the stars and astronomic events; certain people were also believed to be predisposed to disease, because of either their nature or their lifestyle.[19] In the eighteenth century plague was the main disease that physicians examined and thought contagious. Because of the lack of scientific explanations, the epidemics of the plague in the late seventeenth and early eighteenth centuries were often associated with vampirism. In Istria (1672), East Prussia (1710 and 1721), Hungary (1725–30), Austrian Serbia (1725–32), East Prussia (1750), Silesia (1755), Wallachia (1756) and Russia (1772) accounts of vampire epidemics became the source of mass hysteria.[20] One of the explanations for these supernatural accounts, as Christopher Frayling notes, was the epidemic of the plague:

> the symptoms of the victim—pallor, listlessness, fever, nightmares— were thought to be those of the plague.[21] The transmission of the 'vampire's curse' from predator to victim, who then became predator in turn, was a graphic way of explaining the rapid spread of plague

germs. Vampires and rats tended to be close companions in European folklore from an early stage, and there *was* an epidemic of the plague in East Prussia in 1710.[22]

The attempts of contemporary folklorists to understand vampirism and disease of the time are 'attempts by preliterate communities to make sense of what we would today call "contagion"',[23] and are similar to the responses to the AIDS epidemic in post-literate societies.[24]

In the nineteenth century the two dominant epidemiological theories of contagionism and anticontagionism tried to explain the way infectious diseases were transmitted. Contagion theory, which was the dominant view in Western Europe from the sixteenth century, argued that infectious disease was transmitted through human contact by an organism called *contagium animatum* or an animalcule, a microscopic animal that carried the disease. On the other hand, the miasmatic or infectionist theory argued that disease was spread by chemical miasmas originating from unclean conditions. It was the doctrine of contagionism that would triumph at the end of the nineteenth century, and would lead to the germ theory and the establishment of epidemiology as a discipline.

Sheridan Le Fanu's 'Carmilla' (1872) is an expression of the theories of contagious disease prevalent during the nineteenth century, and the ways they relate to a vampiric past that is connected through blood to the present. The novella relates the events in the narrative to the reports about vampire epidemics in the late seventeenth and early eighteenth centuries. While the vampire represents an ancestral past drenched in the diseased blood of aristocracy, the English Laura and her father embody the modern healthy middle class, its mobility and freedom. Their ability to purchase an Austrian feudal residence reveals new possibilities that are no longer dictated by the old privileges of heredity.

At the heart of the epidemic is the miasma of degenerate aristocratic bloodlines. The narrative repeatedly associates contagion with vampirism but also with the infectious nature of information and behaviour. Foreshadowing the theory of the transmission of ideas through imitation, or 'contagions of imitation',[25] that would later be developed by the sociologist Gabriel Tarde, the novella stresses that 'poor people infect one another with their superstitions'[26] while the 'precautions of nervous people are infectious'[27] as Laura begins to imitate Carmilla's habits. The terror of the epidemic, then, is not merely experienced through the real event of disease but also through the contagion of beliefs and stories about infection. While the transmission of infected blood tears the community apart, the transmission of customs and rituals through imitation creates community. The customs of peasants and the folkloric rituals of killing the vampire prove to be stronger than the blood ties of an extinct aristocracy.

The spread of the plague in Styria coincides with the arrival of the vampire Carmilla and her 'ill-looking pack of men'.[28] The diseased countenance of her servants, their 'strangely lean, and dark, and sullen' faces,[29] unveils what lies underneath the 'absolutely beautiful' Carmilla.[30] Like the disease itself that cannot be detected or diagnosed by the doctors, Carmilla's disease is invisible: 'there was nothing in her appearance to indicate an invalid'.[31] As will be examined in Chapter 4, the threat of the vampire, like that of the mulatta, resides in the fact that they both can pass as human and white. However, Carmilla's monstrosity and degenerate nature is glimpsed in images of something other than human: a horrific blackness, a 'black creature' crawling and swelling 'into a great, palpitating mass'[32] and a 'sooty-black animal that resembled a monstrous cat'.[33] Carmilla is not human, but an animal. Racially marked as black and monstrous, her life is inferior to that of humans and thus, dispensable. This is why fears of the possible contamination of race mobilise medical, religious and political authorities.

A passing performer announces how many people 'are dying of it right and left'.[34] As Baron Vordenburg notes, 'It is the nature of vampires to increase and multiply',[35] like pestilence. Symptoms of the plague, such as pallor, fever, lethargy and nightmares, are ascribed in the novella to Laura, Bertha and Carmilla. Laura and Bertha suffer from nightmares, and their spirits and strength wane after their contact with Carmilla. Laura grows pale and languid and, like Carmilla, she complains 'of dreams and feverish sensations'.[36] The strange epidemic is identified as malaria, an Italian term that indicated 'bad air', and which was used interchangeably with miasma to refer to similar diseases.[37] As Carmilla explains to Laura, the charm given to her by the wanderer 'against the oupire'[38] is 'fumigated or immersed in some drug, and is an antidote against the malaria'.[39] Paradoxically, the most scientific explanation of the epidemic disease comes from the vampire Carmilla: 'No, these complaints, wandering in the air, begin by trying the nerves, and so infect the brain, but before they can seize upon you, the antidote repels them. That I am sure is what the charm has done for us. It is nothing magical, it is simply natural.'[40] While Laura's father claims that 'nothing can happen without His permission',[41] Carmilla responds that the disease is natural because 'All things proceed from Nature'.[42]

Avoiding a theological aetiology, Carmilla gives expression to the miasmatic theory of disease and the belief that vapours emanating from marsh miasmatas, decayed animal or vegetable matter and putrid air penetrate the human body and 'vitiate the nutritive properties of the blood and diminish the energies of life'.[43] These poisonous organic or inorganic gases may also be fluids in a gaseous form or corpuscles in the atmosphere. In his 1855 'On Animal Effluvia and their Effects Upon Health' lecturer on physiology at St. Thomas' Hospital, London, R.D. Grainger, points out that animal effluvia can enter the body through blood by inoculation, and through water and air that may contain a volatile substance.[44] He argues that the symptoms witnessed in the dissecting room by anatomy students demonstrate the existence of a poison and are similar to those arising from the exhumation of dead bodies.[45] It is possible to argue that Carmilla infects the community through malarious poisons emanating from her (un)dead body and penetrating the bloodstream when she bites her victims. Ernest Jones states that for many writers vampirism and the plague are commonly associated with stench. The 'horrible stink that invests the Vampire',[46] and which can be linked to necrophilia's anal-erotic origins, is inseparable from the idea of vile filth inherent in the Greek name for vampires. The medieval Greek word for vampire, βουρκόλακας (vourkolakas), originates from the words βούρκο (vourko) and λάκκος (lakos), which refer to black feculent and foul mud and a ditch which reeks of muck, respectively. Bertha and Laura get infected with the disease during Carmilla's stay in their houses. Miasmatic theory associated disease with filthy localities and certain places and, in the narrative, it is the presence of Carmilla within a specific place that causes infection. Similarly, disease is located in the Karnsteins' family tomb where, finally, Carmilla is staked, decapitated and cremated.

It is no coincidence that the plague is here connected to the name Karnstein. It is alleged that in 1422 during the siege of the gothic castle Carolstein or Karlstein in Bohemia the invading forces of Zygmunt Korybutowicz, following medieval tactics of biological warfare, catapulted the decaying and plague-infected corpses of soldiers and cartloads of manure into the castle walls and onto the defenders, where the stench of the mutilated and infested corpses caused an outbreak of fever. The use of biological agents as weapons to spread disease is an ancient strategy and anticipates the horror of contemporary vampire narratives of bioterrorism where the difference between the epidemic disease and the bioweapon becomes indistinguishable. In such cases, life itself is weaponised against the life of the population.

Like the invasion of the castle through the use of weaponised and infected corpses, the plague in 'Carmilla' 'invades' the country through the undead and sick body of the aristocratic vampire. Disease is defined in militaristic language as a 'horrible enemy'[47] that has 'invaded'[48] and 'attacked'[49] the country and its people, while Laura fears 'midnight invaders, and prowling assassins'.[50] In order to immunise the community against the infected blood of the enemy, the vampire needs to be sacrificed. What is sacrificed, however, is not Carmilla herself but what her body and blood represent: the bad and diseased Karnstein lineage. The extermination of the Karnstein plague becomes the remedy of the community. Reduced to a mere vessel bearing the name Karnstein, the body of the vampire is finally released to a death that was already part of her life and was threatening to infect the life of the whole community. The ritualistic stake through the heart, decapitation and burning of the victim then function as the object and the instrument of the cure. In his reading of Dracula's 'salvific death', Roberto Esposito shows that his killing, like that of millions of 'other vampires fifty years later', 'means freeing not only those whom he threatens, but also himself, giving him finally back to that death to which he belongs and which he carries within him without being able to taste it'.[51] No longer 'something black'[52] and half-dead, Carmilla is finally offered to the sacred fire of death.

With the consent of the law and the presence of two medical men, Carmilla's exhumed and burned body is an immunitary procedure and a 'pious sacrilege' to 'relieve our earth of certain monsters'.[53] The theological language of politics transforms the medical men into priests with the divine right to choose the unworthy life to be condemned to death. As the old woodman explains to the General, the extermination of revenants by decapitation, stake and burning were 'proceedings according to law',[54] and Carmilla's death is performed according to these 'formal proceedings'[55] and verified by an official report signed 'judicially, before commissions innumerable'.[56] The bad blood of aristocratic heredity is banished from a community that is now based on its shared preoccupation with health and race.

Like Carmilla, Dracula's infected and degenerate body is associated with animality: 'That horrid thing has the wolves and the rats and his own kind to help him.'[57] Metaphors of disease are present in the manifestation of the packs of rats[58] that follow the Count and which he has the power to command. But Dracula's potential connection to disease is made clearer in F.W. Murnau's German Expressionist film *Nosferatu* (1922) where the vampire Count Orlok is associated with the spread of epidemics and pestilence. The name Nosferatu is possibly related to the Greek word *nosoforos*, which means 'plague-bearer'. Count Orlok brings the bubonic plague to Bremen in a ship swarming with rats.[59] Unlike Dracula, Count Orlok resembles a corpse, and his long fingernails and fangs recall the characteristics of rats rather than of humans. The epidemic of vampirism is linked to the influenza pandemic of 1918 which lasted for two years and is considered among the deadliest in history. The pandemic spread particularly among the young and healthy, unlike most influenza epidemics that usually affect the weak and elderly, and was facilitated by modern transportation and infection by travellers and sailors. In *Nosferatu* the idea of contagion and epidemic, the proliferation of dangerous identities through the packs of rats, and the traffic and blending of blood between native and foreign bodies demonises the mobile nature of the racial other.[60] Whereas in 'Carmilla' blood is symbolic of a stagnant and rotting aristocracy, in *Nosferatu* blood demarcates the racial limits between German purity and the plague-infested nature of the vampire.

The resemblance of Count Orlok to caricatures of Jews in Julius Streicher's Nazi newspaper *Der Stürmer* (1923–45), for example the stereotypical hooked nose, materialistic nature, misshapen physical appearance and Machiavellian character, themselves deriving from medieval prejudices, cannot be overlooked. In addition, the presence of the Jewish innkeeper in Orlok's Carpathian castle, and the use of crosses on the doors as protection from the disease, are evidence linking the vampire to traditional anti-Semitic prejudices.[61] The figure of the other as a wandering parasite,[62] carrying disease and vermin, will be the subject matter of many anti-Semitic films such as Fritz Hippler's pseudo-documentary *The Eternal Jew* (1940) and Veit Harlan's *Jew Süss* (1940).

Thus, Count Orlok's death and the end of the plague are made possible through Ellen Hutter's German purity and blood. The film clarifies that 'only a woman can break the frightful spell—a woman pure in heart—who will offer her blood freely to Nosferatu and will keep the vampire by her side until after the cock has crowed'. In the film vampirism carries none of the erotic elements of Dracula's bite. In the last scene, however, an eroticised aura surrounds Ellen's offering of her pure blood to the vampire. Within this context, the sacrifice of her blood is fetishised because it establishes the limits: the prophecy is fulfilled, and Ellen's offering of her pure blood restores order and destroys the threatening other.

While in 'Carmilla' the diseased blood of an ancient aristocracy is wiped out with the death of the vampire, and the diseased blood of the racial other is conquered by the pure blood of the good German housewife Ellen, in Richard Matheson's *I Am Legend*, on the other hand, the mutated bacteria residing in the blood of living vampires have produced a new order of *bios*. Robert Neville is the last man on earth, the last remnant of a past humanity, after an epidemic that has transformed humans into two different types of vampires: those who are dead and those still living, infected humans who did not die. Bitten by an infected vampire bat during the war in Panama, Neville is immune to the infectious disease. However, this immunisation—both in its medical and its juridical meanings—is a negative form of protection that isolates him from the bonds of community. Placed outside of any circulation and shielded from the dangers that affect both the human and the vampire communities, Neville remains other to both worlds. The novel unsettles and undermines the dichotomies of 'us and them', normal and abnormal, black and white. The question is no longer that between the qualified life of the human and the bare life of the vampire, but also about new forms of qualified life born out of the filthy germs of epidemic disease. While immunisation liquidates community, epidemic disease germinates new forms of being in common.

Blood becomes the medium of scientific inquiry through Neville's examination of medical texts and use of the microscope to identify the germ. The mutation of the germ in the blood of the living vampires has created a new biological species of vampires who have managed to prevent the development of the germ through the invention of a new pill, while at the same time organising themselves into a new society. Neville, the embodiment of American individuality, is set against a collective of vampires who have set new rules and are creating a new state based on their different blood. Blood is the biological means that establishes the norm. While in the beginning Neville's 'normal' human blood is set against the 'abnormal' blood of all vampires, later his and the vampires' blood becomes the marker of abnormality and racial inferiority that subjects them to the living vampires' norm. Blood is then both a biological and a political instrument.

The novel touches upon this difference of blood to convey the reality of a new biopolitical order, where a different political knowledge and the use of biology govern the collective of the still-living vampires. Through new regulatory methods of normalisation, exclusion, therapeutics and optimisation, the new regime of bio-vampire-politics is reorganising social life. This organisation involves not only the optimisation of the new life, but the exclusion of the last human, Neville. Despite his desperate attachment to the history contained in his family house, and to a nostalgic past, he dies alone as the last of his kind.

Matheson's novel is exemplary in its introduction of vampirism as a biological threat in the form of a bacterium. According to Neville, 'Certain kinds of bacilli, when conditions became unfavorable for life, were capable of creating, from themselves, bodies called spores' and 'when conditions were more favorable for survival, the spore germinated again.'[63] The medical language to describe the vampiric disease conjures up that of the founder of bacteriology, Ferdinand Julius Cohn, and his prediction that anthrax bacilli could form bacterial spores. Neville's notes and inoculation experiments also resonate with those used by Robert Koch in his discovery of the bacterium *Bacillus anthracis* that caused anthrax. In his 'The Etiology of Anthrax, Founded on the Course of Development of the Bacillus Anthracis' (1876), Koch asks: 'How could such perishable organisms remain contagious through an entire winter or remain dormant in damp soil for several years?'[64] For him, the proof that the bacteria cause anthrax lies in the possibility that they 'form spores that have the capacity, after a longer or shorter period of dormancy, to grow into new bacteria'.[65] Matheson's bacteriological horror and its connections to the anthrax bacteria invoke the 2001 anthrax attacks and the biological terror of post-September 11 vampire fictions.

The biopolitics of the new vampire state is concerned with the multiplicity of living vampires understood as a biological organism affected by the vampire germ and which needs to be protected from internal dangers.[66] In this respect, after the vampire epidemic biopolitics, as an apparatus of security, will intervene to normalise through a pill. While Neville's failed attempts consist in vaccinating vampires with antibiotics, the living vampires' discovery of the pill succeeds in preventing the multiplication of the germs at the same time as feeding them. The equivalence of the use of science by both the vampires and Neville reveals his dominating medical gaze. Puncturing the arms of dead vampires or cutting the wrists of the still-living vampires, Neville sees, isolates, compares and recognises the ways the germ feeds on the blood, and the ways it can be controlled through haemorrhage or the medium of the air. For him, the diagnosis of the germ becomes a way to experiment ruthlessly on objectified bodies: 'when you cut their wrists the germ naturally becomes parasitic. But mostly they die from simple hemorrhage. "*Simple—*".'[67] He sees his bloody treatment of bodies as a 'natural fact'[68] disengaged from the identity and feelings of vampires. For the vampire Ruth, who is living proof that pills exist, Neville's blatant disregard for the 'humanity' of the vampire body is a 'horrible' reality.[69]

While vampire biopolitics seeks to protect the living vampires, on the other hand racist modes intervene to legitimise killing those subraces that threaten the life of the living vampires. As the living vampire Ruth, whom Neville encounters, clarifies:

> We *are* infected. But you already know that. What you don't understand yet is that we're going to stay alive. We've found a way to do that and we're going to set up society again slowly but surely. We're going to do away with all those wretched creatures whom death has cheated. And, even though I pray otherwise, we may decide to kill you and those like you.[70]

The infected humans seek to improve their race by killing the enemy race: ' "That's exactly why we're killing" ... [Ruth] said calmly. "To survive. We can't allow the dead to exist beside the living. Their brains are impaired, they exist for only one purpose. They have to be destroyed." '[71] Under the Soviet State racism, those who did not agree with its ideology were deemed biologically dangerous, 'sick', 'deviant' or mad and removed from society;[72] *I Am Legend* offers a similar model of racism, where Neville and the true vampires are considered biologically dangerous to the new society of living vampires and are eliminated. Defined as 'wretched creatures', physically 'impaired', dead or biologically dangerous, both the living dead and Neville are not qualified as members of the new race.

In a similar way, Neville believes that his own race is the true race that is entitled to define the norm and to exterminate 'those who deviate from that norm' and 'pose a threat to the biological heritage'.[73] Incapable of differentiating among the different species of living and dead vampires, Neville treats all of them as a biological scourge that needs to be excluded and eliminated. Against Neville's normality, the abnormal vampires are unnamed, referred to as 'filthy bastards',[74] 'dogs',[75] 'dull, robot-like creatures'[76] 'snarling and fighting among themselves',[77] merely motivated by their need for blood.[78] In particular, the vampires are imagined as 'black bastards'.[79] Neville justifies his 'callous brutality' against the vampires by choosing not to see that 'these people were the same as he'.[80] They are monsters that would kill him gladly if they could, for Neville claims: 'You've got to look at it that way, it's the only way.'[81]

The threat of vampirism and infection is of course that of a Communist invasion. The novel's exploration of vampirism as a disease caused by Cold War germ warfare and infecting America resonates with the biopolitical lexicon of the Cold War era.[82] George Kennan, a senior American Diplomat in Moscow, in his famous 'Long Telegram' on 2 February 1946 described the communist dogma as 'bearing within itself germs of creeping disease'.[83] And in his testimony delivered before HUAC in 1947,[84] J. Edgar Hoover, the director of the Federal Bureau of Investigation, said that 'Communism, in reality, is not a political party, it is a way of life—an evil and malignant way of life. It reveals a condition akin to disease that spreads like an epidemic and like an epidemic a quarantine is necessary to keep it from infecting the Nation.'[85]

However, when he is finally the haunted animal, Neville can see the 'methodical butchery' of vampires was that of 'gangsters'[86] and 'brutal strangers'.[87] As Ruth explains, they are young and fallible,[88] no worse or better than Neville. Blood, then, is spilled for a new state that is different from, but no worse or better than, the older one. Blood defines the limits of the new state as well as the identity of the new species.

I Am Legend is unique in the ways it deals with contagion and vampirism as the source of innovation in evolution. The contained epidemic creates the conditions for the creation of new forms of life and community. In attempting to move beyond the human condition, the novella presents a form of germinal life as the result of unnatural couplings between bacteria and human beings. The symbiosis of the germ and the human reveals an understanding of germs not as 'disease-causing' but as 'life-giving entities'.[89] While infectious bacteria are considered as the agents of disease and embody the image of the virulent other to be destroyed, they are also responsible for the planet's life and the genesis of the new. According to molecular biologists Lynn Margulis and Dorion Sagan, 'there is no denying our kinship to this sort of living matter. Humans are integrated colonies of ameboid beings, just as ameboid beings—protoctists—are integrated colonies of bacteria. Like it or not, we come from slime.'[90] The human species and bacteria then share a strong symbiotic relationship: 'Life is the strange new fruit of individuals evolved by symbiosis. Swimming, conjugating, bargaining, and dominating, bacteria living in intimate associations during the Proterozoic gave rise to myriad chimeras, mixed beings, of which we represent a tiny fraction of an expanding progeny.'[91] In *I Am Legend* the human does not survive the epidemic as an indestructible and all-wise being, but as a new mutation born out of infection with a vampiric bacterium. It is through contagion and symbiosis that new and unexpected transformations occur. The deadly bacterium becomes a vital part of the new vampire species. The incorporation of the permanent disease of the vampiris germ not only shows that the origins of life are in slime and bacteria, but also poses a challenge to anthropocentric views of life.

Vampiric viruses and AIDS

While the nineteenth century associated vampirism and blood with the epidemics of the plague, and the 1950s with political and technological threat, 1980s vampire narratives focussed on AIDS.[92] The official use of the acronym AIDS is traced back to July 1982, after two meetings of the US Public Health Service about the rise of the new disease. In the first meeting Dr Bruce Evatt, specialist in haemophilia at the Centers for Disease Control and Prevention (CDC), pointed towards the possible spread of this disease, then known as GRID,[93] through blood. In the second meeting the participants decided on the surveillance of the disease, which they named Acquired Immune Deficiency Syndrome, or AIDS.[94] The reality of bodies suffering and dying of AIDS was soon captured in literature. The first novel[95] with an AIDS-related theme was Dorothy Bryant's *A Day in San Francisco*[96] (1982), published before the disease was given a name. However, Paul Reed's *Facing It* (1984) is considered the first AIDS novel as its central theme is the epidemic. The association of vampirism with AIDS in literature and film came at the end of the 1980s and in the early 1990s. In 1991 and 1992, the publication of vampire novels such as Brian Aldiss' *Dracula Unbound*, Dan Simmons' *Children of the Night*, Patrick Whalen's *Night Thirst*, and Jewelle Gomez's *The Gilda Stories* focussed on AIDS, sickness and corrupted blood through the portrayal of diseased vampires (*Dracula Unbound*), vampires aware of feeding on infected blood (*The Gilda Stories*) or vampires offering a cure for AIDS (*Night Thirst*, *Children of the Night*).

Nicola Nixon argues that Tony Scott's film *The Hunger* (1983),[97] although filmed and released at the beginning of the AIDS epidemic, only one year after the first use of the acronym, can be seen as an allegory of AIDS.[98] In Whitley Strieber's *The Hunger* (1981) allusions to AIDS are evident in the viral language and bad blood. On the other hand, Kathryn Bigelow's *Near Dark* and Joel Schumacher's *The Lost Boys* (1987) postdate the AIDS pandemic, but lack any references to the disease. Both of the films eschew any undesirable commentary on AIDS, retaining the body of American ideals intact and inviolable within celluloid limits.

The association of vampirism with HIV/AIDS lies in their similar nature and propagation through infection. Like the vampire, the virus occupies the ambiguous border between the living and the non-living, and challenges life itself and the tidy separation of the organic and the inorganic. Unable to generate energy or synthesise protein, the virus is not truly alive: 'Living and dead, biological and informational, ethereal and material, natural and artificial', the virus is 'a set of contradictions that can kill.'[99] In a state of suspended animation, virus particles wait for a living cell which they can infect in order to replicate themselves.[100] In this sense, like vampires, viruses cannot reproduce on their own, but require a host which they can infect. After the host cell is invaded and infected it usually disintegrates and dies, while several hundred viruses may be released, abandoning the cell and looking for a new host. In other cases, the virus might fail to infect the host cell and remain within it in a non-replicating mode, or the infected host cell might manage to survive. The vampire and HIV virus then invade a living host through the dangerous circulation of sexual fluids and blood, and reproduce themselves after infecting it. In the following vampire narratives, the inside of the body and blood become the sight of an exhaustive biopolitics that seeks to regulate and contain disease, while marking certain bodies as scientific aberrations, monstrous or diseased.

Vampire texts, in order to make sense of the infection, attempt to frame it within familiar narratives that render it meaningful while inventing ways for its control. Imagined as a foreign primitive virus that invades the modern body politic, HIV is connected to earlier viruses and epidemics that describe the disease in militaristic language while stigmatising its victims as 'enemies within', penetrating and spreading pollution. The Cold War language of sinister invaders is again reanimated with renewed vehemence. Replicating the medical language to define AIDS, these vampire narratives focus on the illicit sexual circulations of blood and virus as they threaten individual and national boundaries, and scientific authority. Blood as a carrier of a promiscuous virus becomes a symbol of criminal sex, while its violence reflects colonial invasion. The contagion of HIV/AIDS in vampire narratives is represented through epidemics associated with the emergence of primitive viruses originating in foreign places such as Africa. The virus justifies scientific exploitation and affirms science's authority against the diseased primitivism of the viral other.

One of the first novels to associate vampirism with AIDS is Brian Stableford's *The Empire of Fear* (1988). Beginning in the seventeenth century and culminating in the 1980s, *The Empire of Fear* traces a history of blood and vampirism, their supernatural origins and their final medicalisation. By juxtaposing two different societies, one based on the blue blood of vampires and the other one based on the norm of vampirism, Stableford's novel offers a critique of the ways vampirism is manipulated by two different powers. In sovereignty, the aristocrats feed off the lower classes; in biopower, the regulation of the vampire life of the population marginalises the human race and treats it as weak and sick.

The associations of vampirism with disease, semen, and blood, and the fact that it has been disseminated through the European vampires' 'unorthodox sexual intercourse',[101] allow the substitution of vampirism for sexually transmitted disease and AIDS. On the one hand, vampirism is spread carelessly by Europeans, but on the other hand, its origins are traced back to the African vampires who have 'created Ogbone, and a race of castrated ancients, and set their faces against the very possibility of progress'.[102] The novel echoes the conventions of the AIDS narrative where the primitive 'African' virus is spread through the sexual networks of European mobility. Disease is rooted in a barbaric and diseased past of African rituals and superstitions, 'as if HIV were a disease of "African-ness" '.[103]

But the connections of vampirism to AIDS are also manifested in medical knowledge, so that the inside of the body becomes the 'colonised' locus where sperms reproduce and spread infection. Michael Southerne explains how, 'Once having colonized the host body, the transformed sperms undergo some kind of crucial change which enables them to produce packets of DNA—including replicates of themselves—wrapped up in a protein coat. These metaviruses operate to make the cell better able to repair itself, and resistant to damage.'[104] The vampire virus replicates the mechanisms of the AIDS virus. Dr Robert Gallo, who in 1984 discovered the virus that caused AIDS, explained that it 'belonged to a family of pathogens called "retroviruses"... rather than kill their host cells directly, these furtive micro-organisms insert their own genetic code into the host's so that it reproduces more of the agent that infected it'.[105] In a similar medical language, *The Empire of Fear* describes the reproduction of vampire viruses in the organism with the difference that they strengthen the immune system. In its inversion of the devastating effects of AIDS, the novel normalises the disease in order to render it perversely sterile. With the total extirpation of the threat of infection, vampirism becomes biologically transparent.

Under the microscope of technological scrutiny vampirism is understood as the transformation of a human into a 'finished' being. The increasing medicalisation and scientific understanding of vampirism leads to the pathologisation of humanity as an aberrant condition. Through the intervention of biotechnology, vampirism becomes a universally valid biological model, a standard which determines whether one's body is biologically 'finished', normal or not.[106] If in the past sovereignty was exercised by the aristocracy, here bioscientists are transformed into the priests of life, administering the right of vampirism. In this respect, through normalisation, vampire identity becomes identical.

Within the new regime of biopower, vampirism becomes the new *status quo* and the norm. Like Matheson's *I Am Legend*, humanity in *The Empire of Fear* is marginalised as an inferior biological condition. The new vampire order, however, does not exterminate otherness, but marks human bodies as weak and sick, imperfect and abnormal. In the novel, as otherness is defined by the human condition, a fundamental line is drawn between the human, frail body and the youthful, physical perfection of the immortal body. The lack of vampirism is seen as a disability, as exemplified by the character of Michael Southerne who is referred to as a 'commoner' and not a 'finished' man, suffering from a damaged leg and a cancerous tumour.

If in Stableford's novel the HIV virus imprisons life within the specific norm of vampirism, in Michael Romkey's *The Vampire Virus* (1997) it colonises and exploits the lifeblood of the body politic. Medical language becomes the topos where anxieties about transgression of boundaries and penetration of the body by a parasitical organism act out the sexual implications of the vampire's kiss. The phallic virus transgresses the limits of the inside and outside of female bodies, penetrating and polluting their pure blood. Metaphors of bodily penetration proliferate; the unearthing of the ancient city of Zonatitucan in Costa Rica by the archaeologist Dr Janis Levy, and her mysterious death caused by a vampire virus, introduce the theme of invasion and the exploitation of native soil. The land of Zonatitucan is a unified, isolated topos that is trespassed by the other, the Spanish conquistadors, and later western scientists. In a similar way, the bodily limits are transgressed by a virus that enters the bodies, pollutes and exploits them. The vampire Lazaro describes it as 'predatory' and Dr Bailey as vampiric.[107]

When Dr Bailey is finally infected with the virus by the bite of a vampire bat, the description of the invasion of the virus into her bloodstream is coloured with disturbingly sexual undertones:

> She could *feel* the virus moving through her system now, crawling inside her arteries like ants, penetrating her capillaries, puncturing cell walls, methodically violating them one at a time, serpentine alien DNA strands corkscrewing their way into the nuclei of her cells. It was the cytological equivalent of being raped—again and again, cell by cell, microscopic assailants penetrating her genetic code with their poison seed.[108]

This explicitly violent pseudo-medical language replaces the eroticised overtones of the vampire's kiss. This, as it is clear, is intended to be understood as a cellular rape and not a mystical seduction.

The penetration of the human body by the virus reflects the violation of the body politic by a foreign power: 'The Zona escaped the conquistadors only to have a virus conquer them.'[109] The theme of colonisation is also entangled with population genomics and the harvesting of biological materials from Third World countries, which is a form of biocolonialism. Dr Harrison is an epidemiologist at the Centers for Disease Control (CDC) in Atlanta, USA. The name of the CDC is closely related to significant discoveries and research projects about blood. The CDC were established during World War II to examine malaria, and had been successful in the prevention of smallpox and polio in the US. The researchers were among the first to investigate the spread of AIDS and reveal the dangers concerned with blood contamination and supplies. In the 1990s the CDC were also related to a blood scandal. It is possible that the text alludes here to a power discourse that involves bioscience, capital and exploitation of indigenous people's blood. Donna Haraway shows that in 1990 the CDC took the blood from a 26-year-old Guaymi woman with leukaemia, which was later exploited to create an 'immortalised' cell line to be added at the American Type Culture Collection.[110] The American organisation not only avoided explaining to the indigenous people the impact of their blood sampling, but also tried to benefit from the project. In a similar way, the Human Genome Diversity Project (HGDP) was characterised by indigenous organisations as a 'vampire project'.[111] The project was seen sceptically by indigenous groups because it involved questions concerned with the people's agency and representation, and sought to profit from their genes without offering any gain to the populations.[112] As Eugene Thacker points out, 'If colonialism historically involved the forced or coerced appropriation of people, land, and economy, *bio*colonialism presents us with a situation in which the bodies of the colonized *are* the land and economy.'[113] This is reflected in *The Vampire Virus* by Dr Bailey's intrusion. When she arrives in Costa Rica she tries to get blood samples from the Indians to build a database, but as she explains, 'They were a little hostile to the idea, to say the least. For a while I thought they were going to be taking blood samples from *me*.'[114] The novel explores the ways scientific knowledge and bioscientific research can disturb the social life of indigenous people, whose beliefs are based on 'superstition' and 'rituals'. Douglas Starr gives an example of how Tanganyikans in Africa feared having 'their soul put into a bottle' because they interpreted the Red Cross workers' attempt to get blood samples as the work of blood-drinkers who invaded their land and wanted to drink their blood.[115] Blood harvesting and sampling involves ethical questions about indigenous people's informed consent for the appropriation and the use of their biological material.

However, biomedicine is not eventually denounced in the novel and is viewed in a positive light. Lazaro confides in Dr Bailey: 'I owe you a very great debt of thanks. Your modern understanding has made it possible for me to think of myself as a scientific curiosity, rather than as a monster.'[116] Scientific research illuminates the mystery of vampirism and demonstrates that it is the virus that gives immortality, and not the superstitious rituals of the Zonas. Assumptions about the primitivism and superstitious rituals of isolated people perpetuate the belief in US intervention in the Third World as a diseased primitive place that needs modernisation. In this respect, what is celebrated here is the heroic epidemiologist and scientific authority that succeeds in civilising the image of the primitive other from a monster to 'scientific curiosity'.

These vampire narratives uncover prejudices, social inequalities and the untold stories of all those who remain excluded from the privileges of white people. The reproduction of the conventional narrative of the presumed African origins of HIV, as well as the fear of vampiric viruses threatening to transform 'us' into 'them', are indicative of a myopic view that regurgitates an immunitary logic and which obsessively seeks to contain disease by demonising the other. On the other hand, the use of HIV as a vampiric virus challenges the familiar scenario of contagion by the racially impure enemy in order to question different forms of 'vampiric invasion' such as biocolonialism or biotechnological interventions in the body that reshape one's somatic identity, while at the same time excluding others as 'unfinished'.

Infectious disease and bioterrorism after 11 September 2001

> The enemy was inside his circulatory system, spreading throughout his organs and wriggling inside his brain.[117]

Like earlier catastrophes and epidemics, the experience of the September 11 attacks on the World Trade Center generated narratives that seek to integrate the events within a historical framework, linking them with other historical events and inventing analogies.[118] Slavoj Žižek notes that immediately after the bombings, 'in these moments of utmost tension', there 'are already the first bad omens' of how the event will be symbolised: the Cold War term 'free world' is resurrected and the 'old division between the Western liberal-democratic countries and all the others is again enforced'.[119] Vampire novels such as Elizabeth Kostova's

The Historian (2005), Justin Cronin's *The Passage*, John Marks' *Fangland*, and Guillermo del Toro and Chuck Hogan's *The Strain, The Fall,* and *The Night Eternal* (2011) are texts that either rework the opposition between West and East, 'us and them' (*Historian; Fangland*), or place the narrative within the pattern of rise and fall, reminiscent of the American cyclical theory of history, evident in post-Cold War narratives such as Matheson's *I Am Legend* (also *The Passage*). In a similar vein, del Toro and Hogan's the Strain Trilogy creates analogies between the vampire pandemic and other historical calamities, such as the holocaust, and Nazi politics, which are facilitated by the power and amoral logic of capitalism.

Unlike in *The Historian*, vampirism in the rest of these vampire novels is presented as the threat of bioterrorism. The terrorist attacks of September 11 and the anthrax attacks that followed seven days later brought national security, public health and the danger of biological weapons to the fore. The anthrax letter attacks[120] of September and October 2001 are considered to be the only successful attempt of third-generation biological warfare.[121] The seven envelopes containing a dry powder of *B. anthracis* spores were sent to two Senators and to the media: American Media International (AMI), the editor of the *New Work Post*, and NBC, CBS and ABC News.[122] Five died and many others were infected, while the cost of decontamination is estimated at $6 billion.[123] The FBI, following evidence found at the United States Army Medical Research Institute for Infectious Diseases (USAMRIID) at Fort Detrick, Maryland, determined that its main suspect was microbiologist and anthrax vaccine researcher Bruce E. Ivins, working in its own laboratories. In addition, the FBI discovered that all samples of the Ames strain of *B. anthracis* could be traced back to a container stored at USAMRIID.[124] This led to the resolution of a national defence strategy against bioterrorism by the Bush administration in 2004, and the approval of funding for biodefence research, called Project BioShield.[125] Infectious disease epidemics and bioterrorism were now considered 'identical threats',[126] with the potential to infect and disintegrate the body politic. As Melinda Cooper notes, for 'U.S. defense, it seems, the frontier between warfare and public health, microbial life and bioterrorism, had become strategically indifferent'.[127] What the Bush administration has achieved is 'the actual institutional conflation of security and public health research, military strategy, environmental politics, and the innovation economy'.[128] War will no longer be waged in the defence of the state, but 'in *the name of life in its biospheric dimension*'.[129] This kind of preemptive warfare results in a permanent state of war, as if war were *'a fact of life'*.[130]

By examining post-September 11 vampire texts through the lens of bioterrorism, the intention is to show the differences between the older notions of infectious disease, analysed in the previous sections, and the transformation of those theories of disease in the twenty-first century. The argument proposed here is that anxieties about the violation of one's body and loss of identity are associated with the life of the population as a species which is endangered from within, by biological and political orchestrated operations or experiments. On the one hand, the focus falls on the growing power of biomedicine, the military, technology and capitalism to control and determine the life and future of the human race. On the other hand, these texts remain concerned with blood and race. The vampire and biological threat originate from the outside, in the form of the foreign and uncivilised other, or as an incarnation of racism, carrying in its blood a history of blood shed in the name of race.

The Passage expresses anxieties about the militarisation of science, which results in the spread of the vampire virus within America, and the unethical application of biomedicine. A team of scientists, guided by Jonas Abbott Lear from the Department of Molecular and Cellular Biology, are sent to the uninhabited jungles of La Paz, Bolivia, to investigate a vampire virus. Here, as in *The Vampire Virus*, a Third World country is identified as the origin of disease, while being penetrated by American bioscientists who want to appropriate its natural resources. Jonas' team is financed by USAMRIID, which also dispatches military support to Bolivia. As he points out, 'it looks like we've been militarized'.[131] In retrospect, the presence of the army reveals their interest in the vampire virus which Colonel Sykes explains is significant, as it can heal soldiers so fast that they can keep fighting 'for God and country'.[132] In order to achieve this, the army decides to use death row inmates as human test subjects. The army's experiments extend to include 300 monkeys, dogs, pigs and homeless people, who end up dead.[133] Those who are deemed inferior—death row inmates (including the African American Anthony Carter), the poor and the homeless—are sacrificed for America's foreign policy. The animalisation of the humans reveals a *zoopolitics* that reduces life to its bare minimum. Here it is demonstrated that while America is waging war against Iraq, Russia and other countries, it also does so against its own racial and class minorities. And it is this war of unequals that will be replicated in the apocalyptic days of the vampire epidemic. Carter and those reified humans turned vampires, will still be defined as inferior creatures, without souls, and referred to as 'smokes'.[134] The monster is imagined as black, without identity, and a slave to its hunger for blood.

It is possible to argue that the novel's portrayal of scientific research financed by USAMRIID, and its fatal results, reflects the real-world perils of USAMRIID's practices which resulted in the anthrax letter attacks in 2001. As Eileen Choffnes in 'Bioweapons: New Labs, More Terror?' and Nick Shwellenbach in 'Biodefense: A Plague of Researchers' show, biodefence research increases the possibilities of biological terrorism since it enables new scientists to access, produce and disseminate such bacteria. For Paul Virilio, 'The accident is the new form of warfare',[135] because the invention of new technologies opens the possibility for a new catastrophe. In the novel Jonas' scientific research is used in the service of military interests, and also against America's minorities. With the vampire virus, humans would become 'weaponized. Think of the American Way as something *truly* long-term. As in *permanent*.'[136] In *The Passage* the hubris of military strategy, facilitated by medical experiments, does not lead to a permanent war between 'Us and Them, between the Haves and the Have-Nots', but to a permanent war of another kind: a war which was 'metastasizing like a million maniac cells run amok across the planet, and everyone was in it'.[137] The enemy is no longer other nations or terrorists, but biological life turned against life itself.

Unlike *I Am Legend* and other vampire novels examined earlier, where the introduction of the bacterium or virus in the organism is the result of contact between bodies and infection through blood, the virus in *The Passage* is first introduced through biological experiments by scientists themselves. From the level of the organic body as a whole, where infection is seen through flows of blood, we have moved to a politics of life at a molecular level. Controlled within the laboratory, the virus is not considered a disease, but is thought to enhance human biological capacities, creating a superhuman organism immune to disease and age. However, with the vampires' escape from the military laboratories, the virus is uncontrolled and creates a devastating epidemic. Within the laboratory, science exercises its power, examining the development of the virus, while outside of this closed space the consequences of the epidemic are counteracted by the regulatory control of the population in order to prevent the spread of the virus: the infected are being shot, while others are held within quarantine zones. Biomedicine and the military seek to control, manage, engineer and reshape the very essence of human beings as living creatures, with all the fatal consequences of such a murderous operation. Life is reduced to bare life without any rights or qualifications.[138] The manipulation of the living creatures' biological constitution with the virus, consequently, results in their loss of identity. Significantly, what is breached here is the border between healing and murder, between strengthening the life of the population and killing those infected humans that endanger that same life. Biopolitics, then, is reversed into its opposite—a thanatopolitics turned against its own body.

In *The Passage* the traumatic consequences of the militarisation of scientific experiments are counteracted by religious symbolism and biblical revivalism connected to the regeneration of history. The novel resuscitates the eighteenth-century cyclical theory of history of American culture, of a cycle of birth, maturity and decline where civilisations reach their zenith, become corrupted and die. The vision of America as a 'redeemer nation',[139] and of Thomas Jefferson's idea of the 'chosen people of God',[140] characteristic of the literature of American mythology, depended on the idea of apocalypse. As John Greville Agard Pocock writes, American apocalypse 'has been envisaged in the form of a movement out of history, followed by a regenerative return to it, so that there have been perpetuated in American thinking those patterns of messianic and cyclical thought'.[141] The infection of the republic was a necessary outcome for virtue to last and rebirth to follow. The epidemic is then an act of God, but one that calls for a new initiative of humanitarian regeneration where scientific progress and military policies are not pursued at the expense of human life.

While in *The Passage* vampirism is propagated by the inhuman use of a militarised science within the boundaries of the US, in del Toro and Hogan's The Strain Trilogy the vampire arrives from Germany at JFK airport. The virus is traced back to Nazi Germany and the extermination camp of Treblinka in Poland where the Master vampire Sardu fed on the blood of Jewish prisoners. In addition, while in *The Passage* bioterrorism is the result of the alignment of biomedicine with the military, in *The Strain*, *The Fall* and *The Night Eternal* bioterrorism and biomedicine align themselves with capitalism. The Master vampire makes a deal with Palmer, an investor and businessman, in Chernobyl, while the Centers for Disease Control (CDC) are compromised following Palmer's orders (*The Fall*). He brings the Master vampire to America, and thus facilitates the spread of the virus, which becomes a 'worldwide pandemic. An extinction event.'[142] Bioterrorism creates a new order informed by the logic of global capitalism and Nazi vampires to control the subjugated hordes of an inferior race: humanity.

Del Toro and Hogan's novels comment on the ways capitalism facilitates the destruction of humanity by chaotically spreading the *'unclean strain'*[143] and violating the equilibrium between humans and vampires,

threatening to expose the ancients' existence and cause ecological disaster. The vampire pandemic unsettles the ecosystem with the mass
exodus of rats from the bowels of the city and updates the associations of vampiric disease with vermin reminiscent of *Dracula* and
Nosferatu. In *The Strain*, however, the rats are not accomplices, but fugi-
tives. For the vampire hunter Setrakian, the rats 'are a sign' and an
'ecological symptom',[144] 'their appearance always coinciding with the
spreading sickness and the corruption of souls'.[145] Rats here herald evil
by equivalence: 'vampires are vermin—an infestation spreading quickly
throughout the city'.[146] The exodus of rats is then a harbinger of the
physical and spiritual corruption of humanity linked to the perverse
and inhuman alliance of capital and evil vampiric powers.

The new vampire order reproduces the inequalities of the capitalist
system. For Palmer, all institutions are obedient to capitalism: 'As with
any bureaucratic institution—say, for instance, the CDC—once you seize
control of the top, the rest of the organization simply follows orders.'[147]
Similarly, he believes that humanity is 'already subservient, and fully
programmed for subjugation',[148] and that humans 'will accept any system, any order, that promises them the illusion of security.'[149] Under
the threatening conditions of bioterrorism, Palmer is confident that his
own ambition will be fulfilled: 'I will be exalted somewhat. Even at the
next stage, there has to be a class system, you know. And I have been
promised a seat at the very top.'[150] In this class hierarchy, Master Sardu
will preside along with Palmer, after his vampire transformation and
the extermination of the rest of the ancients. The second class will consist of the vampires Sardu has bitten—the first-generation vampires; and
the lower class—the second-generation vampires—will comprise those
who were bitten by first-generation vampires (and others infected by
the virus the second night after the plane landing). The new vampire reality is based on a hierarchical system that categorises vampires
according to what strain of the virus they carry in their blood. Similarly, the blood camps establish a *'system of biological castes: the* strigoi
favored B positive'.[151] Resonating with the Nazi belief that different blood
groups proved the existence of superior and inferior races, *The Night
Eternal* shows how 'B positives were the slaves that were more equal
than the others'.[152] While B positives were 'pampered, given benefits
and nutrients', to improve the quality of blood and guarantee frequent
bloodletting and breeding, the 'non-B's were the workers, the farmers,
the true grunts'.[153]

Indeed, the vampire state is based on the establishment of a blood
supply system. The classless, subjugated masses of humanity will be

controlled in 'military-style' concentration camps[154] that will function as 'Human stockyards. Blood farms spread out across the country, the world.'[155] Nazism and capitalism combine their common lust for blood and power in inventing new and efficient ways of managing and controlling life and the blood of the population. As Foucault writes, 'For capitalist society biopolitics is what is most important, the biological, the somatic, the corporeal.'[156] With Nazi Eichhorst's expertise 'in the construction of animal pens and the coordination of maximally efficient abattoirs', and Palmer's financial support in refurbishing 'dozens of meat plants nationwide',[157] the establishment of a brutal society was becoming a reality. On the one hand, blood camps with 'Wrinkled bodies sagged on hooks, flayed skin lying like pelts piled upon the floor'[158] testify to the bestialisation of humanity. On the other hand, birthing camps conjure up the Nazi immunitary procedure of the suppression of birth, here perversely reversed into the realisation of birthing barracks for the production of 'Healthy babies. The vampires needed to replenish the race, and their blood supply.'[159]

The brutality of the new social order is exemplified by the virus' biological rape of human bodies. In this thanatopolitics, the elderly and infirm are eliminated, while the 'meek, the defeated, and the fearful' are left to serve the Master, reduced to animal life: 'We became cattle... the anomaly... We are the vermin.'[160] On the other hand, 'the wilful, the powerful, and the strong' are disciplined by the disease.[161] The virus functions as a biopolitical instrument, creating caesuras within the population and separating the dominant vampire race from the inferior human race. Unlike previous vampires, here the virus cannibalises the human system, in such a way that vampires are 'viruses incarnate'.[162] The virus violently colonises and adapts human bodies from both the inside and the outside, changing their biological and physical appearance: 'the circulatory and digestive systems merge, becoming one. Similar to insects.'[163] No longer human, they have throat stingers that infect through the exchange of a parasite in the form of a blood worm that exists in their white blood.[164] Vampirism is spread through blood worms, driven by their thirst for blood and which can inhabit new bodies even after their host has died. Here biological horror is manifested at the molecular level, in the terrible transgressive traffic of the blood worms which, instead of remaining hidden, are made visible. Capillary worms then embody capillary power:[165] they reach 'into the very grain of individuals', inserting and diffusing themselves everywhere, inside and outside hosts. Blood in this sense disciplines bodies and regulates populations: it is life, food and reproduction. But it also violently excludes, racially separates and condemns to death.

What is at issue here is the pollution of the blood of the whole human race, which results in the new order of subjugated vampire masses, imagined as racial others, inferior and without individual will or soul. After the anthrax attacks and the increasing fears of a future bioterrorist attack due to the development of biodefensive weapons within America, the novels express anxieties about the control and manipulation of biological life, and the consequences for the subjects' identity and the future of the human species.

Conclusion

Significantly, the demonisation of contemporary biopolitics through the representation of evil biotechnologies, the military, capitalism, or Nazism, colonial exploitation in the form of vampiric viruses should not prevent us from grasping the true horror of human injustice. By ascribing horrific events to monsters, vampire gothic narratives risk dissociating the events from their human agents and thus placing evil and vampirism as external forces outside of human grasp and intelligibility. Equally, the pseudo-theological positivism in the end of *The Passage* and its sequel *The Twelve* (2013), the idea of chosen people bound by the sacred bonds of blood, and the mystical message of love and community that follow the vampire apocalypse are vapid celebrations of an immanent community that occlude difference and a history of inequality.[166] Such a vision of community participates in the metaphysics of presence while excluding the horrible realities of those minorities reduced to the status of the animal. What is necessary, then, is the purification of disease from the destructive effects of metaphor and the brutal realities of reductionist biology.

3

' 'Tis My Heart, Be Sure, She Eats for Her Food': Female Consumptives and Female Consumers

One does not always eat what is on the table.[1]

This chapter returns to the theme of disease and vampirism examined in the previous chapter, but this time there is a focus on consumption in order to investigate the associations of vampirism with tuberculosis, consumed and emaciated feminine bodies, and 'bad' eating. Recent critical debates around vampires and consumption tend to follow the position set out by Rob Latham in his monograph *Consuming Youth: Vampires, Cyborgs, and the Culture of Consumption* (2002), where the vampire is understood as an 'insatiable consumer'[2] who metaphorically embodies contemporary society's consumerist philosophy.[3] While consumption in the critical debate over vampirism is seen primarily in this context of contemporary capitalist culture's acquisition of material goods, historically the term is associated with the wasting and eating up of the body as a result of loss of humours and the disease that, in the first half of the nineteenth century, came to be known as tuberculosis. As Bram Dijkstra suggests in *Idols of Perversity* (1986), the two meanings of consumption are by no means completely distinct. Capitalism and disease, but also sexuality and womanhood, are tied to consumption. 'Woman', he writes, 'having been consumed in the marriage market, then having become consumptive as a wife through lack of respect, exercise, and freedom, took her revenge by becoming a voracious consumer.'[4] Indeed, Susan Sontag points out that tuberculosis is described in images that capture the dark, irrational side of nineteenth-century *Homo economicus*: 'consumption; wasting; squandering of vitality'.[5] However, little has been done to examine vampire texts with reference to consumption as tuberculosis. I will begin to investigate the associations of the word with the disease of tuberculosis and vampirism, as well as its associations with eating, cannibalism and sucking blood. In addition to considering the literal meaning of consuming the other, I will focus on the metaphorical understanding of consumption as using up the bodies of others through incorporation, assimilation and sexual appetite.

The figure of the vampire, whose appetite for blood and other non-foods represents the threat of the dissolution of bodily boundaries and the transgression of appropriate consumption, foregrounds subjectivity in terms of being consumed and consuming the other. Inevitably, consumption raises the question of 'eating well' and responsibility towards the other that Jacques Derrida elaborates in his 1988 interview with Jean-Luc Nancy, ' "Eating Well," or the Calculation of the Subject'.[6] For Derrida, eating well is a communion between humans through language and through *'learning* and *giving* to eat, learning-to-give-to-the-other-to-eat',[7] and involves hospitality and generosity. Subjectivity operates through real and 'symbolic anthropophagy', through the ingestion, incorporation and interiorisation of words, objects, of the tongue, lips and breast of the other.[8] If eating well consists of respect and a hospitality that recognises the other's difference, eating badly can be associated with voracious aggression, violence and injustice against the other. The vampire then functions to expose the savage devourer, the exploiter, against whom the other or others are constructed as civilised, healthy and independent subjects, whose identity does not depend on an uncontrolled and monstrous appetite for bad food. But at the same time, through the mouth and acts of consumption, modernity's binary logic of animal and human, feminine monstrosity and masculine humanity, breaks down. Acts of eating and being eaten become images of change, decay and transformation that threaten to dissolve identities.[9]

The mouth of the vampire represents the mouth of the grave, or the grave as a mouth, and voices anxieties about death as a devouring mouth. Fears of vampiric consumption perhaps originate from medieval beliefs in the corruptibility of the earthly body, the corpse, and its digestion and destruction by beasts and the gaping maw of the grave.[10] It is not accidental that death (*mors*) derives from bite (*morsus*), and thus the vampire is a fanged death and an embodiment of the mouth of Hell. The vampire draws attention to the fact that we will all become cadavers and eaten by worms as mere objects. More particularly, the female vampiric mouth represents the threat not only of sexuality, but also of biological processes and decay. Vampire narratives often locate her difference in her body, which is associated with food and nutrition and is considered as a locus of mutability, consumption and physical decomposition. Hungry for food, but also herself food for the foetus and her baby feeding at the breast, woman and her fluids are seen as closer to death and decay than growth and new life.[11] Woman's body then can be understood as the mouth and the tomb that swallows and destroys masculine spirit. She embodies evil because she is not spiritual but physical, mutable and material, subject to decay and corruptibility. The female vampire can only be nourished, then, by blood as food of the soul that replenishes and animates her corruptible flesh.

By looking at the female vampire, her denial of food and her perverse hunger for and consumption of blood, I want to stress the interrelation of consumption to women and identity. If the vampire can be located between a Foucauldian symbolics of blood and an analytics of sexuality, then female and maternal vampires and their voracious appetites are relegated to an inferior position within a system of linearity and bloodlines which they threaten to contaminate, and endowed with a dangerous sexuality that endangers male authority. The control over the feminine is achieved by disciplining her female hunger which signifies desire for 'public power, for independence, for sexual gratification'.[12] The female vampire's uncontrolled thirst for blood represents her thirst for power, desire and sexuality, all portrayed in her deathly, emaciated body hungry for blood. The pathology of hunger and consumption are precisely the result of a patriarchal construction of femininity that is categorised, defined and controlled. Within this context of rational and muscular modernity woman is always defined in opposition to man: norm and monster, mind and body, self and other, she occupies the second and inferior half of the binary.

In postmodernity, however, these monstrous becomings do not only express negative masculine anxieties, but can also express the emerging female subjectivities of the previous minorities.[13] For Rosi Braidotti the postmodern woman is 'a subject-in-process, a mutant, the other of the Other, a post-Woman embodied subject cast in female morphology who has already undergone an essential metamorphosis'.[14] As will be discussed later, for Braidotti issues of embodiment and sexual difference are processes of transformation, of becomings without an ultimate destination. By tracing the cartographies of female subjectivity in vampire literature, it is possible to show the development of the subject of Woman from a disempowered position within the regime of biopower to one that reflects 'a complex and multi-layered embodied subject'.[15]

It is a considerable change, then, to witness emerging representations of embodied subjects who resist patriarchal discourses and reconfigure the positivity of difference. However, beyond celebrations of postmodernist and multiple identities, it is necessary to be aware of post-feminist neoliberal subjectivities that equally embrace a playful fluidity of bodies and desires and processes of transformation that subscribe, however, to the logic of a consumer culture that demands the constant re-invention of selves and of alternative lifestyles. More significantly, the interrogation of the relationship of women to consumption, food and the maternal body is an attempt to understand the development of female identity within culture, but also to emphasise woman's status as the intermeshing of materiality and self-consciousness.

Psychoanalysis, women, consumption

Psychoanalytical theories have suggested the ways in which the infant's relation to the mother through consumption is fundamental for its development and inclusion in culture.[16] Indeed, subjectivity is captured by the image of the open mouth through which one enters the orders of language and culture. The mouth is the place where body and soul unite, where the closed mouth that eats, sucks and feeds at the breast opens up in order to speak.[17] The threatening presence of the vampire's fanged mouth, then, refers to this painful moment when the child rejects the maternal breast for entrance to language. Luce Irigaray has described this suffocating relationship between mother and child as one of 'eating each other' and being reduced to 'consuming and being consumed'.[18] The mother, whose only desire is 'filling up of holes' and offering nothing but 'blood, milk, honey', imprisons the child into a 'stuffed, sealed up, immobilized body'.[19] Paralysed, the child turns to the father with 'mouth gaping on his truth'.[20]

According to Melanie Klein, the oral site is the site where aggressive and sadistic impulses arise from the relation of the infant to the mother's breast. For Klein, the infant's first object is the maternal breast imagined both as a good, nurturing breast and as a bad breast which threatens to destroy the ego. The infant projects its own aggression onto the breast because it hates it: the breast is bad, and thus it attacks it. During this phase, which Klein names as the paranoid schizoid phase, the infant desires to devour the breast (mother) in order to possess what her body contains and destroy her. The guilt, following this phantasy, propels a series of defence mechanisms in order to keep at bay the infant's paranoid fears of being consequently devoured by the mother. These mechanisms are essential for the development of the infant's ego and entrance into language.

Like Klein, Julia Kristeva in *Powers of Horror* (1982) also associates oral activity with the act of devouring.[21] She stresses the necessity of abjecting the mother as a guarantee for entering into language and becoming a subject. While Klein stresses the negativity of the experience of the mother, she also stresses the role of the mother in oedipal tendencies. On the other hand, Kristeva, following Lacan and Freud, expels the mother and turns to the prohibiting figure of the father, the Law and the order of language. She writes: 'Through the mouth that I fill with words instead of my mother whom I miss from now on more than ever, I will elaborate that want, and the aggressivity that accompanies it, by *saying*.'[22] Language, for Kristeva, substitutes and expresses the infantile devouring and aggressive impulses. But it is these long-repressed devouring instincts that the transgressive vocabulary of the gothic's vampiric biting, sucking and consuming renders into language.

In Joan Copjec's influential 'Vampires, Breast-Feeding, and Anxiety' (1991) vampirism and consumption become central themes. Vampirism is connected with the mother's breast, as the partial-object, the part of the mother that the infant rejects in symbolic sacrifice. Following Lacan's seminar on anxiety, Copjec traces the fear of, and anxiety about, vampires to the locus of the breast. According to Lacan, because of the absence of the maternal Thing the subject can get no satisfaction. Pleasure is derived, however, from the process of attaining the object, given that the object itself never satisfies the drive but only opens towards another satisfaction to be attained:

> Even when you stuff the mouth—the mouth that opens in the register of the drive—it is not the food that satisfies it, it is, as one says, the pleasure of the mouth.... As far as the oral drive is concerned, for example, it is obvious that it is not a question of food, nor of the memory of food, nor the echo of food, nor the mother's care, but of something that is called the breast.[23]

Copjec locates vampirism at the point where the fantasy that enables the child's relation to an object of desire disintegrates. Vampirism then warns against the drying-up of the breast as object-cause of desire.[24] Copjec stresses that vampire fictions maintain the real target of attack through the threatening presence of the vampire, its activity of sucking and the victim's female sex, while images of vampirism usually centre upon the female breast.[25] Consequently, the vampire represents the breast as the partial object which we rejected, but also internalised, in order to constitute ourselves as subjects. This *extimate* object, which is inside us, but is not us, creates the uncanniness and anxiety of vampirism when it gets very close to us. Thus, the real danger that the vampire represents is in reality our overproximity to the object of the breast, the *objet petit a*, which the vampire now possesses but as a source of *jouissance*.[26] As Ken Gelder notes, Copjec ignores sexual differ-ence and she considers 'desire as fundamentally heterosexual'.[27] In her analysis vampires are male and their victims are female. It is, however, sexual difference that is at issue in my analysis: the devouring vampire as the other; the female vampire with her consumed body and consuming appetites.

In *Victorian Literature and the Anorexic Body* (2002) Anna Krugovoy Silver connects eating and the female vampires of the late nine-teenth century with sexuality and aggression. Whether the female vampires demonstrate 'excessive consumption or disruptive consump-tion', whether they are voluptuous or emaciated, the 'unruly body' must be controlled and restrained.[28] For Silver, the anorexic vampire's insa-tiable appetite for blood resembles the equally insatiable hunger of the anorexic girl. The emaciation of the body of the vampire represents its uncontrollable hunger for more blood, and not its denial of blood.[29]

I want to draw attention to insatiable hunger that links eating dis-orders to the vampire, womanhood and the maternal. This view is informed by Kim Chernin's seminal study *The Hungry Self: Women, Eat-ing, and Identity* (1985), as well as by the recent resurgence of interest in food consumption and women. Chernin's thesis on consumption has influenced a series of books relating to consumption and is a reworking of Klein's oral phase of infantile aggression that specifically addresses female identity.[30] Chernin's theory, to a certain extent, also resonates with Jacques Lacan's reading of anorexia as a strategy of separation from the Other in order to escape lack by desiring not to desire. For Lacanian psychoanalysis, the anorexic subject is a hysteric whose problem of desire is linked to the mother's desire. The mother, who has fed and loved the child too much, disables the child's desire. Consequently, the child refuses the mother's love by rejecting food.[31] Because the anorexic fails to find the object to fill the lack, she does not merely refuse food but eats the lack itself—no-thing—and keeps her desire in motion. How-ever, following Chernin, the female vampire's consuming and emaciated body can be associated with the primal moment of oral aggression and guilt over depleting the mother. Chernin connects the troubled rela-tionship to food, to female identity and the struggle of contemporary women to separate themselves from their mothers.[32] The woman who feels anger towards the mother and struggles to detach herself from her will express this through 'biting and gobbling and devouring and tearing food'; alternately, if she craves the mother, then through 'sucking and sipping, soft foods and milk foods' she will feel closer to her.[33]

This anxious devouring of the mother-food is understood as an unconscious 'Kleinian memory'.[34] Chernin finds in eating disorders the re-emergence of this archaic childhood fantasy: the pre-oedipal infant's oral aggression toward the mother's breast. During the ego-identity formation phase, Klein stresses the infant's fantasies of devouring the 'bad breast' which refuses to offer milk. Later, the infant will project its devouring fantasies on the breast which it imagines will devour it. A woman's hunger, for example, exemplifies this fear of being devoured by the mother. By controlling the body through self-starvation the woman imagines that her unappetising body will not be eaten by the mother. Women's eating problems can be connected to the guilt arising from this childhood fantasy of attacking, biting and damaging the mother. Seeing their mothers depleted and exhausted in real life, the young women feel guilt for damaging their mothers in their early childhood. A woman's fear of eating and, consequently, re-enacting the oral sadistic impulses, disables her from developing her own selfhood. The emaciated woman's delusions of fat and problematic attitude towards food consumption reveal the idea that 'the woman has been taken over by the mother from whom she is trying to separate and whom she has swallowed down, over and over again symbolically in the re-enacted primal feast'.[35] Eating becomes for these women a 'highly charged symbolic drama of mother/daughter separation and reunion'.[36]

Female vampires, often presented in a troubled relation to food, like the eponymous vampire in E.T.A. Hoffman's 'Aurelia' (1819/20) or Miranda in Helen Oyeyemi's *White is for Witching* (2009), are struggling to separate themselves from the mother in order to become independent and develop their own identity. At other times the mother returns as a devouring and all-consuming female vampire that threatens domestic space. The monstrous maternal, as it has been represented and broken down by Barbara Creed into the monstrous womb, dangerous lesbian vampire and castrating vampire, would also be significant in the analysis of female vampires that threaten male power and sexuality. Their consuming desires and appetites offer a new proposition to patriarchal economies: no longer the objects of consumption, they transform into the subjects of consumption.

But consumption does not need to be defined as negative. Moving away from modernist and psychoanalytic theorisations of gender, which are based on traditional scientific views and dichotomised conceptions of men and women, we arrive at postmodern understandings of woman's position characterised by constant metamorphosis, regeneration and the productivity of difference. Within this context, anorexia can be understood as a strategy that attacks the organism and the constraints of 'lack and hunger at the mechanical mealtime'.[37] In this respect, the subject constitutes herself as self-conscious being by not surrendering herself to her body and its needs but seeking to shed its materiality and its fleshiness by negating to feed and sustain it. As Dorothèe Legrand attests, 'self-transformation may be both at once self-constituting and self-negating'.[38]

The female vampire's consumption, then, should be seen as one of the various manifestations of female subjectivity and as a positive facet of female monstrosity in her becoming a woman. Helen Oyeyemi's *White is for Witching* (2009), the most recent of the texts I examine here, has an agenda diametrically different from the rest of the vampire literature concerned with Woman and consumption. Its potentiality in regards to feminist politics lies in the fact that the text does not come from a genealogy of female writing that understands its difference in relation to the dominant patriarchal power. Following Braidotti's reading of the *Alien* film series, the novel, it can be argued, does not propose 'a morally superior triumphant feminine showing the one-way road to the future'.[39] Instead, the novel introduces a non-unitary and embodied subject as the plane for multiple becomings, that is, a subject that 'endures sustainable changes and transformation and enacts them around him or herself in a community or collectivity'.[40] In this respect, Rosi Braidotti's materialist and anti-essentialist subject is relevant here. Following Luce Irigaray's sexual-difference feminism and Gilles Deleuze's nomadism, she acknowledges sexual difference and the maternal feminine, while advocating transformation, dynamism and nomadism. She does not envision one point or road of resistance, but constant flows of metamorphoses, where becomings are disengaged from dominant modes of thinking and are 'creative work-in-progress processes'.[41] In the novel both Miranda's consuming desires for the female body and her monstrous becoming as a soucouyant address the maternal bond and archaic monstrous feminine, represented by the house as the maternal womb, but they also stress the disengagement from this negative attachment to the mother's body. The metaphor of the soucouyant as the one that sheds her skin can be juxtaposed to Miranda's peeling away of her body through anorexia and eating no-thing in order to constitute her subjectivity and attest to her *no-thingness*. However, by refusing to satisfy her body's nutritional needs 'she ends up mimicking the dead'.[42] Swallowed up by the house, Miranda fails to disengage from the negativity of past ideologies. Ore, on the other hand, the traditional dark other of gothic fiction, has moved on from the negative binary logic of black/white, or evil/good, inhabiting several locations and moving between them. The consuming female body of the vampire, then, a site of devouring and threatening desires, as well as bodily consumption and emaciation, can call into question the normative relations to food and consumption, as well as reveal the possibilities for an understanding of female (vampiric) identity.

Tuberculosis and the New England vampires

From as early as 1398 until the end of the nineteenth century, 'consumption' was a word used for pulmonary tuberculosis.[43] Until 1839 the disease was variously known as phthisis, consumption, scrofula, king's evil, hectic fever and gastric fever. Consumption was used widely to signify any kind of illness that resulted in weight loss and death and the 'catchall term for any and all chronic wasting disease, usually designated emaciation with pulmonary symptoms'.[44] Emaciation was not just a passing stage of losing flesh but 'thanatoid emaciation, deathly thinness, and an ashen skin tone. A weak and wasted physique consumed by disease indicated imminent death.'[45] Tuberculosis, on the other hand, referred to a specific 'condition in which elastic lung fibers, called tubercles, were coughed up. What people called tuberculosis throughout most of the nineteenth century was not the bacterial condition that came to be called by that name later.'[46] Pulmonary tuberculosis, the most usual type of consumption, was understood as an illness of the lungs. Only after the identification of the bacillus by Robert Koch in 1882 did the meaning of tuberculosis change to describe patients that were infected with the bacteria and who produced expectoration.[47]

Tuberculosis, romanticised and feminised, exemplified the feminine flirtation with Eros and Thanatos. The consumptive sexualised woman reflected the late nineteenth-century's binaries of women as virgins and whores, saints and vampires, that Dijkstra has pointed out in *Idols of Perversity*.[48] However, the romanticisation of the disease and its association with the stereotypical representation of the female invalid reflects middle-class preoccupations and was not pertinent to the poorer classes who also suffered from tuberculosis.[49] Such stereotypes were also supported by medical discourse and practice. As Katherine Ott explains, 'the average physician at work practiced a rich mixture of common sense, folklore, popular knowledge, and medical doctrine'.[50] Consumptions, including tuberculosis, existed and disseminated in cultures that produced and invested them with various meanings. The cultural meanings of these wasting diseases informed and determined a discourse that would influence our perceptions about consumption and identity. The vampire, inhabiting marginal zones of existence, became the ideal figure to represent, and therefore through which to discuss, consumptive illnesses and tuberculosis. In particular, ideas about vampirism in folklore are considered to have emerged because of disease.

Historically, consumption or tuberculosis, vampirism and women, are first brought together in late eighteenth- and nineteenth-century New England. Between 1790 and 1890 the disease of consumption or tuberculosis in New England was related to the belief in vampirism. In the New England imagination vampires were young sexual female 'victims turned victimisers' 'draining the vitality' of the community or 'fading away and dying'.[51] The proliferation of vampire superstitions in the area coincides with New England's degeneration and rural decay.[52] Faye Ringel explains that in the second half of the nineteenth century

> most observers agreed that New England's Paradise had been lost to outsiders. Racialist theories of that day foresaw the decay, pollution, and disaster when Irish, French Canadian, and then Polish immigrants replaced first the Puritan farmers and later the Yankee millhands whose blood had produced the patriots and founders of democracy in our land.[53]

Articles in the *Atlantic Monthly* in 1889 document a New England inhabited by mutated freaks and barbarians descended from the noble stock of Puritans. It is in such an atmosphere created by scholarly sources, scandalous journals and newspapers that readers at the time were inclined to believe in vampirism. If New England was inhabited by 'dwarfs, giants, and idiots', then it was logical that these degenerated and unfit creatures would infect and spread their disease to the rest of the New Englanders.[54] Vampirism then became a fitting metaphor for the disintegration of the tubercular female body and the body of New England.

At the end of the eighteenth century Rhode Island was struck by tuberculosis, a disease which would be connected to vampirism and transform the small state of Rhode Island into the 'vampire capital of the New World'.[55] As Bob Curran explains in the *Encyclopedia of the Undead* (2006), from 1796 to 1892 Rhode Island 'was to produce a tradition that was to become known throughout America (and further afield) as "the vampire ladies" '.[56] The first vampire incident occurred in

1796 in the South Country of Rhode Island when the 19-year-old Sarah
Tillinghast, the daughter of Stukely Tillinghast, was diagnosed with and
died of consumption. After her death, other family members wasted
away and, before dying, they claimed that they had dreamt of Sarah.
Her father unearthed her grave and found her 'just as fresh and beautiful as when she had been interred'.[57] He cut her heart with a knife and
burned the body because he thought she was a vampire. It is perhaps not
accidental that nineteenth-century scientific monographs and vampire
literature reveal this awareness of the similarities between consumption
and vampirism.

George R. Stetson was one of the first to draw the connection
between vampirism and tuberculosis in Rhode Island. In his article 'The
Animistic Vampire', published in the *American Anthropologist* (1896),
Stetson writes:

> In New England the vampire superstition is unknown by its proper
> name. It is there believed that consumption is not a physical but a
> spiritual disease, obsession, or visitation; that as long as the body of
> a dead consumptive relative has blood in its heart it is proof that an
> occult influence steals from it for death and is at work draining the
> blood of the living into the heart of the dead and causing his rapid
> decline.[58]

Despite Stetson's desire to categorise vampirism here as spiritual, New
England's folklore and vampire stories were predominantly of a physical
nature, and consumption or vampirism resulted in the physical wasting
of the body and loss of blood. New England's vampires, as documented
in the different vampire texts or accounts, are, unlike the European
bloodsuckers, creatures that are consumed and consume the blood-life
of their relatives, leaving their bodies to waste away. Vampirism is thus
captured by the image of the weakening and emaciated body instead of
the body punctured or penetrated by the phallic vampiric fangs. In particular, the vampire stories of New England focus on the wasting bodies
of females and how these vampire women 'lure' their victims to the
grave. While the reality would point towards the fact that women lived
in crowded domestic circumstances that enabled the disease of tuberculosis to be transmitted more easily, the fictional accounts reveal an
inclination toward the assumption that women were weak and sick,
that their bodies were less resistant to diseases, yet they retained a
threatening and seductive power.

As the belief in vampirism in New England was supported by the fear of degeneration and decay with the invasion of settlers, so the vampire stories set in New England tend to be characterised by a concern with an embodied-vampire being infecting and consuming the community rather than merely a spectre as Stetson notes. The vampire in these stories is very often portrayed as a threatening female; but also as a female threatened to be consumed by the restrictions of a patriarchal and puritan society. Very often, American vampire stories of the late nineteenth and early twentieth century continue to focus on the female vampire. Francis Marion Crawford's 'For the Blood is the Life' (1911) and Henry James' 'Maud-Evelyn' (1900), as well as the New England vampire stories, Mary E. Wilkins Freeman's 'Luella Miller' (1903) and Edith Wharton's 'Bewitched'[59] (1927), are all concerned with female vampires. In particular, Crawford's vampire, Cristina, and Wharton's supposed vampire, Ora, belong to those female vampires who are pathologised and criminalised as different. Cristina is like a gypsy and Ora descends from a family of witches, a degenerated offspring of an incestuous union between cousins. Similarly, 'Luella Miller' investigates consumption and vampirism in relation to the domestication of women and heterosexual relationships in rural New England. In this respect, the young women of New England, outside or within marriage, become the victims of a society that controls womanhood and female desire.

Freeman's feminist project in 'Luella Miller' is shared by another New England writer, Edith Wharton. In 'Bewitched' the real vampire is Mrs Rutledge who desires to control the life of the women whose inappropriate transgressions disrupt the puritan community. Following Barbara A. White's claim that in 'Bewitched' women are consumed and destroyed because of the incestuous marriage and the father's subsequent incestuous relations with his daughters, Gloria Elrich similarly suggests that Ora's vampiric return functions as a catalyst to end the incestuous relation between her father and sister.[60] However, the story does not present enough evidence to support this view. Ora's supposed vampirism is a fictional tale constructed by Mrs Rutledge, a mere invention to victimise a young woman. By presenting herself as a victim, Mrs Rutledge condemns the already dead Ora for sucking the life of her husband. By doing so, she manages to conceal her husband's relationship with Ora's sister, Vanessa, whom she desires to destroy. The story also refers to other female vampires, innocent women like Ora and Vanessa who have been similarly victimised in the past.

Elrich's reading also overlooks the gothic description of Mrs Rutledge, 'a woman of cold manners and solitary character'.[61] From the fixed

features of her face and her voice's 'dead-level tone', to her 'pale spec-
tacled eyes' and her white complexion, she is a bloodless creature.[62]
Whiteness becomes the marker of death: 'the inner fold of her lids was of
the same uniform white as the rest of her skin, so that when she dropped
them her rather prominent eyes looked like the sightless orbs of a mar-
ble statue'.[63] Her withered, cold hands are also 'of the same leaden white
as her face';[64] she looks 'as if the stone-mason had carved her to put atop
of Venny's grave'.[65] This not only connects Mrs Rutledge to whiteness
and death, but also to Vanessa's death as the authorial figure controlling her life and death. Her monstrosity is linked to Bosworth's old aunt
Cressidora, whom he remembers as a 'small white old woman'[66] locked
behind barred windows and strangling a canary-bird that desired its freedom. Bosworth's memory of this, during Vanessa's funeral, suggests that
as his monstrous aunt, denied her freedom, throttles the canary that
seeks its freedom, so Mrs Rutledge desires to throttle and destroy the life
and freedom of women like Vanessa. Her puritanical, cold repression
leads her to destroy the lives of those who have or desire what she does
not possess.

For if Mrs Rutledge manages to manipulate those around her and victimise women, she is, nonetheless, a victim of a puritanical system that
has transformed her into a cold, hateful woman. Her deadly whiteness
and desire to annihilate anything that is different to her puritanical values are juxtaposed to the 'swarthy'[67] Vanessa, whose grave is a 'fresh
black stain in the grave-yard snow'.[68] This is what drives Mrs Rutledge
in the end to 'get a box of soap at Hiram Pringle's',[69] as if her crime, or
Vanessa's dark skin, sexuality and difference can be wiped off and made
pure. But Vanessa's grave, like so many other graves of silenced women,
marks the whiteness of the cold snow and speaks of the crime.

Medical discourse and consumption

While the folklore and stories set in New England have shaped much of
the vampire literature associated with tuberculosis, nineteenth-century
medical discourse has also added to the mythology of tuberculosis.
The fact that the disease had afflicted artists such as Shelley, Keats and
Chopin made it more glamorous and romantic; nevertheless, the focus
of the literature and medical treatises is on the consumptive woman.
Medical treatises of the nineteenth century speculate on the appearance of female consumptive bodies with diaphanous, pale skin and rosy
cheeks. Medicine and literature created a metaphorical feminine body,

a cultural construct controlled by the authority and gaze of the medical practitioner and writer.

Exemplary of this is Samuel Warren's popular *Passages from the Diary of a Late Physician* which was published anonymously as a series of short stories in *Blackwood's Edinburgh Magazine* from August 1830 to August 1837. 'Consumption', published in 1830, describes the disease as a vampire drinking the blood of its victims:

> Consumption!—Terrible, insatiable tyrant! Who can arrest thy progress, or number thy victims? Why dost thou attack the fairest and loveliest of our species? Why select blooming and beautiful youth, instead of haggard and exhausted age?...By what infernal subtilty [sic] hast thou contrived hitherto to baffle the profoundest skill of science, to frustrate utterly the uses of experience, and disclose thyself only when thou hast irretrievably secured thy victim, and thy fangs are crimsoned with its blood?—Destroying angel!—[70]

Warren was not a doctor but his sensational stories examining gothic, scandalous and medical topics were presented as medical papers of a friend detailing his cases as a physician. This use of the genre of medical case history to present his fictional accounts confused the boundaries between medicine and literature, reality and fiction. Indeed, many physicians were deceived by the apparent truthfulness of the medical cases and were infuriated by the use of patients' names and the lack of respect to the code of patient confidentiality. Warren's dramatisation of diseases such as consumption was a response to the already sensational cultural horizon and the evocative symbolisms of consumption.

Medical discourse was not, however, less sensational. Warren's example reveals how frail and indistinct the boundaries between fiction and fact were. This was due to the fact that nineteenth- and twentieth-century divisions between disciplines were not consolidated in the early nineteenth century. For many physicians, consumption was more of a cultural disease than a reality. Physicians talked about blood and the body in poetic terms and their figurative language, manifested in the various medical pamphlets and treatises, idealised the sick body. For many medical practitioners, the surface of the skin became a map of the inside pathology of the body. In *A Treatise on Pulmonary Consumption: Comprehending an Inquiry* (1835) Dr James Clark describes the physiognomy of tubercular patients which is characterised by 'a placid expression, often great beauty of countenance, especially in persons of a fair, florid complexion'.[71] According to Robert Douglas Hamilton, 'in pulmonary consumptions, the mind becomes more acute, and the countenance continues lovely till the last';[72] 'It is in phthisis alone' that 'disease and beauty are blendid [*sic*]; enhancing the most comely features, with that sweetly interesting look, that remains impressed on the mind, when the object that excited it has gone to her long home.'[73]

The nineteenth century's preoccupation with the pale, consumptive body—a result of loss of blood through haemoptysis and in some cases of the physician's experiments with excessive bloodletting—the languid eyes and ephemeral rosy vitality add to the double identity of the victim. As with the fin-de-siècle's binaries of angel and demon, the consumptive woman is also the embodiment of a fascinating evil that consumes her blood from within, while she develops into a spiritual being, negating the horrors of her flesh. In *A Treatise on Pulmonary Consumption* (1830) John Murray's analysis of the disease exemplifies some of the physician's interest in poetical language and the romantic imagination that is captured by the figure of the vampire. He writes:

> Consumption, like the vampire, while it drinks up the vital stream, fans with its wing the hopes that flutter in the hectic breast; the transparent colours that flit on the features like those of the rainbow on the cloud, are equally evanescent, and leave its darkness more deeply shaded. They who are the kindliest and the best it selects for its victims, while it softens the temper to an angel tone, as if it would attenuate that delicate materialism to aërial being, in anticipation of the change it is so soon to assume.[74]

Here metaphorical language flourishes. Despite the fact that this passage does not indicate the sex of the body, the language seems to suggest that women are the victims of pulmonary consumption. They metamorphose here into angelic and ethereal beings by the wasting of blood, made beautiful by the disease and imminent death. The feminine identity of the consumptive was discursively constructed and created a view of woman as weak and inclined to disease. The emaciated and wasted body was mythologised and portrayed as beautiful and more poignant.[75]

Consumption and heredity

In E.T.A. Hoffmann's *Aurelia* the eponymous vampire, the daughter of the depraved Baroness, is awakened by the same necrophilic and cannibalistic appetites that compel her mother to the burying ground for food. At the same time, after her marriage to Count Hyppolitus, she begins to suffer from anorexia. Both mother and daughter are constructed as monsters and cannibals, whose consuming appetites reflect their consumption and exploitation by masculine authority. The story of Aurelia, for example, is served as 'strong meat at table'[76] by the narrator Cyprianus, and consumed by a group of male friends. For the men, the story of female cannibalism becomes a pleasurable meal, 'fearfully interesting, and so highly seasoned with asafoetida[77] that an unnaturally excited palate, which has lost its relish for healthy, natural food, might immensely enjoy it'.[78] Speaking becomes a metonymy for eating, and the feminine is consumed as an exotic and 'repulsive' delight.[79]

The fear and desire of losing herself and joining with death, of becoming one with the corpses she devours, and thus closer to the cannibalistic maternal figure, bring about Aurelia's consumptive degeneration. She goes through a death-like state, during which she resembles more and more her pale and diabolic mother. The rejection of her husband is coupled with her denial to eat as she shows 'the utmost repugnance at the sight of all food, particularly meat. This repugnance was so invincible that she was constantly obliged to get up and leave the table, with the most marked indications of loathing.'[80] As this chapter's opening epigraph remarks, 'One does not always eat what is on the table.'[81] While the Count interprets Aurelia's condition in association with her mother's instincts that 'had begun to awake in her daughter', and the 'possibility of a conjugal infidelity',[82] Aurelia's denial of her husband's food, however, points towards repudiation of his authority and her domestication as a woman.[83] Her refusal to consume what is on the table is a symbolic act that negates her own consumption by masculine power. At the same time, by not offering herself to the other she demonstrates her refusal to eat and be eaten by the other. She denies her husband's food and hospitality, and breaks any possibility of open exchange. In this respect, through her mouth that does not eat, speak to or assimilate the other, she does not participate in her new role and identity as a wife, which includes her rejection, not merely of culinary pleasure, but also of sexual pleasure with her husband.

Consumption of blood and the Báthory ladies

In Johann Ludwig Tieck's 'Wake Not the Dead' (1823), Mary Elizabeth Braddon's 'Good Lady Ducayne' (1896), Arabella Kenealy's 'A Beautiful Vampire' (1896) and Mrs H.D. Everett's (Theo Douglas) *Malevola* (1914) vampiric, aristocratic females drain their young female companions of their blood and energy. The four stories appear to look back in some way towards the infamous Erzsébet Báthory: the monstrous 'Blood Countess' haunts the characters of Brunhilda, Good Lady Ducayne, Lady Deverish and Madame Despard.[84]

The myths surrounding the Hungarian Countess Erzsébet Báthory persist even today in the popular imagination. From Raymond McNally's *Dracula Was a Woman: In Search of the Blood Countess of Transylvania* (1983), to pseudo-historical biographies and fictional accounts of her life, the focus is on Báthory as a bloodthirsty countess who murdered and bathed in the blood of 650 maidens in order to stay eternally young. William Seabrook claims that Erzsébet or Elizabeth Báthory (1560–1614) is the 'world champion lady vampire of all time'.[85] However, not much is known about the actual life and deeds of Báthory, and what is often omitted is that she herself was victimised for debts she was owed by the Habsburgs.[86] Kord explains: 'The fact alone that the only written sources documenting Báthory's guilt were authored by those who had set out to destroy her and who stood to profit from her downfall should make us more suspicious than historians have tended to be.'[87] For Kord, the real story remains unknown. It is possible that Báthory committed the murders and tortured her victims or, alternatively, it is possible that the witnesses' accounts of her atrocities were 'instructed' by those who were against her.[88] However, the number of girls tortured, and the alleged bloodbaths, cannot be supported by any realistic evidence.[89] The legend has become the only reality, and the truth about the Countess' atrocities is probably much less sensational. Kord argues that the literature on her bloody acts, from the first account of her case in László Turóczi's *Tragica Historia* (1729), to Michael Wagner's *Contributions to a Philosophical Anthropology* (1794–6) and Moriz Gans' historical novel *Elisabeth Báthory: The Secrets of Castle Csejte* (1854), sought to control the vampire transgressor 'within the realm of feminine "normality"'.[90] Báthory might have killed virgins and bathed in their blood, but she did so, not because she was a vampire, but because she was a woman. In an attempt to repress her vampiric identity, the literary accounts of her life tried to present her as a woman whose actions were defined by her feminine destructive tendencies. Her beauty and her attention-seeking desire to please men were satisfying explanations for the patriarchal imagination.[91]

Like Báthory, the literary female vampires are presented as degenerate aristocrats, old and desirous of eternal youth and beauty, who consume the blood of their young female servants and companions. In 'Wake Not the Dead' (1823)[92] Walter's passionate love, Brunhilda, returns with the help of a sorcerer as a vampire-bride in order to take the place of the new bride Swanhilda,[93] but she destroys the familial domestic sphere and threatens to consume Walter himself. In order to stay beautiful and young she has to consume the 'potion of abomination':[94] 'Whenever she beheld some innocent child, whose lovely face denoted the exuberance of infantine health and vigour... she would suck from its bosom the warm, purple tide of life.'[95] When her monstrous identity is revealed, after she has devoured the blood of Walter's children, she responds: 'It is not I who have murdered them;—I was obliged to pamper myself with warm youthful blood, in order that I might satisfy your furious desires—thou art the murderer!'[96] Consumption of blood is associated with health and beauty, which are then linked to masculine demands and desires, as well as anxieties about woman's status.

Equally, Kenealy's 'A Beautiful Vampire' emphasises the aristocratic Lady Deverish's unnatural recovery from a consumptive disease and her healthy and 'brilliantly beautiful'[97] appearance.[98] She acquires, through massages, the energy of her nurses in a procedure similar to that followed by Thérèse Despard in Everett's *Malevola*. Having the beauty of a 'vixen' and the ability to bewitch men, Lady Deverish also consumes her two previous husbands who sickened and died consumptive, while her new one, the Earl of Arlington, loses his health and looks pale and moody.

In the context of the nineteenth century, where consumption in the upper classes was romanticised and idealised through representations of passive and suffering women, Lady Deverish embodies the threatening vampire with an 'assertive selfishness' that leads to 'wholesale murder'.[99] But her consumptive appetites are hidden behind the veil of aristocratic behaviour and psychic vampirism. This form of vampirism, which is also represented in other short stories of the time, for example by Arthur Conan Doyle's mind-control vampires in 'John Barrington Cowles' (1891) and 'The Parasite' (1894), and in Freeman's 'Luella Miller', offers a more elegant and aristocratic form of bloodless consumption. Luella Miller and Lady Deverish are stereotypical aristocratic females, their psychic vampirism a consequence of their good breeding. They persist on perpetuating their lives at the cost of others, capitalising on their status, but without revealing their voracious appetites. Blood-drinking signifies dangerous and animalistic consumption, whereas feeding on the psychic energy of others, especially their healthy companions and servants, indicates a more controlled activity, a form of passive consumption more appropriate to aristocratic women than brutal murderesses.

If 'A Beautiful Vampire' represents the tyrannical power and monstrous appetites of a degenerate aristocracy, it does so through the portrayal of feminine desires understood in the male imagination as dangerous and illegitimate. In the 1922 *Married Life and Happiness*, William J. Robinson, referring 'to the wife with an excessive sexuality', argues: 'Just as the vampire sucks the blood of its victims in their sleep while they are alive, so does the woman vampire suck the life and exhaust the vitality of her male partner—or victim.'[100] Woman's hunger for blood and seminal fluid, as Ernest Jones has shown in *On the Nightmare*, is exemplified by Lady Deverish's appetite for young husbands. She is not nurturing, but parasitic.[101]

The consumption of blood-semen-life can be linked to the resurgence of the vital essence theory in the latter half of the nineteenth century. In 1889 the respected physician Charles-Edouard Brown-Séquard reported at a meeting of the Society of Biology that he felt rejuvenated after injecting himself with extracts from the crushed testicles of guinea pigs and dogs. He had earlier speculated that sperm injections would rejuvenate old men physically and intellectually. This observation was consistent with Victorian beliefs in the preservation of man's seminal fluids and thus of his intellectual and bodily alertness. Brown-Séquard's *Elixir of Life* (1889) was an account of this new medical remedy for old age and debility which was coined 'organotherapy' and became the trend of the time. Seminal extracts were used for immunisation to tuberculosis and the cure of various other diseases and, like blood, were considered as life-giving. In the 1918 *Sex and Sex Worship (Phallic Worship): A Scientific Treatise on Sex, Its Nature and Function*, Otto Augustus Wall, blending folklore and medical discourse, discussed the 'sucking' of seminal fluid in terms of vampirism.[102] He wrote:

> Sucking the fresh semen is sometimes now considered a sovereign remedy for wasting diseases, or, as in the houses of prostitution an unfailing cosmetic remedy to produce a fine complexion. Anyhow, when surreptitiously done by night-prowlers, the latter were taken to be vampires and the victim was too frightened to make any outcry.[103]

Depleting their men of their seminal fluid, these female 'vampires' grew strong and robust, threatening to weaken their male victims. Like Lady Deverish, the blood/semen of her husbands is what has kept her beautiful and cured her wasting disease. For Kenealy held the belief that these sexual women not only drew the blood and semen of their partners, but also absorbed their 'blood-traits'.[104] These female predators, desiring and consuming as food their partners' life-blood, not for reproductive use, but for pleasure, were appropriating masculine power while perverting their maternal instinct.

In *Feminism and Sex Extinction* (1920) Kenealy, referring to woman's purpose in life to procreate and receive the male sperm, explains: 'If it be true that she holds these powers in trust merely, they are not hers to spend. To expend them is to despoil her sons; to make paupers and bankrupts of them, humanly speaking.'[105] The vocabulary of commerce and capital, of holding in trust or spending seminal fluid, and the bankruptcy of race, are exemplary of Kenealy's attitude towards the evil woman who has transgressed her 'natural' maternal role and metamorphosed into a sexual predator with masculine characteristics. Lady Deverish's desire to use and consume more husbands grows stronger as she accumulates and consumes more of their vital essence. She is a sexual being, whose masculine predatory proclivities equate her to the vampire: dangerous and all-consuming. But like the rest of the Báthory ladies, she is also economically powerful. Her economic vampirism manifests all those elements—devouring, sucking, draining, consuming—that characterise her transactions with her male victims. The withdrawal and traffic of blood or seminal fluid imitates the accumulation and consumption of capital that was usually the domain of men. Thus, the female vampires that wasted and consumed men's blood and seminal fluid, outside or within marriage, were not only appropriating masculine power, but were also becoming equal antagonists in the capitalist economy. At the same time, their degenerated consumption of vital essence concentrated in the blood, without reproductive uses, promised a future of regressive animality.

Today the demands on femininity and youth seem to return to these early nineteenth-century stories of beautiful vampires through rejuvenation therapies and 'vampire facelifts'. In his *Vampire Facelift: The Secret Blood Method to Revive Youth and Restore Beauty* (2013), the inventor of the vampire facelift, Charles Runels, explains how injecting blood-derived growth factors from the patient's own blood back into her face can rejuvenate the skin as multi-potent stem cells become activated and grow new tissue. By remaining faithful to the 'mathematics of beauty' beginning with Leonardo da Vinci's notebooks, Runels promises to create a younger and natural shape to the face while, at the same time, seeking to enchant medicine with such words as 'vampire', 'youth elixir' and 'magic'.[106] Like the sorcerer that brings Brunhilda back from the dead, Runels is a contemporary magician within a vampire market that excessively devours and regurgitates new products.

From Báthory's blood baths to Brown-Séquard's human rejuvenation transplants and Charles Runels' contemporary cosmetic treatments, blood remains associated with youth, femininity and vitality. Whether consumed by nineteenth-century vampires or injected to contemporary vampire consumers, blood is ineradicably linked to the myth of Báthory and cultural obsessions with beauty and appearance. If, however, nineteenth-century vampires looked unnaturally beautiful by secretly consuming blood in order to 'please man' and subject to phallic standards of beauty, today these vampire procedures subscribe to the feminine norms of youth and beauty enjoyed openly by everyone who can afford them. With the lack of any paternal function, individuals cannot assume responsibility for their actions but become intoxicated and entranced, enslaved into repetitive behaviours. 'Feeling and looking good' becomes the current hedonic model of health that expresses neoliberal capital's lack of morality and celebration of feeling so that individuals can enjoy long and prosperous lives. Evoking the medical subjectivity of contemporary societies examined in the first chapter, women today chose to enhance their appearance through their own biological material so that they preserve their selves and skin intact. Woman, then, becomes not only a consumer of blood but a consumer of products, (re)sculpting her identical self indefinitely.

Maternal vampires in the twentieth and twenty-first centuries

In the twentieth-century manifestations of the monstrous maternal take the form of post-feminist vampires who seek to consume feminism's principles or, more recently, give expression to past ideologies that desire the vampiric consumption of the other's blood. While in their consumerist form contemporary vampire narratives proliferate, spewing homogenous and normalised monstrosities, on the other hand, recent vampire horrors resist such euphoric celebrations, and attempt to offer a critique of those ideologies that vampirise women's identities, while opening the way for in-depth changes.

Unlike the previous female vampires examined here, the vampire-like Zenia of Margaret Atwood's *The Robber Bride* (1993), by repeating the traumas of the past and unsettling the lives of three women, devours their difference and denies any sense of solidarity and common connection to them. The novel uses metaphors of vampirism to describe the character of the 'wolfish, feral, beyond the pale' Zenia.[107] While some critics have celebrated Zenia's new, trendy muscular and aggressive individualism, I want to argue, in contrast, that such a post-feminist identity is isolating and rejects change and difference by reasserting the norm of old and established values packaged and marketed under the label of the new and exciting. Beyond such illusions of a progressive future, Zenia's attractive monstrosity annuls the traditional antitheses of the past, as well as the history of women's struggles, represented by the radical feminisms of Roz, Charis and Tony, by diffusing them into multiple, banal and fragmented positions within which the contemporary post-feminist heroine playfully moves.

Driven by lustful self-interest, Zenia has more affinities with Roz's husband's predatory masculinity rendered through vampiric imagery. He would use and dispose of women, 'Sink his teeth into them, spit them out.'[108] Mitch and Zenia are people that would 'go in for bloodthirsty kink'.[109] Similarly, as the representation of the monstrous maternal, she occupies the role of the evil stepmother, who enters the lives of Tony, Charis and Roz, offers mothering, but soon enough ravages their lives. Zenia's betrayal repeats the mothers' abandonment of their daughters and exposes the economy of phallogocentrism that has dictated the lives of the characters' mothers and haunted their relationships to parasitic men. Zenia's raptorial sexuality and monstrous motherhood are different disguises of a post-feminism that is neoliberal in flavour. Zenia's 'exceptional' womanhood[110] and individualistic consumption undermines inter-connection and generates isolation from the other women.

Today this return of neo-conservative and neoliberal ideologies is performed in a schizophrenic double bind: while it celebrates difference it does so in a deterministic manner so that difference is hierarchically understood in terms of 'us and them'.[111] As Rosi Braidotti argues, 'Post-feminist liberal individualism is simultaneously multicultural and profoundly ethnocentric. It celebrates differences, even in the racialized sense of the term, so long as they confirm to and uphold the logic of Sameness.'[112] In this respect, within neoliberal discourse gender politics is implicated with the discourse of white supremacy given that *our* women are always the Western, Christian, white or 'whitened' subjects raised within Enlightenment tradition.[113]

In Helen Oyeyemi's 2009 novel *White is for Witching*, the maternal returns as the expression of such a national and cultural identity in the form of xenophobia. The maternal breeds and resurrects the white horrors of a colonial past in order to consume and destroy otherness. At the same time, it posits new forms of liberation and cultivates a sense of connection and love through acts of eating that, despite their monstrosity, do not seek to devour difference. Indeed, the formation of feminist, postcolonial and black female identities is an example of those emergent subjectivities that seek to disengage themselves from the nostalgia of the past while moving towards future transformations by embracing a positive ethics.

In *White is for Witching* vampirism, consumption and the Caribbean soucouyant[114] embody essentialist, racist and violent understandings of identity and embodiment. The soucouyant is a witch who, after shedding her skin, transforms into a ball of fire and flies, going through keyholes and crevices until she finds her human victim and then sucks his or her life-blood. The myth of the soucouyant is associated here with eating as a destructive act that seeks to devour difference and the other, but also with the eating disorder pica.[115] Pica is traced through generations, unveiling thus the origins of vampiric behaviour: Miranda and her maternal line are connected through blood to a mysterious woman who would 'bite and suck at the bobbled stubs of her meat. Her appetite was only for herself.'[116] Here the purity of bloodlines is sustained through auto-vampirism, a disorder whose vestiges can be seen in Miranda's unusual eating habits.

Miranda's pica and anorexia testify to her dangerous inheritance of the identity of the soucouyant which finds its violent expression in the attempts to assimilate the racial other. The house orchestrates such desires and invites Miranda to share its destructive appetites with the other matriarchs, in order to celebrate British identity at the expense of the immigrant, as in the episode with the Arab boy Jalil. While Miranda escapes the hunger for blood, she nonetheless attempts to devour her black friend Ore whom she desires and loves. Eating becomes a symbolic feast of sharing and communicating with the other. But it also reminds that acts of consumption are never innocent. What, and with whom, one eats are highly charged political and ethical acts that conjure up images of destruction and change.

Acts of eating and being eaten by the other construct, dismantle and reassemble identities so that essentialist definitions of self and other are never solidified but become worn out through the incorporation and assimilation of difference and through the pollution of blood and purity. The black British Ore, occupying a fluid identity, embodies a 'non-unitary, multiple, complex subject that inhabits several locations and moves between them',[117] always metamorphosing. Her nomadism, vitality and materiality characterise a subject who is not bound by the bonds of the past but struggles in the present to create new alliances and connections that are not dictated by blood. On the other hand, despite her efforts to cut her ties to her maternal past, Miranda remains bound to her vampire identity and the soucouyant. Inseparable from fantasies of blood and purity, vampirism negates change and difference. Devouring appetites expose the dark side of consumption associated with the maternal, whiteness and blood. Like the white towels in the novel that seek to wipe out the black colour of Ore's skin, the presence of black feminist and progressive subjectivities stain the whitened economy of the same, promising change and transformation. In this respect, vampire gothic itself is polluted by the difference and possibilities opened by new monstrous imaginings and powerful identities.

Conclusion

In the vampire novels examined here the vampire females are imagined as bodies open, uncontrolled, sick and dangerous. Consumption and blood are associated with the violence of the female body and her vampiric identity. But her consumption and monstrous hunger for blood can offer a reversal of male order by mirroring back the violence and exploitation she has suffered. When her insatiable and consuming vampire appetite for blood is directed against the other, her desires threaten to confuse the boundaries of bodies under siege, to assimilate and incorporate, to devour the other, their difference and identity. The consumption of blood stages the male fantasy of the dependency of woman on the other. Her sucking and consumption perform the perverse nurturing upon the other. Her maternal power is demonised so that the other will be gloriously celebrated. However, as she crosses boundaries, no longer the Other of modernity but postmodernity's normalised monstrosity, the female vampire becomes a metonymy of contemporary society's post-feminist subjectivity. Aggressive and individualistic, woman's predatory sexuality and playful consumption of products escapes paternal and other disciplinary limits as it evaporates into celebrations of differences that remain, however, highly deterministic and hierarchical. At other times, she sheds her predatory individualism in order to rise above the hierarchies of the past and towards future transformations.

Going beyond gender trouble, vampiric tales of consumption of blood by centring on the cannibalistic act, drinking of blood and the sickness of bodies wasting away stress that identities are formed and dismantled through acts of consumption. Through the symbolic or real experience of eating well, eating-speaking-interiorising the other, giving to and receiving from the other, surrendering to and incorporating the other, ethical reciprocity with the other is established. On the other hand, as *White is for Witching* shows, eating badly and refusing to participate in a good meal with the other, is an unethical rejection of the other. It is this concern with otherness understood in the public imagination as black and biologically determined that the next chapter will begin to examine.

4
'Race as Biology Is Fiction': The Bad Blood of the Vampire

While in vampire narratives the monstrous consumer was gendered, it was also defined in terms of race and ethnicity. If medical discourse has historically demonised certain nationalities with theories of degeneration and race, vampire tales have demonised the racial other as vampiric and all-consuming. In this chapter I am concerned with blood as a symbol of race and the ways vampirism, like foreignness and race, is believed to be something ingrained in the body, and which taxonomises bodies as human/animal and normal/abnormal. Nineteenth-century vampire narratives insist on the chromatics of skin and a 'racial epidermal schema'[1] to define the monster. In twentieth- and twenty-first-century vampire stories, however, the 'racial' body is penetrated and made visible through a biopolitics that plunges deep into the soma to uncover and reshape the individual's identity at the molecular level. If skin and blood were the primary referents of racial discourse, now racial difference is relocated and imprinted by new technologies deep into the recesses of the body. However, vampire narratives retain at their heart the blood for its rich symbolism. Its dangerous circulation underneath the skin is, like blackness and vampirism, hidden but threatening. With its capacity to spill outside the body and pollute white society's categories, blood remains associated with race and the colour black.

For example, from nineteenth- to twenty-first-century narratives, vampirism is located at the intersection of black and white. The fear of the vampire is a blackness that can 'pass' as whiteness. This is why, from 'The Amber Gods' (1860), 'Carmilla' (1872) and *The Blood of the Vampire'* (1897) to the Blade films (1998–2004) and *Fledgling* (2005), the vampire is the individual who cannot be classified as completely black or white. In particular, the vampires in these texts struggle with the stereotype of the tragic mulatto, a person whose mixed-blood inheritance causes personal turmoil, marginalisation and rejection by both white and black groups. As Cherene Sherrard-Johnson notices in her discussion of Nella Larsen's *Quicksand* and *Passing* (1929), the mulatta figures of Denney and Clare are similar to the vampire Carmilla. They both 'possess flawed beauty concentrated in an ultra-whiteness that raises suspicion'.[2] The passing figures of vampires are ideal vehicles to examine the trajectories and dangerous crossings of blood in vampire texts. Their perfect whiteness shrouds a terrifying blackness.

As figures of pollution, vampires have always been associated with race understood at the molar level of organs and tissues, of the tangible body flagellated by the histories of blood, lineage and biology.[3] As John Allen Stevenson argues, Dracula threatens to 'deracinate' his victims by injecting them with 'a new racial identity'.[4] This is why, from the eighteenth to the nineteenth century, race was thought of as an inherited structure that formed the racialised individual's character. In the twentieth century, however, research on the human genome revealed that there is one human species consisting of individuals with physical differences. The fact, however, that the category of race is a fiction, as has been widely acknowledged,[5] does not mean that racism does not exist. Race is a political category that affects the social and biological life of human beings. As Audrey and Brian D. Smedley show, 'In many multiracial nations such as the United States, there are profound and stubbornly persistent racial and ethnic differences in socioeconomic status, educational and occupational status, wealth, political power, and the like.'[6] Despite the fact that race is not a biological category, it is increasingly witnessed in genomic research an emphasis on genetic difference which is supported by biological definitions of race. Sociology and Law professor Dorothy Roberts argues that, from science and pharmaceutical companies to government policies and popular culture, the concept of race as a biological category written in our genes is rearticulated and defended in new damaging and sinister ways that appear innocent, legitimate and humane. For her, this brutal promotion of inherent racial classifications facilitates the creation of a new racial biopolitics that seeks to control and regulate the populations by maintaining racial divisions intact while masking social injustice and inequities. On the other hand, the British sociologist Nikolas Rose locates the contemporary emphasis on race in genomic medicine not within the trajectory of racial science but within the new biopolitics of the twenty-first century. According to him, race does not conjure up a history of slavery and racial reductionism but is understood in relation to the contemporary demands and expectations of biosocial communities for biomedical research to discover the genomic bases of their common diseases and the possibility of treatment.

By writing a genealogy of race I want to bring these cultural theorists into contact with popular culture and, particularly, the vampire so that through the interconnections, oppositions and discontinuities between the high and low, it is possible to understand the present focus on race as the conflicting space of various discourses. In this respect, in this chapter I want to interrogate the crossroads of genomics, race, blood and medicine in contemporary analyses of the use of race in genomic research and in vampire texts. The chapter will first address the ways medicine and genomic science is introducing and legitimating biological definitions of race through the work of Dorothy Roberts. I will then focus on the work of Nikolas Rose and discuss how the new molecular understanding of life reshapes notions of identity by examining the concepts of biocitizenship and biosociality. Thirdly, through analyses of nineteenth-, twentieth- and twenty-first-century narratives of vampires of colour, I want to trace the shift from the essentialising genetics and the rigid categories witnessed in older vampire narratives based on the biology of race, to the new biopolitics of race witnessed in Octavia Butler and Tananarive Due's vampire novels. I locate the interlaced ensemble of genomics, race and medicine within this emergent biopolitics of race characterised by the increasing demands of biosocial groups for their differences to be acknowledged in genomic research, and also by the recognition that racism persists as a trauma at the heart of medicine and genomic research. Within this context, while the figure of the vampire represents difference and the pollution of blood and racial categories, at the same time it points towards the consuming maw of postmodern haemocommerce where blood and difference are marketed as products for black people.

Racial science and the biology of race

Despite the fact that the Human Genome Project (HGP) showed that human beings were 99.9 per cent genetically similar, scientists remained anchored on the 0.1 per cent difference and sought to explain this small amount of genetic difference by resurrecting biological definitions of race. As Dorothy Roberts clarifies, race is 'a political division: it is a system of governing people that classifies them into a social hierarchy based on invented biological demarcations'.[7] As an 'invented political grouping'[8] whose roots can be traced in the institutions of slavery and colonialism, race is 'not a biological category that is politically charged. It is a political category that has been disguised as a biological one.'[9] For Roberts, the new genomic science that is emerging from sequencing the human genome is reinforcing biological definitions of race, giving new legitimacy to old race-based genetic categories, exacerbating social inequities and inflaming racist rhetoric. This shift towards a re-articulation of race-based genetics is not, however, the result only of genomic research, but also of pharmaceutical companies and biotechnologies tailoring drugs according to race, and government policies which favour corporate interests at the expense of minority communities' rights. The new racial politics being shaped by genomic research in America today is a ruthless biopolitics guided by the myth and bloody fantasies of race, perpetrating racial inequality and perpetuating social injustice. Haraway, for example, has expressed fears about the ways biomedicine reproduces essentialist notions of race at the biological level.[10] For Roberts, the new genomic science and technology seeks to naturalise the biological origins of race while masking its effects in a society that is repeatedly defined as 'postracial'.[11] Roberts warns against this new racial biopolitics that insists on racial difference while at the same time seeks to '*de*politicize race' by postulating a colour-blind attitude towards social policies.[12]

While today the new racial science of genomics seeks to rationalise racial difference, in the past eugenics or cultural explanations attempted to mark individuals of colour as inferior. For example, slavery was justified by biological definitions of race that dictated the status of master and slave. This has been historically supported by the association of black peoples' bodies with particular diseases which marked them as biologically different. Instead of locating disease in political inequality, medical practitioners and politicians sought to justify the unequal system of white supremacy by claiming that disease was racially defined and diseased black bodies were inherently inferior. For example, racial policies were preserved and supported by beliefs in African Americans' biological inferiority justified by such diseases as syphilis or tuberculosis which arguably affected them differently.[13] With regard to consumption as defined before Koch's discovery of the tubercle bacillus in 1882, hereditary predisposition and environment, rather than contagion, were believed to be the causes of the disease. Even after 1882 some eugenicists still believed that tuberculosis was hereditary. In their introduction to *Heredity and Infection: The History of Disease Transmission* (2001) Gaudillière and Löwy explain:

The description of the role of Koch's bacillus in the induction of tuberculosis, a feature which theoretically could 'democratize' this disease (everybody can be accidentally contaminated by an airborne pathogenic microorganism) led, paradoxically, to the reinforcement of links between TB and race and to the accentuation of the importance of hereditary traits in TB transmission.[14]

Furthermore, in the 1870s and 1880s in America 'discussions of immunity or tendency to disease often mirrored ethnic and racial fears and prejudices'.[15] In the late nineteenth century tuberculosis was stigmatised as a racial disease as health officials were concerned with the control of racialised groups such as blacks in the US South, Irish and Eastern Europeans in the North, and Asians in the West.[16] Tuberculosis was considered a degenerate disease afflicting the poor and the non-white races. Fears and anxieties about race mixing, immigration and resistance have historically been translated into medical stories of racial difference and disease.[17] This racial stereotyping influences the views of medical practitioners today who treat black people according to race and perpetuate a system of inferior health care. As Roberts argues, with the significance and popularity of genetics and the emergence of the new racial science that confirms the difference among human races at the molecular level, the old racialised notions of disease are now modernised and reinforced. Inevitably, racial disparities in health cannot be separated from medical prejudices and racism.

Roberts sees the interest in using racial categories in biomedical research in order to guarantee greater representation of disadvantaged minority groups and to address inequalities in health care as damaging since it promotes racism and reinforces the belief in biological definitions of race. Celeste Condit has pointed out that 'Differences in hypertension or diabetes that may result in whole or in part from cultural factors are conflated with inherent "genetic" predispositions.'[18] Sickle-cell anaemia and cystic fibrosis are also presumed to be common genetic diseases that affect black and white people, respectively. The misconception that sickle-cell anaemia is a black genetic disease was constructed in the early twentieth century by haematological specialists who believed that 'the capacity to develop sickled cells was an inherent feature of "Negro blood"'.[19] The impossibility of proving scientifically that health disparities are the result of genetic difference is related to the fact that is difficult to separate genetic and environmental contributions to health.[20] Roberts points out that scientists should turn towards environmental causes and not genetic explanations to eliminate the gap in health. She clarifies: 'Race is a political category that has staggering biological consequences because of the impact of social inequality on people's health. Understanding race as a political category does not erase its impact on biology; instead it redirects attention from genetic explanations to social ones.'[21] It is important, then, to be suspicious towards genetic explanations of diseases because these are usually treated with marketable pharmaceutical products.[22]

Indeed, genomic research is inseparable from the production of capital. As Richard Lewontin shows, genetic scientists who participated in the Human Genome Project also had financial stakes in biotechnology industries.[23] Tailoring drugs according to race was soon to become a growing and profitable avenue for personalised medicine. Pharmacoethnicity, or the importance of ethnic and racial differences in drug response instead of genetic traits, is, of course, a faulty way to predict how patients will respond to medication. Marketing race-based drugs gives people the false impression that race represents genetic difference and that racial difference is inherent: people 'can now talk openly about natural distinctions between races...without appearing racist'.[24] For example, BiDil, the first race-based drug for the black heart-failure market, was not in reality a new drug. A combination of two generic drugs, BiDil was not designed specifically for black people or according to any genetic profile, but was marketed according to race for purely commercial benefits.[25] On the one hand, some African Americans condemned the use of drugs marketed for black people because it justified biological explanations of race. On the other hand, many black organisations supported racial medicine in order to address past biases in research and health care and realise African Americans' demands for science to attend to their needs.[26] For Roberts, BiDil should be available to everyone and not racially marketed.[27] Despite the pill's financial demise, the allure of race-specific drugs and therapies remains a promising commercial market. Race is not, however, the place to look for genetic differences: 'health inequities...cannot be fixed by color-coded pills'.[28]

Race, biocitizenship and the new molecular biopolitics

For Roberts, the question relating to personalised genomics is whether it will empower individuals to take control of their health or whether it will be consumed by those that can afford it, reinforcing thus existing social and racial inequalities.[29] While Roberts understands race in genomic research and medicine within the context of a brutal racial science, Nikolas Rose locates the ensemble of race, genomics and medicine within the transformed biopolitics of the twenty-first century.[30] According to Rose, the use of race in genomic medicine does not resuscitate the spectre of racism, but is linked to the 'changing ways in which we are coming to understand individual and collective human identities'.[31] As he writes, with the development of genomics 'race now signifies an unstable space of ambivalence between the molecular level of the genome and the cell, and the molar level of classifications in terms of population group, country of origin, cultural diversity, and self-perception'.[32] Within this space, he writes, 'a new genomic and molecular biopolitics of race, health, and life is taking shape'.[33] As he points out, the molecular genomic biology of the present is not essentialist but open, unlocking the possibilities of transformation and 'not identifying an essential racial truth that determines individuals to different fates'.[34] Rose summarises the controversies, interests and pressures that have developed over issues related to race-based and race-blind genomic medicine. He discusses the demands of racial and ethnic groups for a 'genetically based medicine', and not a 'race-blind genomic medicine', that 'could play a key role in reducing race-based health inequalities'.[35] These identity groups address the necessity to be racially classified in order 'to target the particular diseases suffered by disadvantaged racial groups, and to redress their underrepresentation in medical research, drug development, and access to effective health care'.[36] Rose perceives the contemporary preoccupation with race and ethnicity as linked to the 'hopes, demands, and expectations'[37] of biosocial communities which have 'formed around beliefs in a shared disease heritage, demanding resources for the biomedical research that might reveal the genomic bases of these diseases, and mobilized by the hope of a cure'.[38] Rose points out that the demands on research relating to race, genomics and health do not arise from a racial science, but from these biosocial communities of patients and advocacy groups.[39] In this respect, he locates the molecular biopolitics of race within the context of biolosocialities, and the changing ways in which individuals and communities understand their human identities and govern their differences. No longer determined by fate, individuals are now able to choose to reshape their identities and claim their right to life, health and cure, and that their differences be acknowledged in genomic biomedical research.[40] For Rose, the current debates over race and genomics should be situated within a new biopolitics that nurtures individual life and 'does not seek to legitimate inequality but to intervene upon its consequences. Crucially, it is a biopolitics in which references to the biological do not signal fatalism but are part of the economy of hope that characterizes contemporary biomedicine.'[41]

On the other hand, Dorothy Roberts questions Rose's biocitizen who takes responsibility for his/her own well-being at the molecular level, and the concept of biosociality that connects people around their common health conditions and genetic traits. While biocitizenship is envisioned to open the way towards a new kind of postracial community of people brought together by their genotypes and not their racial identity, Roberts argues that race remains crucial to the new genetic technologies and determines access to them.[42] For her, biocitizenship 'threatens to replace active, collective engagement to create a better society' and eliminate social injustice and racial inequalities by focusing on one's individual life at the molecular level, providing one's genetic information to the biotech industry and consuming its products and services.[43] Even when African Americans seek to uncover their racial roots in genetics, this is understood as dangerous given that science is increasingly defining race in biological terms. Roberts believes in a common humanity and solidarity to fight social injustice, and not confirmation of one's self and identity based on biology.[44] Celeste Condit poses the possibility that the 'willingness of African Americans and other racialized groups to embrace rhetorics of difference' based on genetic definitions[45] might increase the belief in the inherent differences between white and people of colour, as well as contribute to inferior health care and discrimination.[46] For Roberts, the increasing belief in the truth of genetics and the decreasing significance of societal truths leads to biological understandings of race that legitimate and preserve an oppressive politics of race. While, for Rose, the biopolitics of identity in advanced liberal democracies involves choice and individual responsibility, for Roberts the political reality of the new racial science involves brutality and cruelty against minorities.[47] The following vampire stories attempt to negotiate these positions through understandings of blood as a symbol of race, but also as a symbol of transformation and change, that is, however, capitalised by pharmaceutical companies.

Blood and race in vampire texts

Donna Haraway in *Modest Witness* (1997) warns about the dangers of rigid and essentialist categories based on blood in biomedicine that are threatening to the identity of the subject, and offers the figure of the vampire as a metaphor for progressive and anti-essentialist definitions of subjectivities. The vampire pollutes kinship, race and family all tied through blood and thus challenges all hierarchical categories in order to re-imagine a humanity that does not relate to the problematic issues rising from such concepts as identity and reproduction. If the vampire questions biological understandings of race, at the same time it can also call attention to blood and difference as necessary tools to reshape identities and disrupt social structures of inequality.

Vampires of colour appear in literature from as early as 1897 with Florence Marryat's *The Blood of the Vampire*.[48] There are the African American lesbian vampires of Jewelle Gomez's *The Gilda Stories* (1991), the maternal vampire of Toni Brown's *Immunity* (1996), and the Caribbean soucouyants in Nalo Hopkinson's *Brown Girl in The Ring* (1998) and 'Greedy Choke Puppy' (2000) and David Chariandy's *Soucouyant* (2007). There is the exotic sexuality of the black vampire Katrina (Grace Jones) in *Vamp* (1986), but also that of male vampires in such films as the blaxploitation *Blacula* (1971) and *Vampire in Brooklyn* (1995).

In Harriet Prescott Spofford's[49] 'The Amber Gods'[50] (1860), set in New England, the female vampire is associated with racial difference and her family's degenerated race. The narrator is a female vampire, Giorgione Willoughby. Giorgione, or Yone, is a blonde but also an ethnic hybrid, half-American, half-Italian, who does not reveal to the reader her vampire identity until the end of the tale. Like those of the female vampires of New England in 'Luella Miller' and 'Bewitched', Yone's story reveals the limitations of and on nineteenth-century womanhood: she begins wasting from an unknown disease on the same day she is getting married. Unlike 'Luella Miller' and 'Bewitched', however, 'The Amber Gods' links vampirism to the threatening presence of the racialised other, the so-called 'little Asian' and 'dwarf'.[51] The racialised other functions as the beautiful vampire's doppelganger in order to reveal the hidden and dangerous identity of the vampire. Yone's vampirism is connected to a primitive amber rosary, inherited by her mother, and traced back to the Asian small woman, her mother's 'black slave'.[52] Ronald Takaki points out that in the nineteenth century Chinese immigrants were associated with blacks and depicted as 'bloodsucking vampire[s] with slanted eyes, a pigtail, dark skin, and thick lips'.[53] They were 'Africanised' and, like the blacks, were seen as threatening to American society.[54] The Asian woman is described as a 'sprite', an 'imp'[55] and a 'Thing',[56] and her presence is a reminder of Yone's racial difference. While the Asian's monstrosity is located in her non-white skin, Yone's is hidden underneath her white skin. Her whiteness, associated here with consumption, disguises her mixed blood. Yone's disease is related to her 'evil' race.[57] She is 'the last of the Willoughbys, a decayed race, and from such strong decay what blossom less gorgeous should spring'.[58] But her ancestors from their portraits on the walls call her a 'Rank blossom, rank decay'.[59] Her beauty, described in such detail by the narrator herself, is superficial and hides her mixed blood and ethnic difference.

Blackness, Toni Morrison argues, is associated with race in American gothic. Spofford's vampire tale shares with Edgar Allan Poe's vampire tales associations of vampirism with racial difference. Following Toni Morrison's reading of the Africanism in Poe's works in *Playing in the Dark: Whiteness and the Literary Imagination* (1992), and specifically Joan Dayan's reading of 'Ligeia' as the 'tragic mulatta',[60] Poe's eponymous vampire and Spofford's Yone can be seen as portrayals of racialised otherness. In *Gothic America: Narrative, History, and Nation* (1997) Teresa Goddu, following Toni Morrison's argument that American gothic's blackness is related to its social context, and that race should be restored to American literature, attempts to examine how southern gothic, and especially Poe's southern gothic, explores racial difference. For Goddu, the racial discourse of Poe's period was concerned with 'perfect whiteness as terrifying blackness'[61] and reflected a national discourse on race and not only regional anxieties about blackness.[62] Leland S. Person goes further in his essay 'Poe's Philosophy of Amalgamation: Reading Racism in the Tales', which places many of Poe's tales within the context of race and racial difference.[63]

Similarly, blackness and race in Victorian England were markers of evil and dangerous vampiric appetites. In Arthur Conan Doyle's 'The Adventure of the Sussex Vampire' (1924) the black Peruvian wife of the English Mr Robert Ferguson is believed to suck the blood of her infant after she is witnessed biting at his neck. It is discovered, however, that she is not a vampire, but that her English stepson who hates his half-brother has been poisoning the baby. Here it is the dark other that is immediately found guilty, and blackness associated with evil, cruelty and consuming desires. In Sheridan Le Fanu's 'Carmilla' (1872) blackness is also linked to vampiric appetites through its juxtaposition with the white mask of the vampire Carmilla. Laura's governess notices a woman who was with Carmilla in the carriage: 'a hideous black woman, with a sort of coloured turban on her head, who was gazing all the time from the carriage window, nodding and grinning derisively toward the ladies, with gleaming eyes and large white eye-balls, and her teeth set as if in fury'.[64] As noted in the second chapter, Carmilla's hidden disease is unmasked by the presence of the 'strangely lean, and dark, and sullen' faces of her 'ill-looking' servants.[65] Like Yone and Carmilla, the dangerous identity and consuming powers of the vampire Clarimonde in Théophile Gautier's 'The Beautiful Dead' (1836) are juxtaposed with blackness and racial phobia through the presence of her Negro page.

In the British author Florence Marryat's *The Blood of the Vampire*, Harriet Brandt's vampirism is also linked to racial difference. Harriet is a psychic vampire and a hybrid, born of degenerated parents and carrying the taint of black blood. Her mother was a mulatta, the child of a slave, carrying in her bloodstream not only the inherited black and bad blood of her mother, but also the vampire strain. Here representations of blackness are painted through the nineteenth century's cultural ether that imagined the black body as hypersexualised, voracious and uncontrolled. Harriet's mother's gluttonous body and her 'sensual lips protruding as if she were always licking them in anticipation of her prey' are signs of her excessive indulgences.[66] The white medical practitioner, Dr Phillips, constructs her accordingly:

> She was not a woman, she was a fiend... a revolting creature. A fat, flabby half caste, who hardly ever moved out of her chair but sat eating all day long, until the power to move had almost left her! I can see her now, with her sensual mouth, her greedy eyes, her low forehead and half-formed brain, and her lust for blood... But she thirsted for blood, she loved the sight and smell of it, she would taste it on the tip of her finger when it came in her way.[67]

The racist discourse, steeped in eugenics, defines Harriet's mother as a defective, atavistic, mixed racial and degenerated other. Blackness is set against refined whiteness, and is characterised by passivity, sensuality, savagery and greed. Dr Phillips believes that, like her mother, Harriet is cursed to inherit such dangerous appetites.

Indeed, Harriet is similarly imagined as an animal. While her 'white' prey is described in terms of delicacy and helplessness, Harriet is like a 'coiling snake'.[68] Her feeding is bloodless, but the rhetoric describing her hunger emphasises her vampiric qualities. She is like a cormorant,[69] a panther,[70] a sly puss,[71] a lynx, a 'terrier [that] worries a rat'[72] and a tigress.[73] It was in the appearance of Harriet's 'dark eyes' looking for their victim and the 'restless lips... incessantly twitching and moving one over the other'[74] that we can situate her identity as a vampire and a racial other. Similarly, as examined in the second chapter, Carmilla is imagined as a black animal attacking its prey. The inferior race is bestialised and reduced to the status of the animal as a prophylactic measure for white society's purity.

If Dracula threatens to change his victim's racial identity,[75] then Harriet, being a child of miscegenation, threatens to violate and blur the boundaries between black and white. In addition, her hybrid identity enables her to veil her sexually appealing and threatening blackness under her innocent whiteness. In particular, as Howard L. Malchow argues, 'What serves to tie the racial fears of the story to the larger issues of fin-de-siècle identity and social anxiety' is 'apprehension of those who can "pass", who can move with impunity across boundaries of class, gender, race, or ethnicity.'[76] Gothic tropes and medical discourse construct Harriet as a monstrous amalgamation of black and white, a mixing that is all the more frightening because it cannot be detected on the surface of the skin. As with other vampires such as Yone, Carmilla and Clarimonde, racial identity is hidden underneath the seductive and sexual surface of the vampire's skin, made visible through their racially marked companions or servants. Harriet, for example, is repeatedly associated with her mother's bad blood and voracity. As Freud writes, 'individuals of mixed race who, taken all around, resemble white men, but who betray their coloured descent by some striking feature or other ... are excluded from society and enjoy none of the privileges of white people'.[77] Here the doubling of identity and the attempt to relocate anxieties about the vampire's dangerous identity on the bodies of others who are defined as black and diseased reveals a desire to separate black from white and retain clear boundaries. If the figure of the hybrid is threatening because it challenges European modernity's dichotomies and essentialism and holds the promise of transformation and change, at the same time such a liquidation of boundaries opens up towards the fluidity of postmodern markets. As will be examined in the following section, new technologies of genetics offer the promise of improving individual health as they profit from racially marketed products.

Contemporary vampires and genetics

Recent vampire texts such as the *Blade* films (Stephen Norrington's 1998 *Blade*; Guillermo del Toro's 2002 *Blade II*; and David S. Goyer's 2004 *Blade: Trinity*), Octavia Butler's *Fledgling* (2005), and Tananarive Due's African Immortals series: *My Soul to Keep* (1997), *The Living Blood* (2001), *Blood Colony* (2008) and *My Soul to Take* (2011) examine blood and race within the contemporary context of genomic research and medicine.

The *Blade* films bring Butler's multiply transgressive text (race, gender, species) back to a more conventionally en-gendered fold by presenting stereotypical understandings of African American men. The films present essentialist accounts of genetics based on biological definitions of race, thus perpetuating problematic assumptions about race. On the other hand, Butler's female vampire hybrid navigates her complex position within what Nikolas Rose names as race's new unstable space of ambivalence. By juxtaposing these various texts, it is possible to show the reconfiguration of race in genomic science and the ways difference and identity are no longer associated with a racist discourse but with individual choice and responsibility. At the same time, it is important, as Due's vampire texts show, to be aware of the oppressive and violent politics of race and the persistence of social inequities.

In *Blade* and its sequels there is a fascination with science and the biology of blood. Biomedicine and genetic engineering are portrayed in the films as scientific tools that will sculpt and define human selfhood; in particular, they address questions of blood and science in relation to race. In Stephen Norrington's *Blade* (1998) the eponymous protagonist is a genetically modified African American, whose DNA was changed when a vampire, Deacon Frost, bit his pregnant mother. Blade's body, reshaped at the molecular level, becomes '*all the more* biological'.[78]

In the three *Blade* films vampires are preoccupied with pure blood, race and lineage. In the second sequel, *Blade Trinity*, Dracula is considered to be the 'patriarch of *hominus nocturna*', the perfect born vampire brought back to life by the vampires to help them gain the power to walk in daylight and kill Blade.[79] As one of the members of the Nightstalkers—the group of young vampire hunters—explains, 'Dracula is the progenitor of the vampire race, his DNA is still pure. It hasn't been diluted by a hundred generations of selective mutation.'[80] To paraphrase what David Punter says about the literary *Dracula*—at the heart of *Blade* is pure blood.[81]

The narrative of the *Blade* trilogy always returns to the question of purity of race and the creation of a new species that will be perfect and rule humanity. The vampire nation of *Blade* is stratified into the pure-blood vampires and the turned vampires, both of them desiring the perfection of their species through the science of blood. The vampires who are not pure, turned vampires like Frost, see Blade's genomic changes as an opportunity for the vampire nation to ascend as a species above humans. They understand the pollution of boundaries and the mixing of blood, but they are depicted as evil vampires who want to disrupt the traditional function of the vampire family and gain power by their contagious proliferation of vampirism. Deacon Frost tells Blade that he has 'all of our strengths and none of our weaknesses', and that he can't keep denying what he is.[82] Blade and Frost are reflections of each other: Blade lacks and desires pure human blood; Frost lacks and desires pure vampire blood and status.

Even when genetic engineering is introduced in the sequel *Blade II*, it is only to reinforce the discourse of a pure blood race. Genetic engineering becomes, in the hands of Overlord Eli Damaskinos, a tool to repeat the mistakes of the past about the myth of a perfect race and reinscribe the blood as a carrier of race. Damaskinos says to Blade that 'for years I've struggled to rid our kind of any hereditary weaknesses. And so, recombining DNA was simply the next logical step. Nomak was the first. A failure. But in time, there will be a new pure race, begotten from my own flesh, immune to silver, soon even to sunlight.'[83] Damaskinos experiments with genetic engineering in order to produce a vampire species that is not characterised by diversity and that suits his plans for domination and power over the human species. Both the turned vampires and those who are pure bloods fail. The *Blade* films present genetic engineering negatively, not because it is capable of promoting structures of power, or the will to recreate and enhance the genome, but because it is considered unnatural and transgresses the boundaries of pure breeding and lineage. In this sense, blood is the epitome of race and should not be contaminated by genetic experiments or alterations of the genome.

This is related to the ways blood is depicted in the three films. When the haematologist Karen Jenson asks Abraham Whistler why vampires need to drink blood, he responds that 'their own blood can't sustain haemoglobin'.[84] Jenson explains that this is why vampirism is a 'genetic defect, just like haemolytic anemia', and needs 'to be treated with gene therapy, rewrite the victim's DNA with a retrovirus. They've been using it on sickle-cell anemia.'[85] The racial implications of such a statement cannot be ignored. The haematologist, an African American, suggests vampirism can be treated in the same way as sickle-cell anaemia, a blood disorder that is presumed to affect primarily African-American people. The misconception that sickle-cell anemia is a black genetic disease is associated with the presumption that Blade's mixed blood and vampirism is a genetic disease and, therefore, proves that the two vampire races are biologically different. As was mentioned earlier, the belief in racial differences in disease helped to segregate humanity and reinforce blacks' inferior status. This is further emphasised when the haematologist has a conversation with the turned vampire Frost and reminds him that 'vampires like you aren't a species. You're just infected, a virus, a sexually transmitted disease.'[86] Because Frost was not born a vampire, he is not as perfect as the pure bloods who inherited vampire status. Both Frost and Blade have diminished status, as their blood becomes a marker of diseases of sexual and racial impurity. The association of blood with racial purity, and also with corrupted blood and AIDS, reveals fears and anxieties about diseased and degenerated bodies. The medieval notion of the body as a container of identity returns to haunt postmodernity. The viral language that explains vampirism as a 'genetic defect' or infection is used to attack only the turned vampires' otherness.

In *Blade II*, Damaskinos explains to Blade that the vampire virus has evolved into a new virus called 'Reaper' that has found a carrier in the bloodstream of Jared Novak, and compares Novak to Blade as an anomaly.[87] Frost, Novak and Blade are similar in the ways they are presented as dissatisfied by their subjective positions and their relations to the Father. The vampire father, Damaskinos, is the authorial figure that facilitates entrance into the vampire family. However, for Frost, Novak and Blade vampire family represents a purity that is a threat to their identities. To destroy the dichotomy of pure/impure blood they need to kill the vampire father and replace his law with one that does not marginalise their condition. Frost kills the aristocratic patriarch of the vampire nation, Novak kills the overlord, the father who created him, and Blade kills Frost, the man who infected him, and also Dracula as the archetype of all vampires. Their desire to disrupt the lineage of the vampire race and kill the figure of the father is rooted in their unconscious wish to take his place, and in the case of Novak and Frost to re-establish a new order that respects their difference. In the end Frost and Novak have to be eliminated, in order that the vampiric order is restored, while Blade needs to accept that his identity is bound by his blood.

Blade specifically is not only a genetically engineered vampire, but also an African American who has the power to disrupt sameness but has not escaped from the constrictions that bind him to his organic body. In *Blade II* a pure-blood vampire named Nyssa asks Blade 'why do you hate us so much?' and Blade answers: 'it's fate. It's in my blood.'[88] Unlike Blade, Nyssa was born a vampire and that gives her a stable understanding of her self and identity. Blade perceives his genetic modification as monstrous, but later he refuses to accept any treatment because it will change his sense of selfhood. Blade's blood represents for him the violent rape of his African American mother by a white vampire, and the contamination of his species. Blood here carries a history of slavery and domination. His fate is tied to his blood and, despite this negation of his vampire self, he finally gives in to the thirst. The *Blade* films are fascinated with essentialist definitions of bodies and subjectivities, of the purity–pollution, good–evil binaries that are symbolised in the blood. Instead of regarding his self as different, always multiple, unsettling, infecting the hierarchical categories of human/non human, vampire/human, black/white, Blade chooses to settle for what his organic body means in a culture that fails to value such difference. He incarcerates his self in a position that is stable, but is unable to escape feeling resentment about his identity.

While Blade remains trapped by his blood, the heroine of Octavia Butler's *Fledgling*[89] is not confined by notions of purity of blood. She is the first black vampire female of the Ina vampire species. Shori's universe, unlike Blade's, is based on mother figures instead of the Name of the Father. The two elder mothers have integrated human DNA with vampire DNA after experimenting with viruses. As her father Iosif explains, 'Some of us have tried for centuries to find ways to be less vulnerable during the day. Shori is our latest and most successful effort in that direction. She's also, through genetic engineering, part human.'[90] The Ina vampires are another species. They were born vampires and live in symbiosis with humans. But they are sensitive to sunlight and thus the creation of Shori will be their hope for a better future, because she 'carries the potentially life-saving human DNA, that has darkened her skin and given her... the ability to walk in sunlight'.[91] In this respect, Shori is not a cyborg, or what Katharine Hayles would call posthuman.[92] The capacities of her body are not enhanced with prosthetic devices which would make her less biological, but she is all the more biological because genetic engineering has enhanced her biological capacities. As Nikolas Rose suggests, instead of advocating that 'we have become posthuman, I ask to what extent we are inhabiting an "emergent form of life" '.[93] Shori's artificially enhanced body is an example of such an emergent form of life, transformed through biotechnology at the organic level.

Rose's proposition of the concept of ethopolitics, according to which genetic interventions are no longer directed at the body of the population but at the molecular level of individuals, is telling here. According to Rose, ethopolitics 'concerns itself with the self-techniques by which human beings should judge and act upon themselves to make themselves better than they are'.[94] *Fledgling* demonstrates exactly this ethical politics of life, where Shori's enhancement of biological capacities is understood as a responsibility for the future quality of life of vampires.

However, some members and families of the Ina species see Shori's black identity and contaminated blood as a pollution of their vampire race. They burn houses, kill her mothers and attempt to murder her and all the vampires who believe in biotechnology and the alteration of their genomes. The violation of the biologically fixed category of the white vampire race, and the consequent punishment of those advocating the genetic rewriting of this identity, echoes the violent history of lynching in America. Shori and her family are imagined and targeted by white vampires as black and other. Just as the miscegenation Shori represents endangers whiteness, it also reminds and warns against the traumatic emergence of a racist past.

In *Fledgling*, as in previous novels like *Dawn* (1987) and *Kindred* (1979), Butler employs a female character who transgresses the limits of race and species so as to construct the possibilities of a progressive future. While in the *Blade* films genetic engineering is seen as dangerous, Butler proposes alterations of the genome and condemns racial purity in order to undo the dramas of a violent past bound by blood, and of hierarchical categories that eliminate difference. Shori, unlike Blade, accepts the possibilities that her enhanced biological body offers her, but, in doing so, she does not let the fact that she is genetically manipulated determine who she is. In this way, Haraway's affirmation that Butler is a cyborg writer is correct to a certain degree. Indeed, Butler condemns racial purity and any notions of organic wholeness as kinship, as well as the separation between humans and vampires. But she also insists on blood and genetic engineering as ways to change human or vampire biology. Blood and genetics are important as long as they do not serve or reinforce the hierarchical discourse of purity or the dissemination of sameness. In *Fledgling*, Shori's identity and possibilities are celebrated by most of the vampires, and in many cases it is demonstrated that her ability to stay awake during the day has been crucially important for the survival of her people. At the same time, she is driven by her own will and she is responsible for the choices she makes for her family of humans and vampires.

This is what is lacking in the *Blade* films. Blade makes no choices and creates no relations with other people, whether vampires or humans. Shori, while trying to find out the truth about her past, gradually creates bonds and erotic relations with female and male humans. Blood is given to her by her family and this binds her to them, as well as her symbionts to her. Here Butler proposes a family that is centred on multiple relations that are expressed between two different species. Blood as a symbol of kinship between people of the same race is abandoned, and this agrees with Haraway's concept of becomings that are not based on race. Although Butler, like Haraway, is against racial purity, her description of the history of Ina vampires points to a recognition of an originary species that was bound by blood and familial bonds. An Ina vampire explains to Shori their history written in books: 'There was a time when Ina believed that paradise was elsewhere in this world, on some hidden island or lost continent' and that 'Some of us wandered as nomads with our human families. Some blended into stationary farming communities.'[95] Butler's narrative exposes blood relations as a symbol of connection to an original past, not one that is fixated by racial categories, but rather one that is bound by the productive and sexual relations between humans as well as vampires. The family represented in *Fledgling* is the product of multiplicity, of no phallus, and of kinships that resist organisation. Instead of slavery, symbiosis is characterised by the free flow of desires between different species.

Butler offers a vampire subjectivity that takes into consideration the bodily experience and blood, not as a historical discourse of race, but as a tool that will ensure difference for future generations, and, at the same time, she shows awareness of the need for social experiences that will shape the notions individuals have about their bodies. *Fledgling* points towards a new understanding of race and the ethical choices individuals make and the responsibilities they take in order to improve their life and health. Instead of feeling angry and shameful like Blade, Shori chooses to confront the world and remake it. Against phallogocentric assumptions of tortured selves by technoscience and blood origins, and against the utopian vampire subjectivity that Haraway envisions, Butler offers vampiric becomings that are tied through blood and their environment. The novel shows an awareness of biology but condemns cultural constructs such as racial purity or a racialised and essentialist identity in order to demonstrate how blood and genetic manipulation can be seen as significant in the disruption of hierarchical patterns and the reshaping of identities.

While Butler celebrates Shori's unique identity and offers positive understandings of race that are not based on a bloody history of racism, such reconfigurations are in danger of being rapidly absorbed by vampiric capital's tentacles and turned into commoditised subjectivities. Caught in the tendrils of biopolitical production, hybridity and new identities are not only promoted and celebrated, but also become increasingly ordinary and assimilated within a system that devours and corporatises difference. Tananarive Due's African Immortal series, while it recognises that blood is important to the extent that it can improve the quality of life of all human beings, also shows awareness about the dangers of submitting blindly to the logic of individual enhancement and self-actualisation. Such a neoliberal subjectivity, as we have earlier shown, supports the interests of biocorporations. Instead, the novels eschew Nikolas Rose's notion of biocitizenship and the use of genetic technologies and personalised medicine to improve and manage one's health at the molecular level and support collective efforts to end inequality and offer health treatment to every human being.

Due's series presents a new race of African vampires, a community of immortal men bound by their unique blood. The 'living blood' has regenerative powers and has been passed on by Khaldun to the other immortals through a ceremony. However, the immortals remain a secret society of men segregated from humanity. Against the pure vampire blood of the masculine order of the Brothers, there is the promise of change embodied by Fana. She is the first African hybrid vampire, half-mortal and half-immortal. Fana's difference opens the way to a new society where all citizens will have free access to the blood. For Fana, the 'Us and Them mentality' of separating humans into races, 'Mortal. Immortal. Good. Bad. Nothing in between',[96] was tiring.

Due's fiction criticises health care and genomics within the United States as the privilege of those who are wealthy, and supports public welfare and not individual consumption of marketable health products. Circulating in the form of a blood-based drug called Glow, the miraculous immortal blood is available in the South African black market, secretly sold to paying customers who are willing to spend millions for the blood, and distributed by Fana's friends. Indeed, because in the United States the drug is 'classified as a schedule II drug—the most dangerous—because of corporate meddling and fabricated reports of fatalities. There were even new rumors cropping up in the news that Glow was related to terrorism.'[97] However, these laws are created 'because the multinationals don't know how to profit from it. The health corps get richer while people are dying.'[98] The interests of biocorporations are shown to facilitate an unequal system that is apathetic towards the health of its people. The healing blood then becomes the antidote for racial inequities in health care. It is offered free as a cure for blood and other diseases regardless of race, gender, ethnicity and class. The community of people sharing the gift of blood is dedicated to changing biopolitical structures by gaining access to blood, drugs, genomic research and biotechnologies, but also by transforming the ways these new technologies articulate race in order to create a more humane world.

Conclusion

While nineteenth-century narratives and the *Blade* films persist in the idea that blood and genes determine identity, demonising racial others as vampires and monsters, on the other hand Butler and Due's vampire fiction endorses the idea that people can choose their identities and communities without being limited by rigid biological categories. Shori and Fana do not define themselves according to their inherited traits. Instead, they are members of groups that embrace change in order to overcome biological essentialism.

Shori's biological enhancement advocates difference as a form of self-actualisation that transgresses modernity's limitations and the essentialist categories of blood. This celebratory and, arguably, liberating and deterritorialising vampiric transformation, however, naively occludes the realities of race as a political problem experienced by those poor minorities that cannot afford the benefits of new technologies. Indeed, in real life access to individualised health care is not available to everyone, and thus the other remains excluded. If medicine in the nineteenth century identified the diseased vampire as racially inferior or legitimated homophobic policies in the 1980s through the AIDS discourse, today the other can be pathologised in new and dangerous ways through race-based genomics. Shori's difference inscribed within her body and visible on her black skin endangers the belief in the inherent differences between white people and people of colour, contributing thus to the intensification of racial discriminations. The celebration of genetics minimises the significance of racial injustices and preserves an oppressive system intact. On the other hand, Fana's vampirism is not the privilege of an individual but a gift offered collectively to all those who seek to improve their health regardless of race, ethnicity, class or gender.

Celebrations of vampiric identity, hybridity and monstrous becomings, as is evident in Butler's *Fledgling*, might be an antidote to modernity's patriarchal and all too human categories, but they are also increasingly subjected to vampiric capital's control. Its insatiate consuming machine does not respect limits or politics but feeds on a difference that it spits out as another regurgitated banal commodity.

In the same vein, the enterprising individual who is responsible for his/her own happiness and health and participates in new forms of health consumerism is, nonetheless, similar to the privileged customer of neoliberal economics. In the next chapter I will be investigating the predatory networks of exploitation of neoliberal finance through the circulation of blood as a commodity and its associations with capital.

5

'The Sunset of Humankind Is the Dawn of the Blood Harvest': Blood Banks, Synthetic Blood and Haemocommerce

In the passage from modernity's industrial economy based on factory labour to postmodernity's new post-industrial economy based on information, affect, services, communicative and cooperative labour, boundaries collapse. Capital marches through the world ruthlessly subsuming under its control global society and translating previously established forms of status and privilege into calculable economic terms.[1] Through its system of equivalence capitalism inserts all material, biological and cultural products, from ideas to species of animals and blood, into the cash nexus, assigning them a monetary value and making them into private property. Vampire capital no longer exploits the worker as Marx tells us, but engulfs the whole of society, feeding like a vampire squid[2] on anything that might generate maximum profit for least possible cost. No longer embodied by the malign figure of Dracula, capital is not a subject but an abstract 'shadowy, centerless impersonality' that 'would be nothing without our co-operation'.[3] It is a mistake, then, to disavow our own participation within the bloody, rapacious and oppressive networks of capitalist production and circulation by cynically distancing ourselves and demonising gothic Others as evil capitalists.

Over the last thirty years capital has become neoliberal in flavour, characterised by 'strong private property rights and weak labor rights, privatization of common and public goods, free markets and free trade'.[4] As David Harvey points out, the new capitalism is not about the production of the new but seeks 'to re-establish the conditions for capital accumulation and to restore the power of economic elites'.[5] Everything in society is infused by a business ethic so that work and life become inseparable.[6] In contemporary neoliberal economic regimes, deregulated predatory capital subsumes 'not just labor but society as a whole or, really, social life itself, since life is both what is put to work in biopolitical production and what is produced'.[7] The focus shifts from commodity production to that of social relations.

In this respect, neoliberalism is not merely a form of governing economies but also a way of governing individuals and their capacities of communication and creativity now transformed into mere commodities. What is created, invested and exploited today is the very production of subjectivity itself.[8] The previous opposition between labour and capital collapses as the worker is transformed into 'human capital' responsible for his/her own management according to the logic of interest and competition. Individuals become 'companies of one',[9] investing in their own skills and abilities so that anything that 'increases the capacity to earn income, to achieve satisfaction' 'is an investment in human capital'.[10] Even when other parts of human capital such as bodies, brains, genetic material, race or class are concerned, these can be altered through plastic surgery, genetic engineering and other technologies in order to 'transform one's initial investment'.[11] In this respect, in the societies of control external surveillance is no longer corporeal but is transformed into an internal and invisible policing characterised by continuous consumption and development.[12] The neoliberal self-interested subject is at once 'manager and slave of him/herself, capitalist and proletarian'.[13]

It is in such a violent and impoverished world where life is viciously subjugated to financial abstraction and everyone becomes a vampire that contemporary vampire narratives such as the *Daybreakers* situate the dystopian present. Capital depends on what Franco 'Bifo' Berardi calls the cult of energy, a sort of *'Energolatria'* and a dogma of growth obsessed with production, domination and competition.[14] The availability of energy, however, as we hopelessly and depressingly realise today, is not boundless. Similarly, in vampire texts blood's availability becomes limited, ushering the whole of society into a crisis, sharpening appetites and facilitating the privatisation of human blood and the increase of vampire capital. As in recent financial catastrophes, where the threat of debt is inevitable and the consequence for the people remains the same, 'They will be bled to death regardless',[15] so the blood crisis in vampire narratives affects humanity which is, in the same vein, bled to death to feed vampiric society. Exploitation is no longer territorial, taking place in the factory where blood is produced and packaged, but consumes the whole of society, so that all of social relations are structured according to the relation between owners and non-owners of capital, between those who have access to blood and those who have not. The exploitation and packaging of human blood becomes inseparable from the production of subjectivities as indebted to vampire capital.

For Maurizio Lazzarato, neoliberalism is founded on such a power relation between creditors and debtors. It is money/blood that imposes modes of domination, subjection and exploitation, creating and destroying social existence. If in the past we were indebted to the community and gods, now we are indebted to the god Capital.[16] Similarly, if blood was spilled in ritualistic sacrifice creating bonds among human beings, now blood in vampire texts feeds an impersonal and unequal vampire structure that destroys social relations. As Lazzarato argues, the destructive power of debt constructs a particular form of subjectivity, the indebted man. Vampire texts produce a world where there is no alternative to neoliberal capital's predation, no possibility of collective transformation. Instead, the indebted man has to take responsibility for all the evils wrought by capital as if they were his 'investments' to manage while feeling guilty for not managing them successfully. Indeed, debt not only feeds on one's blood life but on the whole of existence, inscribing guilt in the mind and the body, fear and bad conscience, so that life becomes wretched. The indebted man guarantees repayment through his flesh and blood, his morality and virtues, and his personal existence. As Marx points out, it is no longer commodities, paper, metal, but man's moral existence that is evaluated and exploited:

> One ought to consider how vile it is to estimate the value of a man in money, as happens in the credit relationship... In credit, the man himself, instead of metal or paper, has become the mediator of exchange, not however as a man, but as a mode of existence of capital and interest. The medium of exchange, therefore, has certainly returned out of its material form and been put back in man, but only because the man himself has been put outside himself.[17]

Man is turned into money while human morality becomes an object of commerce.[18] As Lazzarato argues, credit exploits not biological life but life as existence. Blood in vampire texts, then, is not only understood as biological material but also as a symbol of life itself and human existence. What is at issue here is not only life in its biopolitical dimension, as it was analysed in the second chapter, but existence as 'self-affirmation, the force of self-positioning, the choices that found and bear with them modes and styles of life. The content of money here is not labor but existence, individuality, and human morality; the material of money is not labor time, but the time of existence.'[19] In this sense, contemporary vampire capitalism indebts one for life, exploiting the very heart of one's being. It is not difficult to discern that the impoverished and hungry vampiric monstrosities in *Daybreakers* are nothing else but the indebted of contemporary control societies, whose very flesh and blood, their existence and individuality, are the price to be paid for capitalism's inhuman rapacity and irresponsibility. In this respect, humans are born in debt, owing their blood and life to the great vampire creditor, capital.[20]

Vampire texts expose the vampiric exploitation of blood as organic capital through the vampires' use of science and technology to produce synthetic blood or create human blood banks and farms. Human needs and individual identity are deemed irrelevant. The vampires represent the voracious nature of capitalism, constantly desiring more blood and inventing new ways to produce and profit from human or synthetic blood. In this chapter I approach vampire texts through the examination of the technologies of blood banking, synthetic blood and the associations of blood with money in order to draw attention to the changing status of blood. While blood is still considered as an intimate part of the body and of the identity of an individual, it is increasingly understood within biotech industries and pharmaceutical companies as a commodified biomaterial that can be exchanged for profit. No longer associated with the gift and symbolic exchange which creates social bonds, blood is now sold as a commodity. Vampire novels expose and offer a critique of an unequal system within which biomaterials, including blood, circulate as economies destined for consumption by those who *own* the capital. The paradox that is presented in the following vampire texts is that whereas human life is devalued, biological materials such as blood become extremely valuable and significant for vampires. In the contemporary vampire society blood/money is what rules and communicates, producing and consuming relations and imposing modes of subjection as it circulates within a network of disequilibrium and difference.

On a more general note, what the proliferation of images of vampire corporations and capitalism shows today is not the distant chaotic future, but the current state of politics and economy. While 'Vampyres, or Blood-Suckers i.e. Sharpers, Usurers, and Stockjobbers'[21] have always existed, now they increasingly define the ravenous subjectivities of the present. From Michael Hardt and Antonio Negri's references to vampire Empire and neoliberal zombies in *Empire*, *Multitude* and *Commonwealth* and David McNally's *Monsters of the Market: Zombies, Vampires and Global Capitalism* (2011) to Hernri Giroux's *Zombie Politics and Culture in the Age of Casino Capitalism* (2011) and the explosion of vampire fiction focusing on money and voracious appetites, what is witnessed is a ruthless vampire economics. This is a 'regime of privatized utopias'[22] where self-interested people invest in their own survival and increase of wealth, while others trudge across the abandoned spaces of bankrupt cities reduced to the status of the living dead. Blood, then, becomes an apt metaphor for money as the 'great wheel of circulation'[23] but also for life as both biological and social existence that is controlled, moulded and dominated by the new predatory capitalism.

Blood banking and synthetic blood

This chapter begins by examining the concept of blood banking and the ways vampire texts problematise issues relating to harvesting human blood. In Russia and Spain in the 1930s physicians experimented with the storage of blood and their success became known around the world. However, the idea of a 'blood bank' was first introduced in 1937 when Bernard Fantus organised the collection and supply of blood at Cook County Hospital in Chicago. As he explained, 'Just as one cannot draw money from a bank unless one has deposited some...so the blood preservation department cannot supply blood unless as much comes in as goes out. The term "blood bank" is no mere metaphor.'[24] Nevertheless, the collection and storage of blood did not escape its ethnic segregation into black and white. For example, in 1941 the American National Red Cross refused to accept blood from African American donors. The categorisation of blood according to race during World War II lasted until the civil rights struggles in the 1950s and 1960s.[25]

In Rod Hardy's 1979 film *Thirst*, the vampires are organised into a corporation collecting and supplying human blood. *Thirst* prognosticates the industrialisation and commerce of blood, a long time before films like *Blade*,[26] *Underworld*[27] and *Daybreakers*.[28] The film presents a 'dairy farm'[29] in which elaborate and scientific facilities are used to extract human blood for consumption by vampires around the world. During the beginning of the film, a guide shows the tourists who visit the blood farm the technological equipment of the farm, and the slave-donors caged like animals behind bars and treated as cattle. As the guide explains, the reason for the 'establishment of the dairy farm in 1939 was the brotherhood's growing concern about the health of its members', specifically the dangers of drinking blood, such as malaria, hepatitis and anaphylactic shock.[30] The establishment of the blood farm in 1939 perhaps reflects the opening of the first blood bank in Chicago in 1937. With the spread of diseases through blood, the farm is prepared to control the purity and quality of the blood. Here the health of the vampire population is predicated on the corresponding devaluation and exploitation of human life. As the guide moves through the areas where the slave-donors are giving blood, the camera focuses on the dehumanising spectacle. The viewer participates, along with the prying tourists and consumers, in a voyeuristic exhibition of humanity reduced to its mere biological functions. The guide praises the farm's policy for the battery humans' 'stringent diet' and 'haematological tests for any blood contaminants'.[31] The blood is under strict medical analysis by vampire doctors and packaged in milk cartons for global distribution. Unlike, for example, the excess violence of vampiric consumption in novels such as Justin Cronin's *The Passage*, here the factory functions as an organised operation controlling the purity of blood of reified humans in order to guarantee the survival of vampires. In particular, it is shown that blood is not merely a biological material, but also a symbol of vitality, youth and race, given that the vampires prefer the pure blood of young, white humans.

The availability of blood for the appetites of the vampire community is, however, dependent upon humans. In films and novels of the 1990s and 2000s vampires are concerned with the idea of blood substitutes or synthetic blood which will allow them to live among humans and gain independence and control over their vampiric condition. The historical context of the publication of such novels as Charlaine Harris' *Dead Until Dark* (2009), or the release of films like *Underworld*, informs such issues. As early as the 1980s, problems arising from blood banking, such as the limited supply of blood for transfusion, the rise of the AIDS epidemic that called upon the threat of banked blood and other pathogenic viruses, along with the prospect of profit, led to the idea of producing artificial blood.[32] However, the quest for an artificial oxygen carrier or red cell substitute has not yet been realised. The first-generation products were perfluorocarbon[33] emulsions manufactured in Japan by the Green Cross Corporation and Alpha Therapeutics in the USA in 1989. The second-generation was stroma-free haemoglobin,[34] and the next-generation was polyethylene glycol haemoglobin. These products were discontinued because of their adverse effects and lack of efficiency. Recently, scientists in Britain announced a new project of producing synthetic blood from embryonic stem cells.[35]

Although in reality the search for synthetic blood is a work in progress, vampires in films and literature have managed to develop blood substitutes for their sustenance. George R.R. Martin's *Fevre Dream* (1984) is one of the first novels to explore the idea of blood substitutes. The vampire Joshua York has developed a potion which kills the 'red thirst' or fever for blood.[36] For Joshua and his followers, the potion not only satiates the thirst for blood, but also supports Joshua's ethical attitude towards the taking of human lives. On the other hand, the vampires in the *Ultraviolet* television series want to gain control and power without depending on human beings through the global production of synthetic blood.[37] For example, in the fifth episode of the series, 'Terra Incognita', a Brazilian man who has sickle-cell anaemia is transfused by vampires with blood that carries the vampire virus Code V. The implications of this process, Dr Marsh observes, will be immense for the medical world, given that the synthetic blood could cure not only sickle-cell anaemia, but also any other blood disorder.[38] However, as shown in the last episode, 'Persona non Grata', the vampires' 'obsession and fascination with blood pollution, their environment, mass infection...[and] genetic engineering to replace recruitment'[39] demonstrates their future project of a world where humanity will be subjugated to vampires. The series expresses anxieties about the inhuman use of science, and views synthetic blood as an unnatural product that, when perfected, will herald the dawn of a new era of vampiric dominance.

Unlike the *Ultraviolet* television series, in Harris' *Dead until Dark* (2009), the first of the Sookie Stackhouse books, the vampires' desire to live among human beings is facilitated by the Japanese development of synthetic blood. In the HBO television series *True Blood*, based on Harris' novel, synthetic blood is distributed everywhere, from shops to bars and clubs. Here the vampires become more human, and some of them, like Bill Compton, aspire to live out of the shadows and among humanity. Moving away from the social and ethical commentary of vampiric science in the *Ultraviolet* series, and the use of artificial blood as potentially harmful, Harris' world presents synthetic blood in a positive light. Synthetic blood is viewed as a product that will facilitate the entrance of a supernatural being into the symbolic order. No longer associated with the hunt for prey, synthetic blood can be bought and enjoyed by the vampire at his/her own convenience. Blood packaged in beer bottles becomes a commodified product. Branded as *Tru* Blood (and not *True* Blood), this artificial blood is a mere semblance of real, biological blood. As a simulation of the real thing, synthetic blood for some vampires cannot be compared to, or substitute for, the sensual materiality of biological blood. While the synthetic blood enables vampires to live in peace with humans in a society where difference is accepted, it does so by transforming vampires into insatiable consumers, and blood into a product exchanged for money. The integration of vampires into society, while giving the illusion that difference is accepted, in actuality facilitates the accumulation of capital through the production of Tru Blood, and creates a new category of consumer. At the same time, vampire difference is further exploited by humans who sell V on the black market. V is real vampire blood, which functions as a hallucinogenic drug and enhances sexual pleasures. While the assimilation of vampires into a consumer society erases their vampiric difference and transforms them into mere consumers, at the same time their difference, carried in the blood, is exploited by humans. Vampires, it seems, are dangerous and need to be controlled and tamed, either by conforming to a consumerist ethos, or by being reduced to mere vessels of blood to be exploited by humans.

In *Underworld* the blood bags that Selene carries with her are filled with cloned blood produced by vampires. Unlike the commercial packaging of the bottles of synthetic blood in the *True Blood* series, the artificial blood used in *Underworld* is contained within medical blood bags and carries the logo of the vampire company Ziodex Industries. Synthetic blood is shown to be a medical achievement of vampire science. In Kerrelyn Sparks' *Vamps and the City* (2006), the second book from the Love at Stake series, the vampires of Darcy's circle drink 'chocoblood', a synthetic mixture developed by Roman Draganesti. In the sixth book, *Secret Life of a Vampire* (2009), vampires drink 'blissky', a whisky-flavoured synthetic blood. While in Harris' novels synthetic blood is categorised by its different types, in Sparks' vampiric universe the vampires infuse synthetic blood with different flavours they enjoyed when they were mortals. Presented with a sense of humour, 'chocoblood', bubbly,[40] and 'blissky' bring synthetic blood into the sphere of the mundane by playfully mingling together the products of science and consumer culture. Similarly, the *True Blood* series' promotional tactics playfully integrate the fictional synthetic blood product into real-life consumer culture.[41] It seems that the blood, circulating from the world of biblical prohibitions and taboos to the territory of scientific research, finally arrives in the hands of everyday vampire consumers. As Giorgio Agamben writes, 'If to profane means to return to common use that which has been removed to the sphere of the sacred, the capitalist religion in its extreme phase aims at creating something absolutely unprofanable.'[42] Blood, being removed from its sacred context through the scientific experimentation and the development of synthetic blood, is repeatedly desacralised by its mixing and dilution with objects of consumption, an empty mockery of that which has ceased to be profane. The introduction of blood, and specifically synthetic blood, into the sphere of the mundane and unprofanable, its production, consumption and distribution through the vampires' corporate, scientific and technological networks in *Thirst*, *Ultraviolet* and *Blade II*,[43] leads inevitably to its commodification, the vampires' increase of economic power and the traffic of blood money.

Blood money

The English philosopher Thomas Hobbes in *Leviathan* (1651) drew the connection between blood and money. Blood, like silver and gold, was reserved to nourish man. He notes 'the reducing of all commodities, which are not presently consumed, but reserved for Nourishment in time to come, to something of equal value... And this is nothing else but Gold, and Silver, and Mony [sic]' which pass from one man to another and results in the 'Sanguification of the Common-wealth: For naturall Bloud [sic] is in like manner made of the fruits of the Earth; and circulating, nourisheth by the way, every Member of the Body of Man.'[44] In Adeline Knapp's *One Thousand Dollars a Day: Studies in Practical Economics* (1894), the chapter 'The Sick Man: A Fable for Grown-Up Boys and Girls' is a lesson in practical economics using metaphors of blood and its circulation inside the body to talk about money. Metaphors of money were also used by physicians to describe blood, at a time when blood banking was still inexistent.[45] In *Flesh and Blood* (2008) Susan Lederer explains that American surgeons were among the first doctors to become 'blood bankers' and talk about loans, deposits and balance sheets.[46] The rise of blood banks was the result of the increase of donated blood and the institution of a 'paid donor system'.[47] As noted earlier, Fantus' concept of a 'blood bank' prospered because it was based on the exchange between blood and money. As Lederer shows, in the late nineteenth and early twentieth centuries, due to medical advances, new possibilities arose for the commercial use of body parts and fluids.[48] She explains:

> In the 1930s, American physicians and surgeons appropriated the language and concepts of financial institutions—deposits, withdrawals, and banking—for the storage of bodily fluids and tissues.

More than a metaphor, banking captured the transactional nature of commerce in the body.[49]

Economic language converged with the language of medicine and the vampiric webs of commerce. Karl Marx in Chapter 10 of *Capital* ([1867], 1976) had used the vampire metaphor to describe capital as 'dead labor which, vampire-like, lives only by sucking living labor, and lives the more, the more labor it sucks'.[50] This analogy is discussed by Franco Moretti in '*Dracula* and Capitalism', where he argues in Marxist language that Dracula is an 'ascetic of terror: in him is celebrated the victory "of the desire for possession over that of enjoyment"; and possession as such, indifferent to consumption, is by its very nature insatiable and unlimited'.[51] He does not waste a drop of blood. Dracula is the capitalist who accumulates more and more blood/money by feeding upon the labour-power of others. Dracula's continuous accumulation of money, his need for the blood of innocent virgins, is contrasted with the men's willing act of transfusion of blood to save the pure Lucy. Unlike the blood that Dracula hoards, the men's blood/money is used for a good cause. And this is, according to Moretti, the 'great ideological lie of Victorian capitalism, a capitalism which is ashamed of itself', a capitalism that aligns itself with religion in order to defend its own ends.[52] In *Dracula* Harker attacks the Count with his kukri knife that cuts through his coat, 'making a wide gap whence a bundle of bank-notes and a stream of gold fell out'.[53] Similarly, in Guy Maddin's film *Dracula: Pages from a Virgin's Diary* (2002), Dracula is cut fighting with his rivals and again bleeds gold coins.[54] Later, he throws Jonathan Harker on a mound of emerald bank notes, puts some of them in his mouth and then a knife in a symbolic gesture that brings together metaphors of blood, money and death. As Moretti explains, for Stoker, Dracula's monopoly capitalism is a foreign threat to the free trade of nineteenth-century Britain,[55] while his enemies' money '*refuses to become capital*' and is intended '*to do good*'.[56] In both *Dracula* and *Dracula: Pages from a Virgin's Diary*, money represents the profane and amoral nature of capitalism which threatens the Crew of Light's benevolent and heroic purposes.

While *Dracula* manifests the '*curse* of power'[57] of the capitalist who is obliged to accumulate without escape, Braddon's 'Good Lady Ducayne' ([1896], 2006) exemplifies the logic of the capitalist to assign to all things an exchange value. The story begins with an emphasis on money, as Bella Rollerston 'was willing to go to any lady rich enough to pay her a salary',[58] and many of Bella's initial comments are telling in hindsight: 'I should be anxious to oblige anybody—who paid for my services.'[59] Indeed, Bella ends up being paid for her blood very generously. Similarly, Dr Parravicini is paid for the transfusions. The medical practitioner aligns himself with capital, and blood becomes a commercial commodity, circulating within a capitalist-medical circuit. The relationship between Bella and Lady Ducayne, based on the exchange of blood for money, raises questions about the quality of such a relationship and of human values. Although the naive Bella is unaware of her blood donations, Lady Ducayne has assigned a price to blood. In a similar way, Lady Deverish in Arabella Keneally's 'A Beautiful Vampire' (1896) offers to her companion Marian fifteen hundred pounds a year for transfusing her own youthful blood to her. In *The Gift Relationship: From Human Blood to Social Policy* (1970) Richard M. Titmuss discusses the ethical consequences of donating and transfusing blood, and stresses the freedom 'to exercise a moral choice to give in non-monetary forms to strangers'.[60] According to Titmuss, the British donor system is characterised by voluntary donation and altruism, and does not depend on any expectations of returning the blood gift. Titmuss draws on Marcel Mauss' anthropological study *The Gift: Forms and Functions of Exchange in Archaic Societies* ([1925], 1969), in which Mauss examines traditional customs of obligatory giving and receiving in older societies, where 'to give something is to give a part of oneself' and 'to receive something is to receive a part of someone's spiritual essence'.[61] The thing that is given is never inert but 'alive and often personified'.[62] These gift relations create positive social bonds which, for Titmuss, are important and necessary for organising the system of blood donation. It is this ethical handling of blood that is absent in the relationship between Bella and Lady Ducayne. The powerful 'social relations set up by gift-exchange' and 'which bind a social group together',[63] are substituted here by relations based on the exchange value of blood as a commodity. The commodification of blood is, for Titmuss, destructive not only in terms of dissolving human relations, but also in opening the market to a new 'institution of slavery—of men and women as market commodities'.[64] If blood is treated as a commodity, 'then ultimately human hearts, kidneys, eyes, and other organs of the body may also come to be treated as commodities to be bought and sold in the marketplace'.[65] Bella's blood, transformed into a commodity, reduces her to the status of a thing. 'Good Lady Ducayne' hints at the commodification of blood and the reification of human relationships, and is instrumental in anticipating issues relating to the marketisation of blood, organs and cell lines in late capitalism.[66]

Whereas Lady Ducayne exchanges money for blood, in Julian Osgood Field's[67] 'A Kiss of Judas'[68] (1894) money and blood become interchangeable. The vampires embody the desire for power and money exemplified by their association with the figure of Judas Iscariot. Dracula does not enjoy taking the lives of others or spilling blood, but only takes the necessary quantity of blood.[69] Field's vampires, however, desire the spilling of blood and the death of their victims. The vampires' bite leaves the mark of the Children of Judas on the neck of their victims. The Children of Judas are lineal descendants of Judas who have to sacrifice themselves first, in a parody of the sacrifice of Christ, before they can harm their chosen victims. Instead of the mark of fangs, the wound of the vampire's kiss is the Latin number XXX which indicates the price of blood: thirty pieces of silver. For these vampires, the taking of a life has a price. Through the exchange of blood as money, and the victims' paying with their blood, the vampire is demonised as the harbinger of currency, and money as evil. Thus, the vampiric appetites of the Children of Judas are opposed to the ascetic and immaterial nature of the good Christian.

Neoliberal capital, vampire consumers and vampiric existence

The nineteenth century witnessed attempts to purify capital and align it with religion (*Dracula*) or demonise it altogether ('Good Lady Ducayne'; 'A Kiss of Judas'). The twentieth and twenty-first centuries, however, have glamorised and exalted the power of capitalism and its products, turning capitalism into a religion of money. In a society of atomised monsters and vampire capitalists locked in brutal competition, life itself is subjugated to and policed by money. Vampirism becomes the subjectivity of neoliberal societies dominated by appetites and selfish interests.

Whitley Strieber's *The Hunger* (1981) juxtaposes Sarah Roberts, a scientist of a gerontology group who works on the cure for old age, and the vampire Miriam Blaylock in order to draw attention to the universal human desire for eternal youth and the impossibility of both science and the ancient vampire to offer it to humanity. In the laboratory Dr Roberts finds that the key component to control age is in the blood and is triggered by drugs, temperature and diet. It seems that science and blood in the service of the subject's desires for beauty, physical perfection and immortal youth have become a fashionable means of a commodity culture obsessed with the body. In the laboratory drugs and controlled diet acquire an uncanny quality as their double power to heal and their association with Hollywood lifestyles, beauty regimes and narcissistic emptiness place them at the vampiric crossroads of bloody capital, science, fragmented subjectivity and a consumer culture of simulation. As Mary Pharr points out, 'our millennial vampiric mythology has transmuted the "blood of the covenant" into the promise of blood as glamour'.[70] The subject of consumption, perfectly embodied in the undead existence of Miriam Blaylock and in the gerontology group working with Dr Roberts, is the subject absorbed in the culture around him/her. They all aspire to feed on the blood, whether blood is, in the case of Blaylock, a necessary life-giving fluid, or in the case of the scientists, the blood of the market and symbol of economic flows that feeds capitalism. Fred Botting writes: 'With the discovery (and patenting, no doubt) of the "Methuselah gene" controlling aging, the line that wavers due to the presence of the double, will find itself erased: humans cross over to the realm of the undead.'[71] According to Botting, the subject of consumption resembles the figure of the vampire, cannibalising the culture around him or her, absorbing and feeding upon a world that becomes frighteningly more uncertain and vague.[72]

Matt Haig's *The Radleys* (2010) celebrates the commodification of blood and the ultimate domestication of the vampire through its representation of the new suburban vampire family. While the older generation of vampires, such as the prodigal Uncle Will, retain their transgressive power through the hunt for human blood and the horror and eroticism of the vampire bite, the Radleys, on the other hand, control their appetites and follow the vampire law set out in *The Abstainer's Handbook*, the disciplinary tool to regulate vampiric instincts and desire. According to *The Abstainer's Handbook*, vampire 'instincts are wrong. Animals rely on instincts for their daily survival, but we are not beasts. We are not lions or sharks or vultures. We are civilised and civilisation only works if instincts are suppressed. So, do your bit for society and ignore those dark desires inside you.'[73] For the vampires to integrate into human society they need to control their thirst for blood. Unlike Harris' *Dead Until Dark*, where humans are aware of the existence of vampires living among them, Haig's vampires keep their condition a secret while living and behaving like humans. Thus, as *The Abstainer's Handbook* explains, vampires are not allowed to drink blood: 'Blood doesn't satisfy cravings. It magnifies them.'[74] Consequently, the Radleys abstain from blood. The children, Rowan and Clara, are unaware of their condition, while the parents strive to keep their thirst under control. Blood is substituted for Night Nurse liquid and ibuprofen tablets. Like the medical products the vampires consume, the vampire hunter, Jared

Copeland, consumes Lazy Garlic, a ready-made garlic paste to protect himself from the vampires. Both humans and vampires are indistinguishable. The dangerous magic of the forbidden, folklore and the fear of the supernatural have been eradicated in favour of the mundane and consumer products. The vampire no longer resembles a monster: 'Our monsters', writes Jean Baudrillard, 'are all manic autists.'[75] They have all become the same, identical, sterile, without any of their hereditary otherness. The vampire father, Peter Radley, recognises this: he is 'trapped inside a cliché that's not meant to be his. A middle-class, middle-aged man, briefcase in hand, feeling the full weight of gravity and morality and all those other oppressive human forces.'[76] The Radleys embody the contemporary vampiric condition: domesticated, homogenised and without difference, they resemble too much the humans they once desired to consume.

It is within this network of consumption that, ultimately, with the commodification of vampire blood, the Radleys are able to enjoy blood without sacrificing the benefits of their suburban lifestyle. Black Narcissus, a vampire nightclub in Manchester, sells vampire blood for 'Twenty quid a bottle'.[77] The 'Accessible, guilt-free blood-drinking' offers the contemporary vampire consumer the convenience of the supermarket: 'You didn't have to be unfaithful, or steal, or kill someone to get a fix. You just went to a place in Manchester and bought it and drank it, and you could be happy again.'[78] If everything can be bought, then vampirism itself can become a bottled commodity.

This is the triumph of capitalism, of a society ruled by commodity fetishism and where tradition or symbolic institutions have been replaced by 'processes of recoding': 'bureaucratization, the nuclear family, and consumerism'.[79] According to Eugene Holland, it is the 'abstract calculus of capital itself' that organises social order through decoding (deterritorialisation) and recoding (reterritorialisation) processes.[80] Following Gilles Deleuze and Felix Guattari, Holland explains that under capitalism the symbolic order has 'no fixed center' and 'no established authority figure'.[81] There are no 'traditional meanings and preexisting social codes', he writes, 'nor the priest, king, or god' to organise and understand social life.[82] What governs the symbolic order under capitalism is the semiotic process of 'decoding': 'market society's aggressive elimination of all preexisting meanings and codes',[83] and the recoding of 'libidinal energy back onto factitious codes so as to extract and realize privately appropriable surplus value'.[84] In *The Radleys* the vampiric family is transformed into a functional, nuclear family after the dismissal and substitution of the fictional and ineffectual symbolic vampire law, represented by *The Abstainer's Handbook*, with commodified vampire blood. The vampire, integrated into the symbolic order of capitalism, embodies the perfect consumer.

If blood is bought and consumed, then it is no longer a material substance that is exchanged in private between lovers, humans and vampires. It becomes a marketable commodity, and in *The Empire of Fear* ([1988], 1991) it is manipulated by genetic scientists in the laboratory, a factory that produces blood combined with vampire DNA. In this respect, blood is not experienced as a transgressive or vital warm fluid, but as an unprofanable, cold product. Dr Chadwick, a leading genetic scientist in Nova Scotia, explains that in the age of modern biomedicine 'we extract the relevant molecule on a commercial scale from blood donated by humans and by chimpanzees, though we hope to move over in the near future to manufacturing techniques based in genetic engineering'.[85] When vampirism becomes the dominant form of life, then the products of consumption change: 'you create too great a demand for human meals. Blood economics.'[86] Vampiric consumption is intertwined with the consumption of commodities. However, blood as the ultimate commodity is not associated with choice or ownership, but with compulsory consumption, and one that will be eternally repeated.

Blood in a consumer culture is also exemplified in the non-productive activities of the vampires in *Blade*. The enjoyment of excess is captured in the film in the camouflaged nightclub in which the vampires indulge in a carnival of wasted blood. During the vampires' dancing and excessive sexual energy, blood sprinklers shower them in blood. The blood bath under the meat factory is the quintessential image of the animalistic and collective spending of energy of the postmodern consumer. Here the artificial theatricality is the product of the technologies of modern entertainment. Blood is artificially spent: a product circulating inside the modernistic, underground geographies of pipes and coming through the sprinklers, it no longer carries its positive life-giving powers. The arterial circuits of global capital feed off the excess energy of the vampires, who in turn feed on the marketable product that is blood. The exchange is exemplary of the economic structures of late capitalism.[87] Admission to the space of the nightclub is given to the vampires by the simple confirmation of their vampiric identity, thus enabling them to exchange, like consumers, their identity for acceptance to the club. Inside they indulge in the hedonistic enjoyment of mass consumption of blood that gives the illusion of a momentary absolution of any ethical responsibilities. Vampiric identity and blood become accordingly the mere products of an exchange-value system.

Even when the original vampire Dracula enters the world of the second sequel, *Blade Trinity*, his sense of selfhood is provoked by a vampire culture of simulations that feeds off his image. While Dracula enters a gothic shop selling vampire merchandise, the seller tells him: 'We've got Dracula lunchboxes. Did you see those? There's bobble heads, key chains. We've got just about anything. Even vampire vibrators.'[88] As a pure blood vampire and the progenitor of his race, Dracula is faced with limitless simulations of his original image. The pure blood of Dracula is presented against the new blood-life of the market. As Nick Land playfully writes, 'vampiric transfusional alliance cuts across descensional filiation, spinning lateral webs of haemocommerce'.[89] The vampire no longer controls his vampiric reproduction; the market diffuses his image into multiple reproductions. In a culture that feeds upon its recycled images and spreads its viral vampiric products, Dracula is left with nothing else but revenge. The film reconfirms the status of blood and authority of the archaic Dracula as he feeds on the vampiric merchant and consumers.

In del Toro and Hogan's *The Strain*,[90] *The Fall* and *The Night Eternal*, the capitalist Palmer, by controlling the markets, is able to sustain his personal wealth and power, while destroying the lives of others. As a capitalist, he invested in a vampire future where he would be the only powerful and wealthy immortal. Like vampire capital, Palmer's orchestration of, and refusal to invest during, financial crises resonates with Dracula's ascetic logic. As Moretti writes, Stoker's vampire is 'the capital which, after lying "buried" for twenty long years of recession, rises again to set out on the irreversible road of concentration and monopoly'.[91] Palmer's interests in the vampire virus and blood reflect the similar investments by corporate capital in the life sciences and the profiting from genetic innovations.[92] Palmer is an abstraction of a vampiric capitalism that sucks the lives and money of society in order to keep on living forever: 'an abstract parasite, an insatiable vampire and zombie-maker; but the living flesh it converts into dead labor is ours, and the zombies it makes are us'.[93] Following Deleuze and Guattari's argument that capital is the 'unnameable Thing', Mark Fisher similarly understands capital as an 'abomination', 'a monstrous, infinitely plastic entity, capable of metabolizing and absorbing anything with which it comes into contact'.[94]

In this new vampire society, 'All currency is blood'[95] and humans are subjugated to an oppressive and hierarchical regime based on different blood types for vampire consumption. The new vampire state is stripped back to its core military and police functions and is unable to

generate anything new: 'everything a repeat', 'nothing new was produced. And...people like it.'[96] Like neoliberal regimes, the culture is
given over to retrospection and the security of the old, unable to create new memories. The humans surrender like 'cattle' and are in danger
of being at any moment 'devoured by the concrete structure of the
closest farm'.[97] The world of the vampire 'Master, a being marshalled
by no morality or code. A virus, and a ravenous one at that',[98] is a
deracinated one, of bloodletting camps, capitalist accumulation and
dehumanisation.

The economic exploitation of the masses and the thirst for power and
profit in times of economic recession becomes the focus of the Spierig
brothers' *Daybreakers*. The future is overpopulated with vampires,[99]
while humans are farmed for their blood by vampire corporations. The
dystopian vampire society reflects the present financial crisis and ecological disaster, and is a world that is moving towards an extinction event.
'These are desperate times' for the vampires.[100] This is a world where
after the plague the crisis has been normalised and where capital and an
authoritarian state are inseparable: blood farms of forced bloodletting
co-exist with franchise coffee-blood bars. It is a world of contradictions.
As the film shows, beyond sleek billboards and the indifferent coolness
of vampire youth smoking, the dehumanised poor beg for blood.

The new vampire state is experiencing an escalating global blood crisis: blood rationing leads to crime in the streets, while the poor vampires
who cannot afford blood feed on other vampires or on themselves,
mutating into bat-like monstrosities called Subsiders. Meanwhile, the
remaining humans are captured and given to Bromley-Marks pharma-
ceuticals to be farmed. Wealthy vampires enjoy the highly priced human
blood, while Bromley-Marks searches for a blood substitute which, for
the capitalists, means 'repeat business'.[101] Neoliberal capital is about
the restoration of power to economic elites and their accumulation
through dispossession of the poor. The corporation is here striving to
solve problems of supply by finding a blood substitute with the help
of biotechnologies. This is a world where production can no longer
satisfy the insatiable hunger for consumption. From human blood to
blood substitutes, vampire corporations adapt to new conditions in
order to maximise profits and preserve the order on which their wealth
depends. As Evan Calder Williams notes in his reading of zombie films,
'When you can no longer squeeze a profit from your workers, the
point is not to squeeze harder. It is to change the nature of the work.
To change the nature of the workers, of the structure of exploitation
itself.'[102]

Daybreakers and *The Strain Trilogy* focus on the evil vampire corporation or the capitalist Eldritch Palmer, demonising these fictional others and absolving us of any involvement in capitalist networks of exploitation. What is being disavowed here is our own cooperation, as well as that of the humans in the texts who seem passive, submissive and too atomised. Addicted to a hypermediated consumer culture, they retreat into the safety of their own homes, their addictions and rerun television programmes, unable to resist. In *Daybreakers* wealthy vampires watch indifferently the public spectacle of the wretched vampires burned in the sun, while in *The Night Eternal* humans passively return to the normality of everyday life without any possibility of collective change. Of course there are resistant groups in both of the texts whose sense of trust, obligation and morality counters the self-interested world of vampiric capital. However, their celebrated attempts are interpreted through an American, white, Christian lens *restoring* society to the safety of older regimes and not opening towards *new* possibilities outside of the devouring maw of capitalism.

Conclusion

The examination of blood capital in vampire texts presents us with ethical questions regarding the manipulation and exploitation of blood as an intimate part of the self and one's notion of a stable identity. At the same time, it demonstrates that the vampire metaphor in contemporary culture is solidified and stabilised around the figures of the vampire consumer and capitalist. As blood is increasingly commodified, desacralised and separated from one's body, so does the vampire resemble more and more the capitalist and the passive, apolitical and indifferent consumer. Contemporary vampire narratives are reactions against the inhumanity and voracity of postmodern capitalism and against the objectification of humanity. If the vampire is Capital itself transforming us into zombies and insatiable consumers, then vampire narratives point towards the search for an alternative course where humanity will be able to follow its own line of flight and create new cartographies outside the control of capitalism. A different world is possible beyond capital and beyond the vampiric subjectivity of interest and competition that will produce a new alternative political subject liberated from consumerism and working in common with its fellow beings.

6
'Many People Have Vampires *in* Their Blood': 'Real' Vampire Communities

This chapter will examine blood in contemporary vampire communities and demonstrate how the symbolic meanings of blood analysed in previous chapters evolve in the realm of hyperreality and simulations. In postmodernity blood circulates from the symbolic to the simulated, and arguably becomes a mere accessory for the vampiric lifestyle. As examined in the previous chapter, all ethical values, beliefs and cultural objects are subsumed by capitalism and are turned into aesthetic objects assigned an economic value. Within the reality of capitalism, blood is no longer veiled by symbolic significance, but shamelessly stripped of its religious and social meaning and aestheticised. As Avery Gordon points out, 'In a culture seemingly ruled by technologies of hypervisibility we are led to believe not only that everything can be seen, but also that everything is available and accessible for our consumption.'[1] In this respect, blood is not only a metaphor for capitalist circulation, fluidity and liquidity in the network society but also a product that circulates like any other commodity.

At the same time, however, the proliferation of contemporary vampirism should be understood not only as a mere problem of simulation but as indicative of contemporary capitalist relations. From vampire television shows such as *Buffy the Vampire Slayer* and *True Blood*, to films such as the *Twilight* series, popular culture is replete with images of predation, danger and compulsion. The attraction to, and fascination with, vampires points towards the omnipresent and generalised pattern of parasitic relations and the threat posed by those predatory humans caught in the spell of voodoo economics and compelled to feed on each other, maximising their human capital at the expense of others.

Indeed, the ubiquity of the metaphor of vampirism in contemporary fictions and relations suggests a world in which predation has become a compulsion. The antagonistic, competitive and predatory relationships that neoliberal capitalism encourages paralyse contemporary subjects who are either compelled to become predators themselves or surrender to the appetites of other predators. As Noémi Szécsi writes in her novel *The Finno-Ugrian Vampire* (2012), 'You must suck out their blood before they suck out yours.'[2] In a similar way, the Temple of the Vampire defines vampire identity in terms of predation: 'The hierarchy of living beings on earth is based upon the food chain. Ultimately everything is reduced to the issue of who eats whom. To achieve the Vampiric Condition, the Vampire must come to a predator's perspective toward human beings. It is impossible for one to become Vampire if one is unwilling to prey upon the vital life force of humans.'[3] As examined in the first chapter, for these neoliberal individuals, vampirism is a celebration of individualism, freedom and empowerment through management of one's assets.[4] Neoliberal vampires, then, are entrepreneurs of themselves, fashioning themselves and profiting from their own labours.

In this respect, contemporary manifestations of vampirism may be considered as expressions of a vampiric neo-individualism in the light of neoliberalism. The normalisation and aestheticisation of predatory behaviour, of individual self-fashioning and selfish explorations of identity, are symptomatic of the neoliberal governmentality of the self. The entrepreneurial subject responsible for his/her self and obsessed with his/her self-improvement and development reflects the contemporary selfish individual who embraces the seductive surface of vampiric identities and lifestyles.

At the same time, beyond a seductive but alienating individualism, the neoliberal vampires desire to create strong and meaningful collective relations and community bonds. On the one hand, personal and individual freedom, well-being, and material possessions are considered valuable. On the other hand, vampiric rituals and communal bonds are expressions of alternative social forms that substitute for the failure of social and political institutions and the withering of civil society.

Hyperreal vampires

Prior to the premiere of the HBO vampire series *True Blood*, a promotional campaign was launched consisting of viral marketing and an alternate reality game, where different websites like BloodCopy.com, the RevenantOnes.com, and Chishio.jp created and disseminated information about the mysterious existence of 'real'[5] vampires. This strategy involved emails and letters sealed with a TB logo,[6] sent to selected individuals, including bloggers, and containing a text in cryptic language. The campaign also included web links to a MySpace account under the username 'BloodCopy' with the videos 'Vampire Taste Test— True Blood vs. Human' and 'BloodCopy Exclusive Interview with Samson the Vampire'.[7] At BloodCopy.com many other similar YouTube videos were uploaded testifying to the existence of vampires, including videos from real vampires from Russia, Germany and Japan, images of adverts about the synthetic blood found in public spaces, and various other news from around the world, such as 'Vampire Plague Real, Says Downing Street'.[8] This marketing strategy confused the boundaries of reality and fiction, normalised the vampire and opened the way to unending simulations and merchandising. From *True Blood* clothing and jewellery, to the commercialisation of Tru Blood, 'an exact replica' of the 'delicious blood orange carbonated drink inspired by Bill's favorite synthetic blood nourishment beverage',[9] the *True Blood* series transformed the vampire of fiction into a simulated reality, and blood into a product to be bought, sold and consumed.

But what is more important, one day before the premiere of the show on 7 September 2008, two documentaries were broadcast for the promotion of the series: *True Bloodlines: Vampire Legends* and *True Bloodlines: A New Type*. While *Vampire Legends* presented the vampires of folklore, literature and film, the second one, 'A New Type', portrayed the real vampire communities and vampire clubs. The latter included Michelle Belanger and Patrick Rodgers, both self-identified psychic vampires.[10] On the one hand, these promotional tactics helped to stir the interest for the new vampire series; on the other hand, they problematised the idea of reality and made almost indistinguishable real vampires from their fictional counterpart. This framing of the fictional universe of the television series with the so-called real, while giving a sense of realism to *True Blood*, fictionalised and dramatised the vampire community, infecting both reality and fiction.

It is within this endless, viral simulation of events and products that we can partly situate the contemporary phenomenon of real vampirism. The individual's belief in being a real vampire and drinking blood is a result of postmodernity, where there are no taboos, no clear boundaries or safe categories, where fictional monsters permeate everyday life without the power to disturb or pollute but express uncertainty about their status as human beings. If with the death of God in modernity there is not a transcendent guarantor of values and meaning and, consequently, the value of Truth is questioned, in postmodernity the real world becomes 'weightless' and a 'gigantic simulacrum'.[11] With the advent of the death of the real, metaphor is replaced by the metonymic orgy of signifiers.

The existence of vampire communities is consequently perhaps a sign of our times: 'the incredible coexistence of the most bizarre theories and practices, which correspond to the improbable coalition of luxury, heaven, and money'.[12] It is no coincidence, then, that the twentieth century saw the creation of real vampire communities by people who identify as real vampires, and who believe that drinking small amounts of blood or absorbing the psychic energy of others is necessary for their physical and mental well-being. These are the sanguinarian[13] or psychic vampires, respectively, while those who practice both name themselves hybrid vampires. However, there are other vampire groups within the community that follow a religious path and condemn the above forms of vampirism. For them, vampirism is a form of 'apotheosis achieved through occult knowledge and willpower'.[14]

As Arlene Russo[15] points out, 'There are endless categories of vampires—and many new sub-categories are invented regularly, such as medical vampires and astral vampires.'[16] It is not surprising, she says, that with so many definitions of a vampire, some people believe themselves to be vampiric.[17] Establishing one definition of what it means to be a 'real vampire' is problematic, as vampiric identity is always 'self-designated' and describes the individual's specific condition.[18] More generally, real vampires or real vampire communities, are part of a larger vampire network, a multi-faceted group and an 'acephalous' entity,[19] that embraces the various real vampire groups, vampire religions and their social networks, as well as donors, lifestyle vampires and other non-vampires who are considered vampire allies.[20] Vampire identity, however, is embedded within the structures of capitalist society and culture, and is influenced by the cultural representations and meanings of vampirism, or what the vampire groups describe as 'vampire milieu', and also their ideas, regulated and disseminated in books or on virtual spaces. As the psychic vampire Michelle Belanger explains, 'The reflexivity of fiction and fact have made it nearly impossible to separate the reality of the vampire from the archetype: One feeds into the other in a loop as complicated and infinite as the orobouros.'[21] For Belanger, the representations of fictional vampires have 'left an indelible stamp' upon the vampires' imaginations and influence their vampiric rituals and the communities' rites.[22]

The existence of vampire communities and, in particular, of sanguinarian vampires raises questions about the significance of the insistence on vampirism as a medical condition or need based on the idea that blood is a life-giving substance nurturing the body. Blood is treated by sanguinarian vampires as a material extracted from willing donors to sustain their physical and mental health, and is arguably divested of any other cultural meaning. There is no official medical condition or explanation about vampirism to support this view, and the fact that blood as a bodily fluid is indigestible by humans reduces the sanguinarian need for blood to the realm of fiction. What connects the self-identified sanguinarians and allows them to develop the bonds of community is the belief in blood and vampirism as a necessary or innate part of their identity. Like the self-identified psychic vampires, sanguinarian vampires are trying to separate themselves from the religious and occult vampire groups by claiming that their vampire condition is something that they are born with, and is manifested as the need for energy or blood in the early years of their lives, in puberty or even earlier on in their childhood. The attempt to define vampirism as *something in the blood* is one of the ways these vampires are trying to appear more 'real' and believable than the occult groups' vampire definitions, while giving the illusion that their vampirism is not derived from vampire representations in literature or other cultural influences.

But vampires who claim to need blood for medical or health reasons are also individuals already enmeshed in a culture oversaturated with vampire imagery, and who have consumed and regurgitated literary and cinematic representations of vampires. The choice of such an identity is arguably a gesture of participation in the cultural representations of vampirism and blood consumption. In particular, by choosing specific vampire representations from culture, such as Anne Rice's fictional vampiric personae, they produce a sanitised vampire identity that shares nothing with the reanimated corpses of folklore. In such identities, blood is no longer a transgressive fluid, but a perilous matter that is first, controlled through medical analyses of the donor's blood, and secondly, attained by vampires through careful procedures and sterilised needles.

On the other hand, vampirism in the occult and religious groups is explained as a spiritual development through esoteric practices, knowledge of which is exchanged for money. These vampire religious groups can be placed within a wider context of religious groups selling apocryphal and spiritual knowledge and other Salvationist fantasies, through, among other things, the production, advertising and selling of various holy books and jewellery. This is a form of capitalist vampirism and describes the consumerist logic of contemporary capitalist society with its obsessive pursuit of health and happiness and the hedonistic promise of an afterlife.

With the establishment of a global society of control and the withering of disciplinary institutions arises the phenomenon of vampire communities of like-minded people, understood as a response to this contemporary lack of authority. With the failure of symbolic authority, the subject does not take pleasure in the way s/he would in the presence of the Father. Instead, s/he is left with a feeling of anxiety, since from the moment s/he is instructed to enjoy without limits and prohibitions, when everything is permitted, nothing is desired. This is why we believe that desire is controlled by 'a despotic figure which stands for the primordial *jouisseur*: we cannot enjoy because *he* appropriates all enjoyment'.[23] With the return of the obscene father transgression is no longer possible. Thus, the vampire communities, by constructing a hierarchical system of priests or elder vampires, writing and distributing their own books and codices, try to create a vampire identity and an ordered tradition: in the case of vampire religious groups, the belief in old vampire gods; in the case of psychic and sanguinarian vampires, the return to a premodern symbolics of blood through rituals, New Age pop-wisdom, holistic health beliefs and vampire deities in order to appeal to some order and find meaning within a culture that has lost its faith in the big Other. The existence of vampire communities creates a phantasmatic sense of unity which does not exist in postmodernity. On the other hand, the imitation of, and playful experimentation with, bloodletting, initiation and S/M rituals questions notions of a stable identity. While vampires try to find in the reality of blood and the body something more truthful and stable, this remains anchored to simulacra and the sensuality of vampire spectacles.

Blood changes its meanings according to its use by different vampires or vampire communities, and in different contexts. If in postmodernity blood and the vampire myth function as symbols without any power to unsettle boundaries and reduced to mere simulations, then, in order for blood to be transgressive and symbolic, the vampires have to appeal to the spectre of the law. By returning to the premodern 'symbolics of blood', where 'nothing was more on the side of the law, death, transgression, the symbolic, and sovereignty than blood',[24] vampires call forth the old symbolic law that guarantees *jouissance* in the post-oedipal age of no authority.

For religious scholar Christopher Hugh Partridge, the vampire generation is indeed 'in search of spirituality, in search of that which transcends history'.[25] From holistic health practices, to New Age, Pagan and vampire spiritualities, Partridge claims that the world is experiencing a surge of re-enchantment, an antidote to the loss of order in a society of boredom. However, such re-enchantment seeks to affirm and justify a meaningful existence within a world that is subordinated to the exigencies of atomism and apathetic consumerism.

In this chapter I will focus on the vampire communities' emerging vampire identity, and discuss how the meaning of real blood changes in different contexts. Blood, with all its symbolic and cultural values, may invest meaning or create an organised community, or participate in the discourse of postmodernity as a simulation of a 'fantasised reality'[26] and an accessory to the vampiric lifestyle. The proliferation of the vampire identity in contemporary culture designates a preoccupation with predation, unrestrained self-interest and rampant individualism that has become the widespread subjectivity of our desperate and brutal neoliberal times.

Naming the thing

While vampirism and blood consumption in literature and film is represented as inhuman, a way to define otherness or to expel the other from the community, within the vampire communities vampirism is a desired, self-designated term to which different groups lay particular claim. Whether sanguine or psychic, self-claimed vampires insist on designating that they are 'real' or more real than other vampires. Like the realism of neoliberal capitalism, where all symbolic and ritual meaning is stripped off,[27] vampirism is no longer metaphor but metonymy. It becomes an aesthetic reality without the magic of fiction.

But while the 'vampire' is the figure with whom every one of these individuals chooses to identify, the definition of a vampire bleeds into various subjective characterisations that share the common idea of *belief*. The belief that there is something in the blood, some inherent quality that nurtures the organism and sustains health and mental balance, is associated with the symbolic fictions and representations of vampires and their thirst for blood, and is shared by real-life vampires. Such belief in the blood or the energy it contains is supported by similar beliefs in New Age spiritualities and Chinese medicine held by many of these vampires. As the Atlanta Vampire Alliance claims,

> there is a popular but not universally-held theory within the vampire community that the life force energy or 'prana' contained within the blood is the source from which they feed, rather than any physical

component of the blood itself. This theory is supported by the notably small amount of blood that vampires consume to alleviate their hunger; usually one to two tablespoons.[28]

Although, as the Atlanta vampires explain, such a fact is usually counteracted by the dissimilarities between psychic and sanguinarian vampires—the first demonstrate 'psychic tendencies', and the latter 'more physical symptoms'[29]—this definition still remains within the boundaries of pseudo-intellectualism and New Age spirituality. According to the VEWRS and AVEWRS statistics, 21.43 per cent of sanguinarian vampires would disagree with this formulation and support the idea that blood is needed as a biological food. On the other hand, 42.88 per cent of sanguinarian vampires agree with the idea expressed by most psychic vampires, that blood contains energy and life force.[30] These non-western, alternative religious beliefs, integrated in western capitalist society, have become widespread commodities which along with the consumption of popular vampire literature and other vampire-related products help create a belief in blood as food or a source of energy.

By removing the vampire and its consumption of blood from its fictional context, they made real and material what was once a mere fictional element. While sanguinarian vampires and Laycock argue that it is not because of a belief in blood, since 'There is no organization or text within the vampire community that prescribes the drinking of blood or attributes special properties to this practice,'[31] the fact that they have reduced the supernatural undead to the mere act of consuming blood, the only quality of the fictional vampire individuals can emulate today,[32] manifests not only a belief in vampire fictions, but also an attempt to believe in something real and palpable. Within the symbolic order of capitalism, the belief in the power of images and signs, of vampiric commodities and other spiritualities, has sold them the dream of vampirism. But the desire to believe itself has been perverted into a desire or need for something real behind the fictions. The metaphors of blood and vampirism are snuffed out in the real, realised and disillusioned. Symbolic notions of blood are replaced by the biological need for blood.

The belief in vampirism is inseparable from a sense of narcissistic individuality and self-fulfilment that Christopher Lasch demonstrated as early as 1979 in *The Culture of Narcissism: American Life in an Age of Diminishing Expectations*. For Lasch, the dominant disposition in the 1970s was 'To live for the moment...to live for yourself, not for your predecessors or posterity.'[33] The contemporary pursuit of personal improvement was already evident in that generation of Americans interested in 'getting in touch with their feelings, eating health food, taking lessons in ballet or belly-dancing, immersing themselves in the wisdom of the East, jogging, learning how to "relate", overcoming the "fear of pleasure" '.[34] This collective narcissism was, according to Lasch, characterised by a fixation on 'private performance', and of becoming 'connoisseurs of our own decadence' and cultivating a 'transcendental self-attention'.[35] Laycock rightly observes that the Americans' withdrawal into narcissism in the 1970s was accompanied by the growing interest in vampires,[36] with Anne Rice's publication of *Interview with the Vampire* (1976) reflecting and participating in, as Rice herself has claimed, 'a protest against the post World War II nihilism' of the era.[37]

Indeed, the freedom of choice and of embracing diverse lifestyles, modes of expression and different cultural practices is characteristic not only of postmodernism but also of the current spirit of neoliberalism that arose in the troubled years of the 1970s. With its emphasis on freedom, consumerism and narcissistic exploration of self, sexuality and identity, neoliberalism 'proved more than a little compatible with that cultural impulse called "postmodernism" which had long been lurking in the wings but could now emerge full-blown as both a cultural and an intellectual dominant'.[38] The celebrity vampire Don Henrie states: 'I have always been interested in the occult and anything that helps fortify my image and spirituality.'[39] This self-aggrandising and unbridled individualism forms the bedrock both of postmodernism, with its play of identities, and of the neoliberal market-based culture of consumerism.

Neoliberal subjectivity is compatible with the so-called real vampires' self definitions. Flexible, spontaneous, nomadic and oriented towards feelings and appearances, the neoliberal individual pursues his/her own desires and their immediate gratification. Today individuals are fascinated with tradition and the past, unable to create new memories. The neoliberal privatised individual is concerned with the emancipation of his/her entrepreneurial freedoms and skills and with the promotion of his/her own well-being. Neoliberalisation celebrates, in unison with postmodernism, ephemerality and the short-term contract.[40] In the endless pursuit of profit, the atomised individual prefers the temporary rather than the sanctity of unbreakable bonds such as marriage. Individual needs, desires and responsibility for one's own life dictate the seductive but alienating world of neoliberal consumer culture and 'fleeting existences'[41] as opposed to the strong bonds of community and solidarity. Contemporary vampirism's insistence on freedom of choice, exploration of different spiritualities and the illusion of a unique vampiric identity are expressions of the neoliberal governmentality of the self.

What is obvious now, for Baudrillard, is not the old heroic bourgeois individualism, but a neo-individualism where 'Everyone is ready to turn themselves, depending on their various advantages or handicaps, into an autonomous micro-particle. And why not? This is the age of the daily invention of new particles.'[42] This radical individualism, or 'terroristic fundamentalism of this new sacrificial religion of performance',[43] leads, according to Baudrillard, to a metastatic and self-identical individual.[44] The demand to be different from him/herself and others has made the postmodern liberal individual a 'victim of that psychological and philosophical theory of difference which, in all spheres, ends in indifference to oneself and others'.[45] Today, the individual's identity mania has led him/her to conquer otherness by being different. But this difference has resulted in the boredom of the same. Similarly, self-identified vampires have become imitators of a monster that used to be other and different.

Many definitions of real vampirism can be situated within neoliberalism and postmodernism's freedom to choose and play with identities. Lady Nightdancer[46] uses language derived from alternative medicine and pseudo-science to convey her own definition of vampirism. She explains:

> There is a possibility that the flow of energy through the body's energy meridians is disrupted in some way and this would be something that could not be found by allopathic medical practitioners... This could be an inborn condition natural to the vampiric thus making it necessary to take energy from various sources. It depends on the individual as to what works best for them. None of us come out of a mold so there are differences. I don't classify vampirics. Therefore, a vampire is a vampire is a vampire. I don't get into feeding styles describing them.[47]

While alternative medicine supports her belief in the deficiency of energy in the vampires' bodies, it cannot wholly account for their feeding methods, such as blood-drinking or energy-feeding. For this reason, her language moves away from pseudo-medical ideas into postmodern openness, as she explains that every vampire is different, and tries to support this view through the use of rhetorical devices such as 'a vampire is a vampire is a vampire'. Paraphrasing Gertrude Stein's saying 'Rose is a rose is a rose is a rose', she describes the vampire as simply what it is: the name of a figure that conjures up all of its symbolic representations and meanings. A characteristic of postmodern and neoliberal rhetoric about identity is evident in Nightdancer's claim that vampirism should be based on the individual's freedom to express her/his own difference accordingly. While avoiding blood issues or 'feeding styles', she insists on reproducing traditional Chinese medical beliefs, holistic health and non-scientific knowledge to give credibility to her definition of vampirism. Despite her claims that she does not 'classify vampirics', she is, in fact, explaining vampirism through appeals to authority which dismiss western medical science as 'allopathic'.

For Mike Future,[48] who claims to be 'a scientific person', sanguinarian vampires can also be explained scientifically: they 'have digestive issues and the answers to our questions will be found within dusty old medical journals. I think we are on the verge of exposing the truth about vampirism and we may find the answers to be very simple.'[49] Despite claims to pseudo-medical explanations, here vampirism is associated with esoteric knowledge hidden in 'dusty' libraries.[50] He believes that behind the veils of everyday reality lies a different truth that can explain the ancestral origins of the few and select vampiric individuals. However, this call for a past that never was is another effect of postmodern capitalism's interest in the antiquated, the exotic or the unusual. The inability of neoliberal subjects to create new possibilities for action and mark alternative paths of existence results in their nostalgic return to the security of the old and the hollow call for old traditions used merely for effect.

A more romanticised view of vampirism overegged with clichés is offered by Lady Onyx Ravyn.[51] For her, vampirism is an empowering identity for the subject. Here the identity of the vampire gives the illusion of a special and unique being that separates her from the rest of humanity. She says:

> I am a vampyre [sic] because I possess certain qualities that set me apart from a standard being on this planet. I am predatory by nature, I adore the night and find that I am most alert during the late evening/early morning hours... I possess something within me that draws people unto me like moths to a flame. I sense things in others that often go unnoticed. I hear whispers from across a room. I move fluidly and often go unnoticed in a crowded room. I am in tune with currents that run throughout this planet as well as throughout

other people. I have the ability to heal[52] or to harm... Vampyrism for me, is not merely a physical state, but a mental, esoterical, ethereal, and all encompassing existence. Rudimentary, it is simply... I think, therefore I am. I walk between the darkness of night and the brightness of day. I balance in the twilight, where nothing is black and white, but varying shades of gray. How do any of us know we are vampyres/vampires? For the words in and of themselves were created by other beings of mortal making. The mind and the lessons we have been given while traveling this course determines what labels we choose to take upon ourselves. Others may label us, but it doesn't make their labels anymore valid than those we create for ourselves.[53]

Ravyn's vampirism resembles the idealised and fictitious nature of the vampire in literature, and echoes Anne Rice's Lestat's poetic soliloquies, thoughts and somewhat quaint, vaguely archaic language. Like other definitions of vampirism, Ravyn's vampirism is an identity choice that embraces a world of fantasy and avoids logical explanations. Her soliloquy relies on clichés that sustain the illusion of facticity, but when analysed logically there is little proof offered here. This neoliberal obsession with self-definition and narcissistic individuality, the 'mania for identity—for saturation, completion, repletion',[54] has created a fantasy of the self, the lethal illusion of being a unique individual. The superiority and predatory nature of the 'vampyre' are aspects of the contemporary malaise of selfish individualism driven by rapacity, and are enveloped by layers of esoterism that is solidary and isolating. Blood becomes an accessory, an empty symbol and a fashionable material substance that is used to sustain the illusion of vampire identity.

Vampirism in the culture of enjoyment, or selling the thing

The rise of vampire identity is inextricably associated with the contemporary culture of enjoyment, where every intimate fantasy becomes a reality, where choices of identity, lifestyle and commodities proliferate. Within this context of consumer culture, boundaries blur, and commodities influence and shape identities to the extent that it is no longer possible to differentiate between fiction and reality. The sanguinarians' desire for blood can be associated with the mouth as the site of sexual enjoyment and pleasurable consumption of food. Meanings of consumption proliferate: from consumption of blood, to consumption of food, pleasure and commodities.

The real vampire individual of consumerist post-democracy, preoccupied with issues relating to his/her shapeshifting identity, feeds on commodified images without the need to participate in a traditional community: 'Images, fashions, and lifestyles manufactured by the media industries become sources of self-image and vehicles by which the self perceives others.'[55] Axel Honneth asserts that 'there is a *process of the fictionalization* of reality taking place which allows the atomized individual to become an imitator of styles of existence prefabricated by media and which, corresponding to this on a wider scale, leads to an artificial pluralization of aesthetically shaped lifeworlds'.[56] Honneth sees that the individual, exposed to the fabricated images of media, is unable to discern reality and fiction and thus is conquered by images that instruct him/her to simulate unfamiliar lifestyles.[57] Vampiric identity is formed within a consumerist culture and thus influenced by the prefabricated and commodified image of the vampire. It is characterised by a mix-and-match logic of already commodified lifestyles and images: cinematic representations of vampires, gothic sensibilities and aesthetics, eastern spiritualities and healing practices. It combines the literary vampire's vitalistic and immortal associations with the neoliberal consumer culture's persistence on life, well-being and youthful looks. While not all real vampires can be reduced to the mere act of consumption of objects to define their identity (commodity fetishism), there are evident within the vampire community tendencies of commodification of vampiric products or texts that are characteristic of a society of generalised perversion.[58] With the neoliberalisation of culture and the commodification of all aspects of existence, vampire identity is an expression of a narcissistic consumerism and decadent market individualism that momentarily satisfies desires but is empty at its core.

An international survey entitled 'Twentieth-Century Vampire Census', conducted by Dr Jeanne Keyes Youngson with the help of Martin Riccardo and Jerome Miller between 1998 and 1999, while referenced here with caution and the opinions expressed taken *cum grano salis*, revealed, nonetheless, that sanguinarian vampires sometimes purchase their blood from paid donors.[59] For example, Cayne, a sanguinarian vampire interviewed by Jeff Guinn and Andy Grieser in *Something in the Blood* (1996), admits that she traded sex for blood; she did not, however, consider this to be the same as prostitution.[60] Another sanguine vampire, Thia, uses advertising online to attract possible donors who are willing to exchange blood for sexual and S/M practices or money.[61] Vampires are mimicking the system of transfusion of blood by calling those who offer their blood 'donors' and thus perverting the act of donating blood. While, as noted previously, blood donation was an altruistic act that connected people and reinforced social bonds, here, however, as in the nineteenth-century story 'Good Lady Ducayne', there is an exchange of blood for money, where the donation or the gift of blood enters economic relations and becomes a commodity. In particular, according to Richard M. Titmuss, the American system of blood transfusion, unlike the British altruistic system of blood donorship, was individualistic and commercialised.[62] Titmuss' argument is telling here in order to draw parallels between the American individualistic system of blood 'donation' and the American vampires' use of blood as an exchangeable commodity.

In Youngson's survey another sanguinarian vampire referred to taking 'three drops of blood from my finger mixed with a shot glass of Diet Coke',[63] while in Lady CG's *Practical Vampyrism* (2005) Pepsi is a recommended substitute for blood.[64] This resonates with the use of blood in Kerrelyn Sparks' vampire novels, where, as noted in the fifth chapter, synthetic blood is mixed with champagne or chocolate, and in *Daybreakers'* franchise coffee bars where drops of human blood are mixed with coffee. These sanguinarian blood 'recipes' exemplify the ways blood has been integrated into contemporary lifestyles and is enjoyed casually like any other drink. What this shows is the mixing of a vital fluid and Coca Cola, the 'ultimate capitalist merchandise' and the personification of surplus-enjoyment.[65] According to Žižek, because Coke does not quench one's thirst, it has no use-value, but functions as the embodiment of 'the pure surplus of enjoyment over standard satisfaction, of the mysterious and elusive X we are all after in our compulsive consumption of merchandise'.[66] The more Coke we drink, the thirstier we get and our thirst is never quenched. The paradoxical quality of Coke, that the more you have, the more you need, makes Coke a commodity whose properties are already those of a commodity: 'every satisfaction opens up a gap of "I want more!" '[67] In the case of caffeine-free diet Coke we 'drink nothing in the guise of something', which is 'Nothingness itself, the pure semblance of a property that is in effect merely an envelope of a void'.[68] Blood, then, mixed with a capitalist product, becomes a property devoid of any ritualistic or mystical qualities. It is a mere ingredient in a diluted drink that has no use-value and does not offer anything. Within the logic of compulsive consumption, blood, it can be said, becomes that elusive X that consumers who have tried and bought everything are after. Blood mixed with diet Coke, like the *objet petit a*, always eludes your grasp, since the more you have, the greater the lack.[69] In this respect, vampires do not drink nothing, but desire to consume the void itself, the object-cause of desire. This is consistent with Lacan's anorexic subject, who, as mentioned in the third chapter, desires to eat the void itself and keep desire unsatisfied.

As noted previously, beliefs in alternative medicine and the health-transformative powers of blood are products of a capitalist America that has integrated non-western philosophies into marketable commodities. Blood itself becomes something like a commodity, a product that so-called vampires can acquire for free, after signing a contract with their donors, or even purchase. In the previous chapter, it was shown how the marketing campaign of the HBO television series *True Blood* promoted the show's synthetic blood, Tru Blood, as a real-life commodity. Tru Blood is marketed as the vampire Bill's 'favourite synthetic blood nourishment beverage' and is sold in bottles that are the 'exact replica of bottles featured on show'.[70] The marketing of Tru Blood—an otherwise regular carbonated drink—is utilising the fantasised reality and qualities of this blood drink within the show in order to manipulate and direct the consumer's desire towards the specific product. In vampire communities the fantasised reality of blood is constructed not only through vampire texts, but also through Chinese medicine and eastern ideas, which have transformed blood into a health product to fill the emptiness of the addict-consumer.

Many sanguinarian vampires claim that they feed on the energy included in the blood, which they call *chi* or Qi (Chinese term) and *prana* (Indian term), terms adopted from Chinese medicine, holistic therapies and eastern philosophies. Fantasies of blood as a life-giving fluid are then sustained and supported by this widespread obsession for being healthy and feeling good, of transforming the body and mind, of eating healthy food and consuming eastern ideas. As the general definition of real vampirism offered in the 'Vampire and Energy Work Research Survey' (VEWRS) clarifies, vampires are 'individuals who cannot adequately sustain their own physical, mental, or spiritual well-being without the taking of blood or vital force energy from other sources; often human'.[71] For vampires, blood becomes the embodiment of all those qualities holistic culture is selling to western consumers: physical, mental and spiritual well-being. Blood matters as long as it is endowed with qualities that improve the vampires' physical and spiritual condition, and it can be replaced by other products that well-being culture considers good for one's health. For example, in VEWRS and 'Advanced Vampirism and Energy Work Research Survey' (AVEWRS), conducted by Suscitatio Enterprises between 22 March and 1 August 2006, responses to the query about blood substitutes[72] vampires preferred included vegetables, fruit, vitamins, herbal tea, meditation or yoga, and juices.[73] The absurdity of replacing blood with these fashionable and commodified practices and products of well-being culture is a sign of the logic of consumerism: as long as these products are advertised as being good for the consumer's well-being they can replace anything else that equally is thought to promote health and happiness. Real vampirism can therefore be understood as a form of health culture that offers personal transformation through the mimetic consumption of alternative, non-western practices. Such personal transformation also speaks to the American tradition of individualism which characterises and defines American vampires. Blood as matter becomes less important and its significance is constructed within a well-being discourse that renders what is inside the blood—the immaterial energy—as good for the individual's body, mind and spirit.

Vampires today have integrated the popular and commodified forms of well-being culture and eastern spiritualities into their beliefs about blood, consequently, returning to those nineteenth-century notions of blood as a vitalistic substance which were analysed previously in such novels as *Dracula*. At the same time, other vampires have created commodified forms of religion: online spiritual communities based on the 'Blood'.[74] While the vampires who turn to holistic well-being practices and express ideas about the vital powers of blood reject conventional medicine and science, religious vampires such as those of the Temple of the Vampire turn to science to support their belief in physical and spiritual immortality. Such notions of vampiric immortality are based on symbolic references to blood as a carrier of the unique and superior identity of the vampire. The Temple of the Vampire sells its own version of spiritual transformation to those who are different from the human 'herd' or 'slave mentality',[75] promising through the purchase of Vampire Bibles[76] physical immortality, health and personal finance.[77] Of course, 'This is a religion that requires study and application, instead of faith'; that is why those of a superior blood and predatory nature should purchase the various vampire bibles to acquire the vampire knowledge and learn the vampiric practices.[78]

This is appealing to today's individuals whose spirituality can be easily purchased and expressed through commodities that function as fetishised sacred objects. For Marx, capitalism is a religion of money and money the 'god of commodities' that satisfies spiritual and material needs.[79] In the capitalist society of commodity fetishism, 'instead of immediate relations between people, we have social relations between things', where people act as 'rational utilitarians, guided only by their selfish interests'.[80] The commodities, the things themselves, then, become the embodiment of their beliefs: 'They no longer believe, *but the things themselves believe for them.*'[81] Similarly, the vampire religion does not depend on belief or faith but is determined in practice by the exchange of material goods. Belief is replaced by the purchase of the vampire bibles and other vampiric religious products. The Temple of the Vampire combines capitalism and religion to produce a religious vampire commodity. It is in particular through this ritualistic trans-action based on money that the superiority of the vampire blood is reinforced and reserved for the few. The vampire religion is not for every-one to practice for free, but the privilege of those unique individuals whose claims to vampiric superiority rest on the materialistic ground that they have the money to buy immortality and status. Stripped of religious or ethical sense, contemporary individuals lay emphasis on the intrinsic value of money and their financial salvation with-out any concern for other humans. Like Dracula's ascetic Protestantism that facilitates his accumulation of capital, the entrepreneurial vampire individual's contemporary market radicalism, characterised by innova-tion and the promotion of new products, facilitates the expansion and growth of private empires.

While symbolic notions of blood haunt the Temple of the Vampire's capitalist ethos and scientific agenda, other vampires utilise notions of blood in order to add flavour to a more fashionable vampire iden-tity and transform their commodities into sexually appealing symbols. From reality shows to television news, vampires are manipulating their status as fashionable curiosities, turning themselves into entrepreneurs and profiting from their human capital. Sebastiaan Van Houten, well aware of the economic potential of the vampire identity, has become a famous member of the vampire community. He began as a 'fangsmith' for his company Sabretooth, specialising in making fangs and contact lenses as well as organising major vampire events. For Father Sebastiaan, the vampire identity is both glamorous and profitable. In the *Vampyre Sanguinomicon* he explains that fangs are 'a symbol of the Blood and our primal nature'.[82] By creating a pseudo-ideology of kinship and family bonds through the association of fake symbols with blood and vampiric identity, he has transformed fictional imagery into a marketable com-modity, where simulated fangs become glamour and identity accessories for the modern vampire. While Father Sebastiaan's fangs are sexually appealing, blood as a potentially dangerous and polluting fluid is wiped out from his sanitary vampire fantasy world. Blood as matter is nega-tively associated with disease and is of course bad business for a vampire who wants to retain a clean public and alluring persona. As examined in previous chapters, blood in the eighteenth and nineteenth centuries was associated with disease and later, in the 1980s and early 1990s, with AIDS. These associations with AIDS and infectious disease are threatening to the American vampire dream of consumer enjoyment; thus blood is relegated to its mere invocation through simulations such as fangs or the idea of vampiric kinship. In order to avoid controversies over blood issues, blood is no longer a significant element of the vampire identity.

As noted in the previous chapter, blood in recent films such as *Blade Trinity* or *Daybreakers* becomes a commodity for vampires. Similarly, within a universe of fantasised and commercialised subjectivities, blood haunts neoliberal consumer culture as fantasised matter. Whether blood is a *thing* to be exchanged as a commodity, imagined through eastern spiritualities as 'good' for the vampires' well-being, conjured up as a symbol of kinship, or even disconnected from its threatening associations with disease, it is never real blood, but its spectral qualities that are invoked here as a strategy to maximise profits.

Genealogies of blood

The effects of neoliberal capitalism are visible in the ways blood and vampire communities as a contemporary phenomenon can be understood. However, in the self-definitions of the self-fashioned vampires, there is an attempt to create order and stability by associating blood and vampirism with heredity and bloodlines, by creating a tradition of vampirism and binding it to premodern forms of belief in blood as a symbol of kinship and family. The claims for blood genealogies are questionable and mostly fictitious: many of the vampire groups have constructed their histories, laws and beliefs on White Wolf's role-playing game, *Vampire the Masquerade*, and have been largely influenced by Anne Rice's vampire novels. Laycock observes that, despite the anecdotal evidence of certain vampire groups possessing texts known as grimoires that enclose 'carefully guarded histories', no one has shown him any of these vampiric accounts.[83] Whether vampire houses and families have knowledge of their fantastical histories has less bearing than their desire for stability, coherence and order. In the construction of their families vampires create fictional relations based on blood. Vampire houses, families and clans form a system of alliance, where a member acts as a mother or father, a governing or administrative principle, and where the structure of the coven or clan is ordered into castes and descent lines are sometimes invented to produce a pseudo-genealogy of vampires.

Foucault argues that the nineteenth century saw a passage from a symbolics of blood to an analytics of sexuality. In the premodern society, relations were centred around blood and kinship, where 'the systems of alliance, the political form of the sovereign, the differentiation into orders and castes, and the value of descent lines were predominant'.[84] Unlike the withered boundaries of contemporary society, here Foucault describes a society controlled by blood where limits are clear and the old symbolic law is present. In this system of sovereign power blood was '*a reality with a symbolic function*'.[85] In particular, blood's fundamental role in defining one's identity and status, as having a certain blood or being of the same blood, is telling here. Contemporary vampire communities return to this old regime of sovereign power based on 'sanguinity', which is not present in the homogeneous space of postmodernity, in order to create and structure their families and identities on blood.

This turn to the past, however, is not a recent phenomenon. According to Eric Hobsbawm, 'when a rapid transformation of society weakens or destroys the social patterns for which "old" traditions had been designed', there is the appearance of 'invented traditions'.[86] The edifice of many institutionalised traditions stands upon fictitious histories, myths and the creation of an idealised past that never was, and these have become the cornerstones of cultures. An 'invented tradition' refers to a 'set of practices, normally governed by overtly or tacitly accepted rules and of a ritual or symbolic nature, which seek to inculcate certain values and norms of behaviour by repetition, which automatically implies continuity with the past. In fact, where possible, they normally attempt to establish continuity with a suitable historic past.'[87] This historic past, Hobsbawm clarifies, 'need not be lengthy, stretching back into the assumed mists of time', and any reference to the continuity with such a past is mainly inauthentic.[88] Invented traditions are created to serve a particular ideological system or established social order. While clearly modern, they make claims to a collective past in order to ascertain a sense of cohesiveness, collective identity and shared ideology. Invented traditions are also characterised by invariance: 'The past, real or invented, to which they refer imposes fixed (normally formalized) practices, such as repetition.'[89] In particular, such practices or objects acquire symbolic and ritual value when they lose their practical use.[90] Thus, invented traditions are constructed by recourse to older traditions, official rituals and symbolism, religion and folklore, which are then modified and ritualised for the novel purposes of a new community.[91] For example, historical and archaeological facts are modified by vampire communities through the addition of fictional elements, or falsified through different interpretations. This is evident in the Temple of the Vampire's references to a vampire past, a vampire tradition and an ancient bloodline of vampires in order to legitimise their actions and practices. The vampires' invented pasts of ancestral connection to mythological figures such as Lilith, or historical personae such as the Merovingian Kings, function as invented traditions: to support the idea of a shared vampiric identity and belief, produce cohesion and create a familial heritage. As Hobsbawm notes, despite the fact that certain traditions are novel and invented, they 'claim to be the opposite of novel, namely rooted in the remotest antiquity, and the opposite of constructed, namely human communities so "natural" as to require no definition other than self-assertion'.[92]

For the vampire House Dark Haven, because 'modern society has lost the sense of reverence, wonder and anticipation that comes with established standard and rituals', they have created a vampiric family, where the 'patriarch holds absolute control and wields it for the benefit and protection of his family'.[93] Real vampire communities are attempting to create a patriarchal or matriarchal system of vampires, sometimes based on their own mythology and history, or blood rituals and ceremonies in order to construct a family or lineage of vampires. House Quinotaur, Ordo Strigoi Vii and Clan of Lilith, for example, call their vampire groups families and refer to their founders or close members as fathers or mothers. Clan of Lilith's Viola Johnson and Temple Sahjaza's Goddess Rosemary are both the mothers of their vampiric family. Goddess Rosemary is the founder of House Sahjaza—later a temple, including both male and female members—a matriarchal family of vampires. In particular, House Quinotaur has a system of nine ranks or 'cousins'.[94] The member who is appointed as 'first cousin' is considered to be a descendant of Merovech and s/he has allegedly traced her/his lineage back to Merovech.[95] For the House supports the idea that its members and all vampires in general are descendants of the Merovingian Kings.[96] They also prefer the term 'Quinotauri' instead of vampires.[97] Here House Quinotaur has created a fictional hierarchical system and a family based on the prestige of blood. Blood plays an instrumental role in organising a social class system founded upon the aristocratic particularities of blood, where the individual's supposedly 'Merovingian' blood places him/her at the top of the House Quinotaur's ranks. At the same time, it is assumed that the blood of the Frankish royal dynasty of Merovingians flows into the blood of the vampiric Quinotauri, creating thus an aristocratic bloodline that ultimately connects all vampires together as a family. The aristocratic blood that is infused into the vampiric bodies, consequently, separates vampires from ordinary humans. Their beliefs, of course, are based on the legend of Merovech's birth and the mythical creature Quinotaur documented in the seventh-century *Chronicle of Fredegar*. According to the chronicle, the sea monster Quinotaur impregnated the wife of the Frankish king Clodio, who gave birth to Merovech. House Quinotaur claims that Merovech's descendants were considered to be vampires. While such a theory is evidently fictional, House Quinotaur is researching the genealogies of its members to prove the verity of the theory.

Viola Johnson, an American activist and leatherwoman, in her book *Dhampir: Child of the Blood* (1996) has created a similar fantastical lineage but one that plays with and subverts elements of Judaism. The heritage of the Clan of Lilith is based on the legend of the first wife of Adam. Being a more superior and knowledgeable creature than Adam, Lilith is offered certain opportunities and freedoms by God, who understands and supports her interest in learning, to leave her companion and pursue the knowledge she craves. Over the passage of time, 'Lilith found that her body began to adapt. Her aging process slowed, allowing her to maintain the strength and stamina of youth.'[98] She began drinking the blood of others, and procreated by giving her blood to the chosen children who were loved and taught by her. Later, when Cain came to her, she nurtured him with her blood and he went on to create his own lineage, who are the cousins of Lilith's line. What Johnson creates here is a benevolent and inquisitive Lilith, a figure completely different from the malevolent Lilith, the female demon of Jewish mythology. The monstrous mother is turned into a good mother. Akasha in Anne Rice's *Queen of the Damned* (1988) and Lilith in Whitley Strieber's *Lilith's Dream: A Tale of the Vampire Life* (2002)[99] are the matriarchs of the vampire race. Similarly, Johnson's vampiric pseudo-genealogy is based on maternal blood. In literature, as noted in the third chapter, maternal vampires are linked to fears of the abject maternal body. Viola and her female vampires believe themselves to be connected through blood to the matriarch Lilith and desire to devour and incorporate the mother through blood. In the absence of symbolic figures, Viola produces a new symbolic order based on the maternal principle. There is a possible re-emergence of a desire to reconnect with the mother through the perverse act of biting and drinking blood in order to fill the void and hunger for total unity with the mother. In particular, it is through such acts of drinking blood that Viola becomes a mother and creates her family: by offering her 'vampiric' blood she 'turns' women into her lovers and children.

While Viola constructs her queer family based on maternal blood, the Temple of the Vampire invents a pseudo-genealogy whose bloodlines are traced in the mythic past of ancient Greece. The Temple has produced a history that is inauthentic, but historically well-researched, offering its own version of vampiric gods and history, while drawing parallels from historical events to justify its claims. In its attempts to praise vampiric identity and the superiority of vampires from the human 'prey',[100] the Temple traces its bloodlines back to the ancient Cimmerians, whom the Greek historian and geographer Strabo references in his *Geographica* (c. 1469). Although their exact origin remains unknown, the Temple situates them in Greece, living underground at the banks of river Acheron. The Temple follows Philipp Vandenberg's *The Mystery of the Oracle* (1982), in which he discusses the Homeric references to the inhabitants of Oceanus, the Cimmerians, situated near the dark and gloomy entrance of Hades.[101] In *Odyssey* 11.13–19 Homer describes the land of the Cimmerians 'wrapt in a fog and cloud. Never on them does the shining sun look down with his beams' and 'deadly night is spread'.[102] The Temple's invented history of Cimmerian vampire priests, who 'were conducting the highest rites of Communion to feed the Undead Gods' underground,[103] is also connected to the archaeological discovery of Necromanteion by Sotirios Dakaris, a Greek temple of necromancy where pilgrims would communicate with the world of the dead. The Temple constructs a new religion from an older one, borrowing and modifying the official rituals and symbolisms of Christian religion such as 'Communion' and 'blood sacrifice',[104] to refer to the sacred ritual of offering energy or 'blood' to the Vampire Gods. In addition, Plato's allegory of the cave is interpreted by the Temple of the Vampire as 'a literal description of Vampiric Enlightenment for controlling the world. The humans, who are imprisoned in shadows, are eventually led into the light (the Undead Presence) where they then recognize the truth of their world (Vampiric control)'.[105] The Temple has invented this pseudo-history in order to connect contemporary vampirism to ancient mysteries and, consequently, convey a sense of superior mentality and philosophy that goes back to the mists of time, to Greek civilisation: the foundation of all civilisations. In this way, the pseudo-tradition of vampirism appears to be as 'natural' and as old and original as the ancient civilisation of Greece.[106] Thus, the Temple, through its own interpretation of historical facts, establishes historic continuity with an archaic and mystical Greece and legitimises its practices.[107] However, as the *Vampire Priesthood Bible* (1989) reminds the reader, 'Within lies fact and fancy, truth and metaphor. Discriminate with care.'[108]

Despite their invention, familial ties and traditions are fundamental to the vampires' identity. For the vampire Sanguinarius, because real vampires do not have a heritage as an identity group, they are creating it for themselves. She writes: 'we vampires, having no actual common cultural past, traditions, or social structure—and therefore, no identity as a people—are creating our own identity out of group/ cultural/ social necessity'.[109] According to her, 'the only "existing cultural heritage" or knowledge base that could be said to exist are the social/cultural aspects of vampiric fiction, at least those few fictional works that are adaptable to real-life situations'.[110] However, she does not refer to the early accounts of vampirism in Europe, of revenants and living-dead corpses, which of course self-identified vampires like Sanguinarius would avoid claiming as their cultural heritage. On the other hand, if they do adapt vampire fictions they are very selective, choosing only those texts that are fashionable and not characterised by difference or diversity.

For Sanguinarius, vampires desire their own culture: 'Unity. Cultural identity. Social conventions and structures. Traditions. Think of this all as a social gold mine. Everybody else has their culture/lifestyle/social system. Why can't we?'[111] Indeed, Sanguinarius compares such inventions to other minorities' attempts to define their own heritage. 'What we are doing is similar, in a way', Sanguinarius writes, 'to what the African Americans have done.'[112] Such comparisons, of course, eliminate the differences between a pleasurable search for a vampire identity in postmodernity, and the impositions of racial discourse and forced migration. The construction of an ethnic minority's cultural tradition is manipulated here to express the perceived similarities between racial difference and vampire identity, between an African American culture and a vampiric one.

Vampire rituals, anachronistic customs such as courtly titles and duelling, and the separation of houses into castes, are important facets of vampiric tradition and identity. Blood circulates through these practices and organising principles, investing them with symbolic meaning. While vampire rituals create kinship, the organisation into castes and the use of courtly titles and duelling assert the hereditary social status of vampires. The vampires' status is reflected in such titles as 'Lord "O" MacPhee Orion' or 'Sir Shaolin Z. MacPhee of House Sabretooth MacPhee',[113] while their surnames indicate their descent from the bloodline of MacPhee.[114] The aristocratic and medieval institution of duelling is possibly referred to in symbolic terms to denote upper-class status, gentility and the courage of natural aristocrats. It is unlikely that actual violence is pursued between vampire clans.

While vampire rituals connect the members of a vampire community,[115] they are also regulated and based on the Indian caste system. During vampire rituals, different castes are assigned specific roles, and Belanger's vampire house, House Kheperu, has its own Kheprian castes of Warriors, Concubines or Counsellors and Priests.[116] As she notes, the castes are not only associated with a social hierarchy, but are 'formalizations of three fundamental relations to energy'.[117] The paradox here is that while there are castes, a vampire can choose to perform any role s/he desires without being delimited within one caste. The freedom of choice is exemplary of the playful limits vampires set within their practices and which they can transgress whenever they desire. While these playful and simulated transgressions enable the vampire participants to enjoy different roles, that are otherwise lacking in real life, and experience camaraderie, they nonetheless reassert the absence of limits. On the one hand, the vampires' fictionalisation of reality offers a sense of organisation and control of their own life and identity, a life which is, outside the parameters of vampire life, mundane. While for the vampires the choice of castes becomes a postmodern plaything, on the other hand the caste system is a problematic foundation, not based on choice, but associated with blood and social hierarchies, inequalities and restrictions. A symbol for India, caste is, as Nicholas B. Dirks argues, 'a modern phenomenon' and 'the product of an historical encounter between India and Western colonial rule' which has produced 'caste as the measure of all social things'.[118] Thus, a caste system, associated primarily with blood and which, according to Dirks, facilitated the British colonial administration in India, is not an innocent system to be naively imitated by postmodern vampires. In particular, by imitating exactly those stereotypical roles of masculine authority such as the warrior or priest caste, and making use of anachronistic concepts such as the concubine, usually used to denote a restricted social status and gender inequality, the vampires repudiate social realities based on blood and insist upon the pleasurable imitation of concepts reduced to ahistorical symbols.

In vampire rituals blood is used symbolically or literally to create or affirm bonds within the vampire house or community. However, the use of blood in these rituals is essentially influenced by older religious practices. In particular, vampires conjure up the Christian symbolics of blood through the use of concepts such as 'sacrifice' and in the vampiric ceremonies of 'Communion' and 'Sanguine Mass'. Following the Temple of the Vampire's rituals, Father Sebastiaan's Ordo Strigoi Vii refers to the exchange of energy/life force (and not blood) as 'Communion' and the offering of life force to the ancient vampires as 'Sanguine Mass'.[119] Rituals and ceremonial tools are transformed within the space of the vampiric ceremony into symbolic and sacred instruments. For example, chalices symbolise the blood of the family and life force, while ankhs[120] function as the cross. Like the drinking of Christ's blood that is shared by all faithful Christians, the drinking of wine during certain vampire rites symbolises the bonds of spirits and blood.[121] In the 'Sanguine Initiation' the ritualistic exchange of blood between mentor and student, or between vampire and donor, initiates one into the vampiric life, and through their 'sacrifice' of blood mixed with red wine the initiates are bound symbolically to their mentor.[122] The blood that is made sacred is then used in the consecration of ankhs, and mixed with water in the consecration of havens, places where the vampire community congregates. While vampires turn to the East for their definitions of energy, on the other hand they remain bound to a symbolics of blood associated with Christian notions of sacrifice and communion. The highly symbolic notions of blood within Christian tradition, their prevalence in western thought, and especially their use in popular culture and vampire texts, from Stoker's *Dracula* to Anne Rice's The Vampire Chronicles,[123] make them an ideal material for the construction of vampiric pseudo-rituals. Blood's symbolic qualities of creating community and blood relations, witnessed in premodern forms of initiation and blood rituals, is used by vampiric individuals to create a sense of unity through an appeal to some kind of symbolic order.

Creating fictitious universes and pseudo-blood relations to an imaginary past, so-called vampires can feel part of a family. As Hobsbawm argues, the repetition of rites of passage in invented traditions, such as the vampire rituals mentioned here, emphasises the unchanging character of these traditions.[124] In this respect, while the invented traditions of vampires are novel, vampires claim that they are rooted in an ancient past. Specifically, some sanguinarian vampires feel that their condition is a real genetic trait that has been passed down from older generations. To justify the need for blood and demonstrate that blood drinking is not just a modern phenomenon, Lady CG claims that her grandfather, great-grandfather and other members of her family were blood drinkers.[125] Blood drinking is presented by contemporary vampires as a genetic proclivity, something that they have inherited from their family or bloodline. By tracing vampirism and blood drinking to some figure of the past, fictional or not, to whom they are associated through blood, sanguinarian vampires attempt to justify their vampirism as a natural phenomenon carried in their blood and which is not a cultural experience or imitation of fiction. However, despite the vampires' desire to create traditional vampiric communities, these remain bound to fabricated histories and bloodlines, fashionable and playful constructions, offering a temporary sense of stability in a world that recognises no limits.

Conclusion

The concept of vampire communities conjures up ideas relating to a vampiric search for roots, blood, identity and belonging within the insecure conditions of a postmodern and globalised universe. On the one hand, it reveals the desire for a common vampiric cultural heritage, a common tradition and vampiric values, common vampire religion and language. On the other hand, the construction of vampire communities is understood as an expression of individual interests where vampiric identity is considered as a self-sufficient entity, a totalising form of identity that exists as and for itself. Paradoxically, vampire communities thirst for a mythic past while, at the same time, celebrating a vampiric atomistic individualism. This is, however, related to postmodernity's fragmented knowledge and truth that propels a search for origins and an idealised past, and to neoliberal globalisation's emphasis on individualism, self-interest and a rationalistic understanding of the world. In this sense, vampire communities are works[126] that seek to emulate primordial communities and the primitive communion of individuals by creating a vampire fraternity connected through mythological bloodlines and, thus, sharing a common essence. Postmodern practices such as bloodletting and blood drinking embody a return to a sacrificial aesthetics, to a Bataillean universe of archaic communities of ritualistic sacrifice. At the same time, such a return is betrayed by a glorification of a self-sufficient, self-referential vampiric identity that is driven by a capitalist ethos and seeks to homogenise the vampire through the eternal repetition of its self by denying its own history and difference. This is the Cartesian conception of subjectivity that emphasises the unique and independent individual with limitless possibilities and is manifested today as the Western liberal norm of the individualist subject without any responsibilities towards the other. The neoliberal and autonomous vampire is then an unproblematic subject, whose multiple and different dimensions of identity are deemed irrelevant.

Essentialist communities based on a common 'blood' as well as the creed of modern western politics, neoliberal individualism, are bound by a denial of ecstasy. Only rupture can break up the totality of both individuality and pure collectivity in order to envisage a different community of communication where singular beings, and not individuals, are constituted by 'the sharing that makes them others' and not same.[127] In a similar way, blood drinking and the imitation of vampirism are caricatures of sacrifice that do not create communal bonds. Sacrifice is impossible when everything is given to us for our instant gratification. If in precapitalist societies blood was made sacred through communal and unproductive expenditure, now it is a thing to be privately consumed in a rationalist and useful way. Moreover, because the entrepreneur individual consumes pleasures liberally and enjoys comforts and luxuries that in turn allow for the development of production,[128] it is impossible to separate productive and calculable consumption from sacrificial and insane squandering. Blood is today consumed and exchanged in empty acts that lack the ecstatic promise of transformation. Vampires subscribe to a hedonic model of consumption that has nothing, however, to do with the old grandeur and spectacular consumption of the accursed share.

Conclusion

The Blood of the Vampire: Globalisation, Resistance and the Sacred

> It is time for our culture to abandon Dracula and pass beyond him, relinquishing him to social history. The limits of profitable reinterpretation have been reached.[1]

The diversity of a symbolics of blood circulating through different texts and contexts shows the double-edged power of blood to give and take life, and pollute and sanitise racial boundaries and bloodlines, as well as form and destroy the bonds of community. Haemorrhaging from within the body politic and percolating global networks, blood challenges the fixity of boundaries while at the same time creating caesuras within populations, and resuscitating the corpses of old hierarchies and racial categories. While its liquidity and mobility are symbolic of the very conditions that make possible the movement of postmodern anti-essentialist discourses, identities and differences, at the same time such circulations of differences and commodities multiply within the world market. As blood transmits and generates new identities, infecting life with germs of possibility, such a viral potential is easily tamed and consumed by the mouth of the vampire capital. At other times, dangerous becomings and the flows of metamorphosis are equally prevented through prophylactic measures that immunise communities against the threat of difference. Meanings of blood bleed into one another, colouring our attitudes about subjective, corporeal, national and transnational boundaries.

While theorists such as Haraway and Deleuze dismiss the essentialism of blood and biology altogether, blood as a vital fluid spilled in the passage to Hardt and Negri's vampiric Empire remains important. Blood in films such as *Daybreakers* and vampire novels of bioterrorism, from *The Passage* to *The Strain*, *The Fall* and *The Night Eternal*, is considered significant as food and a powerful commodity, but also as life destroyed and wasted in the war and epidemics orchestrated by vampire capitalists and monstrous bioscience. Within this context, the vampire becomes the figure of the capitalist, the exploiter and devourer of human labour, blood and life.

In particular, blood in vampire narratives and practices is shown to be a metaphor for life itself in its various dimensions. In this respect, they reflect contemporary debates in the humanities and the social and biological sciences that concentrate on the question of life and the shifting boundaries between life and death. The question of life circulates from the eighteenth- and nineteenth-century vitalisms, to capital and biotechnology's productivity and vitality, to vampire cryonics. The understandings of the life that permeates biopolitics (biological life, the monstrous and creative living labour of the multitude, or life as existence and intellect) and the real vampires' belief in the life of the blood emphasise blood, and not the vampire, as the generative force behind fictions and practice. Vampiric blood moves, like capillary power, within and outside bodies, transforming them at the molar and molecular levels. However, the productivity of life, as examined earlier, is the site of financial investments. The ability to intervene and improve life through technology does not solve social inequalities and structures of exploitation, but exacerbates them. The optimism of vampire novels such as *Fledgling* does not erase the fact that female and racial others remain excluded from the benefits in advances in biomedicine or genetics.

At the same time, the politics of life can transform into a politics of death, as witnessed in *The Passage* and The Strain Trilogy. Epidemics, biological warfare, viruses and terrorism are associated with vampiric life that turns against human life. The intensification of metaphors of blood and vampirism in bioterrorism texts after the September 11 attacks is linked to an auto-immunitary logic whose victims are quintessentially American. Here, the vampire as a relic from the past becomes a metaphor for death and the return of old fears relating to race. But the symbiosis of machinic and biological life, vampiric viruses and human life, reveals another relationship between life and death. While technologically enhanced bodies promise immortality, they also betray fears about contagion and death. Vampirism then points towards contemporary fears about the generation and extension of life, but also its opposite, extinction.

The recent trend in investing in one's identity is characteristic of contemporary neoliberal regimes in which individuals are immunised from the community by choosing their future genetic programming. The Temple of the Vampire's fantasies of immortality surrounding cryonics testify to this neoliberal pursuit of self-transformation, self-preservation and immunisation from death that separates neoliberal individuals from those humans they consider inferior. This inevitably conjures up Nazi eugenics' preservation of life through its protection from the contagion of those considered diseased or inferior. Such forms of immunisation seal the self from the other and avoid any possible risk of wounding. Conversely, for Georges Bataille, communication is possible when members lose a part of themselves which connects them while separating them from their identity. Only by risking one's ontological integrity is it possible to communicate with the other. In this respect, the metaphor of infection and blood mixing can be considered as a form of communication and transformation.

It is this negative inflection of neoliberal biopolitics in relation to Nazism's horrors that Michael Hardt and Antonio Negri do not take into account in their analyses of the new world order. This deadly genealogy is demonstrated by the negative conceptions of biopolitics in Esposito and Agamben (thanatopolitics). In contrast, Hardt and Negri envision a vampiric biopower, Empire, that is resisted by an affirmative biopolitics connected to the monstrous flesh of the productive and creative multitude and the emergence of democratic sovereignty. While the multitude is the blood/life of the parasitic Empire, at the same time its excess and productivity can resist Empire's exploitation and control. If the multitude's pack of vampires offers a celebration of transformation and possibilities of resistance, vampiric Empire is parasitical, aristocratic, amoral and individualistic. The series of films and novels examined in Chapter 5 reveal this tension between the exploited and the vampire capitalists. In particular, vampire narratives show that biopolitics is not radical but deadly, given the fact that the life of the vampire race is strengthened through the death of humans who are either bled to death or exterminated like animals. It is shown that life is not stronger than the vampiric power that besieges it.

While Hardt and Negri celebrate the potential of the multitude, its difference and revolutionary desire, Butler's *Fledgling* shows that such difference can be genetically engineered and produced technologically. It is then difficult to distinguish between the multitude's vampires and vampire-Empire as different vampires and monstrosities proliferate and multiply through networks of biotechnology, commodification and exploitation. In the smooth spaces of contemporary neoliberal capital, subjectivities slide and differences are suppressed.

In this respect, corporate capital and the world market depend on circulation, mobility, mixture and diversity to maximise their profit and not on the old modernist structures of racism, biology and fixed boundaries. However, the global politics of difference are not equal but hierarchical. Capitalism always functions through an intense deterritorialisation together with a violent authoritarian, racist and patriarchal reterritorialisation. As people of different cultures move towards the open mouth of corporate culture, new brutal hierarchies arise through a differential racism that integrates others within its order and then subordinates them according to their degree of difference from whiteness.[2] With the rise of neoliberal capital and its inability to ground a territory or sociality, the return to neo-archaisms such as racism functions as an evil necessity that fixes identities and delimits territories, securing thus the exercise of biopower.[3] It is this fear of blood contamination and viral transmission of disease through the figure of the vampire and blood that has become the widespread metaphor for global mixing and circulation. The flows of vampires, immigrants and racial others pose, in reality and fiction, one of the worst dangers for contemporary societies. Incorporated within the national body, they are controlled through immunitary measures that safeguard against their difference. This is, however, what bleeds and destroys individual and collective existence.

Indeed, difference is now accepted. No longer experienced as monstrous, the other is normalised and assimilated. As the last chapter on vampire communities demonstrates, vampires become increasingly normal, otherness banal, and blood, removed from the sphere of the sacred, is repeatedly desacralised by its mixing and dilution with objects of consumption. Circulating in everyday life through the real vampires' use, blood becomes as common as Diet Coke. Within the cult religion of capitalism, the profane and the sacred become indistinguishable, while insane forms of expenditure are replaced by cautious consumption. No longer associated with glorious useless consumption, blood is considered as a necessary thing with a practical value to be exchanged between consenting individuals. Once a metaphor for life, identity and redemption, blood is now literally a healthy substitute, good for one's well-being. However, even when it is wasted in ritualistic acts or made to flow uselessly to satisfy the perverse tastes of liberal individuals locked in selfish pursuits, blood does not have the power to give birth to community. Such calculated acts exhibit little of the violence of excess and sacrifice. As the line between what is necessary and useful and what is redundant and useless has receded, vampire practices are mere imitations of sacrifice.

The vampire, then, becomes the embodiment of a neoliberal subjectivity for these gothic times we live in. Predatory and thirsty for blood money, the vampire embodies the neoliberal entrepreneur investing in his or her own human capital and driven by selfish interests. Youthful and glamorous, mobile and cosmopolitan, the vampire woman or man, like the vampires in *The Radleys*, enjoys a successful life. The ubiquity of vampires in contemporary culture attests to the fact that capitalism and the human relations it produces are based on predation. Such a compulsion results in the normalisation of vampiric and rapacious behaviour and destroys solidarity and human relations. The creed of hyper-individualism, characteristic of neoliberal societies, and the pervasive presence of vampires reveal a culture that no longer recognises the other as monstrous but as the image of its self. If Dracula was in the nineteenth century the representation of an ascetic capitalism, now the vampires participate in a capitalist culture that consumes and expends without limit. This aggressive and violent explosion of greed and predation is dramatised in a characteristic scene from *Daybreakers* where the recently turned humans are immediately devoured by the vampires who in turn transform by the bite into humans and are eaten by other vampires. In this dog-eat-dog world, the vampire epitomises brutal appetites.

In a world that is increasingly defined by the short contract, impermanent employment, insecurity and precarity, time becomes the measure according to which life is organised. For example, whereas wealthy vampires have all the time in the world, the poor subjugated masses of humanity do not have enough time, living within uncertain conditions. From Guillermo del Toro and Chuck Hogan's vampire fictions to *Daybreakers*, human existence is exhausted. With the 'slow cancellation of the future'[4] nothing is produced or created. Culture looks back to the past, nostalgic for older periods. The anachronism of our contemporary culture with its restoration of old values and the disappearance of the new finds expression in the very anachronistic nature of the vampire. The vampire is its own repetition in the future; it is the past preserved again and again, indefinitely. Living in the insomniac, apathetic landscapes of neoliberal capitalism is similar to human existence after the vampire apocalypse. Without any solidarity between people, some are left to beg for blood in the streets while others are leached by vampire corporations profiting from their bloodlife.

Because the vampire is part and parcel of capitalism, it is impossible to purge him of his connotations of evil and connection with money. Metaphors of vampirism give expression to the current necropolitics where human existence is reduced to the status of the living dead. In an immoral world populated with flesh-eating zombies and ravenous vampires, it is difficult to associate social responsibility, democratic values, imagination and creativity with the indifference, cruelty and parasitic existence of monsters. If 'everything is reduced to the issue of who eats whom',[5] then it is impossible to envision the vampire brimming with revolutionary potential. Instead, his individualism, cool indifference and rapacity are necessary tools to navigate within an atomised and market-driven society. Similarly, real vampire practices are calculable consummations that do not challenge identities or capitalist structures.

On the other hand, and despite calls to abandon Dracula to the past, the vampire is reinvented and appropriated to define new shifting realities in different parts of the world. Unlike western representations of predatory and vampiric subjectivity, the emergence of vampiric and occult phenomena all over the world reveals forms of resistant and disobedient subjectivities that are different but also in conversation with each other.[6] The appearance of vampires, monsters and other occult phenomena in post-apartheid South Africa, Indonesia, Russia and Latin America becomes a way to understand the contradictory effects of globalisation and neoliberalism. Neither global nor local, but parochial and translocal, modern and postmodern, these supernatural cases and stories are symptoms of the rapid economic transformations effectuated by global capital. Not a return to tradition, they are new forms of magic to make sense of new situations.[7] In these countries, the promise of wealth coexists with the despair of unemployment. The hope of enjoying the freedoms of postcolonial societies beyond limits is crushed by the logic of the market and the freedom to consume. While vast amounts of wealth in postcolonial societies are amassed by a small number of citizens, many experience desperation and poverty. This gives the impression of mysterious forces guiding the market towards selfish goals. New magic is pursued for impossible ends while others are killed because they are believed to be vampires and witches enriching themselves through occult means, illegally using the bodies or things of others or the forces of production and reproduction.[8] For example, the living dead are believed to monopolise all employment. The parochialism of vampires becomes a global phenomenon, linking translocal processes to local situations, the supernatural and gothic with the mechanisms of the market: 'Postcolonial Africa is replete with accounts of the way in which the rich and powerful use monstrous means and freakish familiars to appropriate the life force of their lesser compatriots in order to strengthen themselves or to satisfy consuming passions.'[9] This is not, however, merely an African, but a global phenomenon experienced by people in its different local guises. As Hardt and Negri argue, monsters are means to understand in these various contexts this 'plural collective planetary condition.'[10] For them, these phenomena attest to the emergence of the multitude that consists of singular forms of life that share a common global existence. Community then is no longer based on the old dualisms of us and them, identity and difference but on commonality-in-diversity.

Conclusion

The problem of neoliberal biopolitics, the privatisation of individual lives and their immunisation against the other's difference, is made legible through recourse to the premodern past and the story of first-century philosopher Apollonius of Tyana who is credited with saving the ancient Greek city of Ephesus from pestilence. In the *Treatise on Vampires and Revenants* (1746), published in English as *The Phantom World* (1850) and a possible influence on 'Carmilla',[11] Dom Augustine Calmet uses the specific incident as an example of demonic activity in Ephesus.[12] Apollonius of Tyana identifies in the form of a blind old beggar the demon that was responsible for the plague in Ephesus and thus instructs the Ephesians to stone him to death. The old man is transformed into a mad dog, justifying thus that he was the disguised demon of pestilence. In the face of the old beggar the community recognises the enemy and the victim that needs to be sacrificed so that the people are immunised against the plague. Reduced to a dog, the man is dehumanised and demonised. His life is sacrificed so that the community lives on. This 'demonic' life that circulates through the man and the dog is, however, the same life, and no more or less worthy than the Ephesians' lives. The phantom of the enemy as a plague carrier, a diseased vampire and an animal that needs to be exterminated is what haunts the idea of community.

Against this immunitary apparatus that seeks to isolate human life from its contact with the other and encage life within borders that recognise no outside or otherness but only the logic of the One (one race, one God, one ideology), there is the possibility of thinking about life in its multiplicity.[13] In attempting to move beyond the dualism of *bios* and *zoé*, of the qualified life of the human and nonhuman or animal life, it is necessary to understand life itself as '*a* life', and thus as singular and multiple, 'neutral, beyond good and evil',[14] that courses through the organic and the inorganic, through plants, animals and humans. No longer considered either as the life of the dominant race or that of the inferior race, every life should be understood as a form of life so that no part of it can be sacrificed for another. In this sense, the blood of the vampire, and,consequently its life, is equally as important as that of the human and thus should not be subject to a particular norm of life that marginalises difference. Life, then, becomes the primary source for the institution of norms. Vampire texts, then, are exemplary of the ways they force us to reconsider subjectivity in terms of the positivity of life and thus redefine the relationship between self and other.

Equally, the blood that circulates through different bodies and crosses somatic, national and political boundaries spreading disease is of the same colour and affects in similar and disastrous ways the lives of communities. From an ethical point of view, the blood spilled in wars and epidemics should not be accepted in some places and condemned in others. Drenched in the blood of race and the diseased blood of the other, vampire texts remain trapped in the poisonous dualisms of us and them that threaten to close down the possibility of thinking an affirmative biopolitics where all life has the right to exist. Against fears of invasion and contamination by difference, and the obsession with immunity and purity, it is necessary to think of a community of diversity that in times of plague does not seek to ostracise others but cultivates being in common while striving for rejuvenation and growth.

Notes

Introduction: Blood Bank: A History of the Symbolics of Blood

1. Guillermo del Torro and Chuck Hogan, *The Night Eternal*, London, Harper Collins, 2011, p.304.
2. See Fred Botting, 'Metaphors and Monsters', *Journal for Cultural Research*, 7.4, 2003, pp.339–65.
3. Ibid., p.360.
4. Michel Foucault, *Discipline and Punish: The Birth of the Prison*, trans. Alan Sheridan, New York, Pantheon Books, 1977, p.31.
5. Michel Foucault, 'Nietzsche, Genealogy, History', in Donald F. Bouchard (ed.), *Language, Counter-Memory, Practice: Selected Essays and Interviews*, Ithaca, Cornell University Press, 1977, p.140.
6. Ibid., p.146.
7. Ibid., p.148.
8. Kenneth C. Hanson, 'Blood and Purity in Leviticus and Revelation', *Listening: Journal of Religion and Culture*, 28, 1993, pp.215–30. K.C. Hanson is a biblical scholar belonging to the Context Group, a group of scholars who merge historical exegesis with social sciences to read the Bible in its social and cultural contexts.
9. The Nuer people lived in Southern Sudan, in the East Upper Nile Province around the junction of the Nile river with the Bahr el Ghazal and Sobat Rivers, and extending up the Sobat across the Ethiopian border. The centre of the Nuer area is around Lake No.
10. René Girard, *Violence and the Sacred*, London and New York, Continuum, 2005, p.35.
11. William Keith Chambers Guthrie, *History of Greek Philosophy: The Presocratic Tradition from Parmenides to Demokritus*, vol. 2, Cambridge, Cambridge University Press, 1965, p.303.
12. Empedocles (c.492–c.432BC) was born in Acragas, Sicily. He was a Greek philosopher of the Presocratic period and a contemporary of Protagoras the Sophist, Pericles, Sophocles, Socrates and Euripides. Only two poems are acknowledged to be his own work, *On Nature* and *Purifications*.
13. Quoted in Valentina Conticelli, 'Sanguis Suavis: Blood between Microcosm and Macrocosm', in James Bradburne (ed.), *Blood: Art, Power, Politics and Pathology*, London, Prestel, 2002, pp.55–63.
14. Leviticus, 17:11, 'Atonement by the Life in the Blood', *The Holy Bible: New International Version*, <http://www.biblegateway.com/passage/?search=Leviticus% 2017:11&version=NIV>.
15. Quoted in William K. Gilders, *Blood Ritual in the Hebrew Bible: Meaning and Power*, Baltimore, The John Hopkins University Press, 2004, p.12.

16. Caroline Walker Bynum, *Wonderful Blood: Theology and Practice in Late Medieval Northern Germany and Beyond*, Philadelphia, University of Pennsylvania Press, 2007, p.162.
17. Bynum, *Wonderful Blood*, p.162.
18. Ibid., p.163.
19. Melissa L. Meyer, *Thicker than Water: The Origins of Blood as Symbol and Ritual*, London, Routledge, 2005, p.8.
20. Meyer, *Thicker than Water*, p.8.
21. Ibid., p.171.
22. Ibid., p.166.
23. Jaroslav Černý, 'Reference to Blood Brotherhood Among Semites in an Egyptian Text of the Ramesside Period', *Journal of Near Eastern Studies*, 14.3, 1955, pp.161–3.
24. Ibid., p.161.
25. Dennis J. McCarthy, 'Further Notes on the Symbolism of Blood and Sacrifice', *Journal of Biblical Literature*, 92.2, 1973, pp.205–10.
26. Quoted in Bettina Bildhauer, *Medieval Blood*, Cardiff, University of Wales Press, 2006, p.155.
27. Bynum, *Wonderful Blood*, p.187.
28. Ibid., p.214.
29. Ibid., p.18–19.
30. Meyer, *Thicker than Water*, p.144.
31. Bynum, 'The Body of Christ in the Later Middle Ages: A Reply to Leo Steinberg', *Renaissance Quarterly*, 39.3, 1986, pp.399–439.
32. Julia Kristeva, *Powers of Horror: An Essay on Abjection*, New York, Columbia University Press, 1982, p.105.
33. Bynum, 'The Body of Christ', p.427.
34. Ibid., p.435.
35. Ibid., p.434.
36. Ibid., p.436.
37. Mary Douglas, *Purity and Danger: An Analysis of Concept of Pollution and Taboo*, London and New York, Routledge [1966], 2002, p.150.
38. Ibid., p.154.
39. Michel Foucault, *The History of Sexuality, Volume1: The Will to Knowledge*, trans. Robert Hurley, London, Penguin Books, [1978], 1998, p.147.
40. Ibid., p.147.
41. Ibid., p.148.
42. Ibid., pp.148–9.
43. Ibid., p.147.
44. Ibid., p.124.
45. Ibid., p.106.
46. Ibid., p.107.
47. Ibid., p.147.
48. Foucault uses the terms 'biopolitics' and 'biopower' interchangeably and it is difficult to distinguish between the two. Michael Dillon and Julian Reid make the distinction between biopower and its politics: biopolitics ('Global Liberal Governance: Biopolitics, Security and War', *Millennium: Journal of International Studies*, 30.1, 2001, pp.41–66). Michael Hardt and Antonio Negri

distinguish between the all-consuming vampiric biopower of neoliberalism and the realisation of a productive biopolitics of the revolutionary multitude dedicated to democratic ends.

49. Foucault, *History*, p.139.
50. Michel Foucault, *Society Must Be Defended: Lectures at the Collège de France, 1975–76*, in Mauro Bertani and Alessandro Fontana (eds.), trans. David Masey, New York: Picador, 2003, p.249.
51. Foucault, *History*, p.136.
52. Ibid., p.137.
53. Ibid., p.142.
54. Ibid., p.138.
55. Ibid.
56. Ibid., p.147.
57. Ibid., p.126.
58. Ibid., p.146.
59. Ibid., p.145.
60. Ibid., p.146.
61. Ibid., p.124.
62. Ibid., p.125.
63. Ibid.
64. Elizabeth Grosz, *Volatile Bodies: Toward a Corporeal Feminism*, Bloomington, IN, Indiana University Press, 1994, p.206.
65. In his lectures at the Collège de France Foucault discusses the emergence of race in the seventeenth and eighteenth centuries which is not yet associated with biological meanings (the racist-biological discourse as it is currently understood will appear in the nineteenth century).
66. Foucault, *Society*, pp.254–5.
67. Ibid., p.255.
68. Ibid.
69. Ibid.
70. Ibid.
71. Ibid., p.81.
72. Foucault, *History*, p.149.
73. Ibid.
74. Ibid., p.150.
75. Foucault, *Society*, pp.82, 83.
76. Maurizio Lazzarato, 'Neoliberalism in Action: Inequality, Insecurity, and the Reconstitution of the Social', *Theory, Culture and Society*, 26.6, 2009, pp.109–33.
77. Nikolas Rose, *The Politics of Life Itself: Biomedicine, Power, and Subjectivity in the Twenty-First Century*, Princeton and Oxford, Princeton University Press, 2007, p.3.
78. Ibid.
79. Donna Haraway, *Modest_Witness@Second_Millenium*, London, Routledge, 1997, p.222.
80. Catherine Waldby and Robert Mitchell, *Tissue Economies: Blood, Organs, and Cell Lines in Late Capitalism*, Durham and London, Duke University Press, 2006, p.22.
81. Foucault, *History*, p.149.

1   A Matter of Life and Death: Transfusing Blood from a Supernatural Past to Scientific Modernity and Vampiric Technology

1. John Murray, *Considerations on the Vital Principle*, London, Relfe and Fletcher, Cornhill, 1838, p.27.
2. Mary Elizabeth Braddon, 'Good Lady Ducayne', in David J. Skal (ed.), *Vampires: Encounters with the Undead*, New York, Black Dog & Leventhal Publishers, [1896], 2006, p.182.
3. Ibid., p.183.
4. Ibid., p.196.
5. Ibid., pp.179–99, p.195.
6. See Eugene Thacker, 'Biophilosophy for the Twenty-First Century', *CTheory.net*, 2005, <http://www.ctheory.net/articles.aspx?id=472>.
7. See Michel Foucault, 'The Politics of Health in the Eighteenth Century', in James D. Faubion (ed.), *Power: Essential Works of Foucault, 1957–84*, vol. 3, London, Penguin, 2002, pp.90–105, and Michel Foucault, *The History of Sexuality, Vol. 1: The Will to Knowledge*, trans. Robert Hurley, London, Penguin, 1998, pp.142–7.
8. John J. Jordan, 'Vampire Cyborgs and Scientific Imperialism: A Reading of the Science-Mysticism Polemic in *Blade*', *Journal of Popular Film and Television*, 27.2, 1999, pp.4–15.
9. With the development of biomedicine and the understanding of the body at a molecular level, biopolitical interventions extend to include the inside of the body, what Nikolas Rose calls 'molecular biopolitics' (*Politics*, pp.11–12). Life itself, at the molecular level, is now open to politics (Rose, *Politics*, p.15).
10. Nikolas Rose, *Politics of Life Itself: Biomedicine, Power, and Subjectivity in the Twenty-First Century*, Princeton and Oxford, Princeton University Press, 2007, p.3.
11. Michael Dillon and Julian Reid, 'Global Liberal Governance: Biopolitics, Security and War', *Millenium*, 30.1, 2001, pp.41–66.
12. Ibid., p.56.
13. Rose, *Politics*, pp.11, 12.
14. Donna J. Haraway, *Modest Witness*, London, Routledge, 1997, p.222. Haraway in *Modest Witness* analyses the concept of race in biomedicine, which she sees as 'a fracturing trauma in the body politic of the nation' (p.213). She argues that blood ties have been 'bloody enough already' and that we should learn 'to produce humanity through something more and less than kinship' (p.265). Thus, she playfully takes the side of those vampires who pollute essential categories such as race.
15. Catherine Waldby and Robert Mitchell, *Tissue Economies: Blood, Organs, and Cell Lines in Late Capitalism*, Durham and London, Duke University Press, 2006, p.22.
16. Michel Foucault distinguishes between anatomo-politics (individualised body) and biopolitics (population as a biological species). He writes: 'Unlike discipline, which is addressed to bodies, the new nondisciplinary power is applied not to man-as-body but to the living man, to man-as-living-being;

ultimately, if you like, to man-as-species' and this 'new technology [biopolitics] that is being established is addressed to a multiplicity of men, not to the extent that they are nothing more than their individual bodies, but to the extent that they form, on the contrary, a global mass that is affected by overall processes characteristic of birth, death, production, illness, and so on.' See Michel Foucault, *Society Must Be Defended: Lectures at the Collège de France, 1975–76*, in Mauro Bertani and Alessandro Fontana (eds.), trans. David Masey, New York: Picador, 2003, pp.242–3.

17. Organic materials become, to a certain extent, 'immortal' since they transcend living human bodies. Blood, for example, after its removal from the body, can exist in the bodies of others in order to improve their lives or save them from dying. In this way, even after an individual is dead, s/he may live on since his/her blood or organs continue to exist in the bodies of others. See Sarah Franklin and Margaret Lock (eds.), *Remaking Life and Death: Toward an Anthropology of the Biosciences*, Santa Fe, NM, School of American Research Press, 2003.

18. Richard Doyle, *Wetwares: Experiments in Postvital Living*, Minneapolis, MN, University of Minnesota Press, 2003.

19. Colin Milburn, *Nanovision: Engineering the Future*, Durham and London, Duke University Press, 2008, pp.165–6.

20. Ibid., p.65.

21. As Foucault writes, 'Up to the end of the eighteenth century in fact, life does not exist; only living beings' (Michel Foucault, *The Order of Things: An Archaeology of the Human Sciences*, New York, Vintage Books, 1973, p.175).

22. Xavier Bichat, *Physiological Researches on Life and Death*, trans. F. Gold, London, Longman, Hurst, Rees, Orme and Browne, 1815, p.1.

23. J.S.C., 'Vitality of the Blood', *Lancet*, 2, 1829, pp.139–40.

24. Ibid., p.140.

25. John Hunter, *A Treatise on the Blood, Inflammation, and Gun-Shot Wounds*, London, Sherwood, Gilbert, and Piper, 1828, p.113.

26. John Jones, 'Pathology of Fever, &c. Founded on the Blood's Vitality', *The London Medical and Physical Journal, January 1825–June 1825*, LIII, pp.108–15, pp.289–93.

27. Samuel Cartwright, 'The Haematokinetic or Blood-Moving Power of Inspired Air, Proved by Further Experiments on the Crocodile', *Boston Medical and Surgical Journal*, 46–7, 1852, pp.392–8.

28. Ibid., p.396.

29. Sarah Kember, Mariam Fraser and Celia Lury, *Inventive Life: Approaches to the New Vitalism*, London, California and New Delhi, Sage Publications, 2006, p.1.

30. Catherine Keller, 'Process and Chaosmos: The Whiteheadian Fold in the Discourse of Difference', in Catherine Keller and Anne Daniell (eds.), *Process and Difference: Between Cosmological and Poststructuralist Postmodernisms*, Albany, State University of New York Press, 2002, pp.55–72.

31. Kember, Fraser and Lury, *Inventive Life*, p.3.

32. Life is matter in flux and a technological lineage of natural or/and artificial materiality. See Gilles Deleuze and Felix Guattari, *A Thousand*

Plateaus: Capitalism and Schizophrenia, trans. Brian Massumi, London and New York, Continuum, 2004.

33. See Thacker, 'Biophilosophy', 'The Shadows of Atheology: Epidemics, Power and Life after Foucault', *Theory Culture Society*, 26.6, 2009, pp.134–52, and 'Darklife: Negation, Nothingness, and the Will-to-Life in Schopenhauer', *Parrhesia*, 12, 2011, pp.12–27.

34. Christopher Langton, 'Artificial Life', in Christopher Langton (ed.), *Artificial Life*, Redwood City, California, Addison-Wesley, 1989, pp.1–47.

35. Harvey G. Klein and David J. Anstee, *Mollison's Blood Transfusion in Clinical Medicine*, 11th edn, Malden, MA and Oxford, Blackwell, 2005, p.19.

36. Nicholas J. Vardaxis, *Immunology for the Health Sciences*, South Melbourne, Macmillan, 1995, p.80.

37. Douglas Starr, *Blood: An Epic History of Medicine and Commerce*, London, Little, Brown, and Company, 1998, p.35.

38. Gustave Lemattre, 'On the Transfusion of Blood', *Popular Science*, 2.41, April 1873, pp.679–95.

39. Ibid., p.694.

40. See Kim Pelis' analysis of Blundell's therapeutic beliefs in blood transfusion and the idea of re-animation of women by transfused blood, in 'Transfusion with Teeth' in James M. Bradburne (ed.), *Blood: Art, Power, Politics, and Pathology*, Munich, Prestel, 2002, pp.175–91.

41. Starr, *Blood*, p.36.

42. Mr. Callaway, 'London Medical Society', *The Lancet*, 2, 1829, p.120.

43. Henri Milne Edwards, 'Blood', in Robert Bentley Todd (ed.), *The Cyclopaedia of Anatomy and Physiology*, vol.1, London, Longman, Brown, Green, Longmans, & Roberts, 1835–6, pp.404–15, p.409.

44. Pelis, 'Transfusion', p.186.

45. James Blundell, 'Lectures on the Theory and Practice of Midwifery', Lecture XVI, 'Management of the more Copious Floodings', *Lancet*, 1, 1828, pp.609–14.

46. Blundell, 'Management', p.614.

47. Pelis, 'Transfusion', p.176.

48. James Blundell, 'Experiments on the Transfusion of Blood by the Syringe', *Medico-Chrurgical Transactions*, 9, 3 February 1818, pp.56–92.

49. James Blundell, 'Observations on Transfusion of Blood By Dr. Blundell. *With a Description of his Gravitator*', *The Lancet*, 2, 1828–9, pp.321–4.

50. See J.S.C., 'Vitality of the Blood', pp.139–40, pp.151–2.

51. Starr, *Blood*, p.37.

52. Kim Pelis, 'Blood Clots: The Nineteenth-Century Debate over the Substance and Means of Transfusion in Britain', *Annals of Science Fiction*, 54, 1997, pp.331–60.

53. Pelis, 'Blood Clots', p.332.

54. Ibid., p.357.

55. Ibid., p.360.

56. Susan E. Lederer, *Flesh and Blood: Organ Transplantation and Blood Transfusion in Twentieth-Century America*, Oxford, Oxford University Press, 2008, pp.51, 52.

57. Starr, *Blood*, p.40.

58. Lederer, *Flesh and Blood*, p.52.

59. Marcel Mauss, *The Gift: Forms and Functions of Exchange in Archaic Societies*, 1925, trans. Ian Cunnison, Oxford and New York, Routledge, 1969, p.16.
60. Mauss, *The Gift*, p.15.
61. Ibid., p.16.
62. In his reading of 'Good Lady Ducayne' Fred Botting observes: 'With its capacity to penetrate and alter living bodies, science receives Gothic treatment' (' "Monsters of the Imagination": Gothic, Science, Fiction', in David Seed (ed.), *A Companion to Science Fiction*, Malden, MA and Oxford, Blackwell, 2005, pp.111–26).
63. Braddon, 'Good Lady Ducayne', p.194.
64. As Mary Wilson Carpenter writes, 'more upper-class Victorians were almost obsessed with their own health. They complained of dyspepsia (indigestion), sleeplessness, headaches, melancholy, and many other symptoms that their doctors typically found very hard to cure' (*Health, Medicine and Society in Victorian England*, Santa Barbara, CA, Praeger, 2010, p.23).
65. See Jules Law, *The Social Life of Fluids: Blood, Milk, and Water in the Victorian Novel*, Ithaca, NY, Cornell University Press, 2010.
66. Braddon, 'Good Lady Ducayne', p.196.
67. Ibid.
68. Ibid.
69. Ibid., p.187.
70. Jules Law notes that in the Victorian period emerged an 'intensification of the opposition between the science of fluids *out* of the body and the fetishization of fluids within. As fluids out of the body are subjected to progressively greater rationalization, analysis, and manipulation, bodily fluids become increasingly the emblem and the vehicle of that which is inalienable, irrational, and individual' (Law, *The Social Life of Fluids*, p.4).
71. George Henry Lewes was a British philosopher and critic (1817–78).
72. In *The Physiology of Common Life, Vol. 1* ([1859], New York, D. Appleton and Company, 1860, 2 vols.) Lewes refers to the work of Virchow (p.167). Lady Ducayne's awareness of Rudolf Virchow's work points out that the author was possibly acquainted with other medical analyses such as Lewes' analysis of blood, but also with scientific developments in general, especially Virchow's research on cellular pathology and epidemic disease.
73. Lewes, *The Physiology*, p.225.
74. Ibid.
75. Ibid., p.226.
76. Braddon, 'Good Lady Ducayne', p.182–3.
77. Ibid., p.190.
78. This is because the compatibility of blood types with the discovery of the ABO blood grouping in 1901, the use of sodium nitrate to prevent clotting in 1915 and the *Rhesus factor* in blood types in 1940 were still undiscovered and unknown.
79. Bram Stoker, *Dracula*, 1897, Rev. Ed, London, Penguin, 1993, p.160.
80. Stoker, *Dracula*, p.160.
81. Ibid., p.159.
82. Ibid., p.163.
83. See Pelis, 'Blood Clots', p.359.
84. Stoker, *Dracula*, p.132.

85. Ibid., p.135.
86. Ibid., p.145.
87. The sexual associations with blood transfusions have been discussed and analysed in depth in Glennis Byron's *Dracula*, New York, St. Martin's Press, 1999. See particularly the following chapters: Christopher Craft, ' "Kiss me with Those Red Lips": Gender and Inversion in Bram Stoker's *Dracula*', pp.93–118; Phyllis A. Roth 'Suddenly Sexual Women in Bram Stoker's *Dracula*', pp.30–42; and Rebecca E. Pope's 'Writing and Biting in *Dracula*', pp.68–92. Also see Ernest Jones', *On the Nightmare*, New York, Liveright, 1951.
88. Stoker, *Dracula*, p.138.
89. Ibid., p.187. The 1912 American silent film *The Hospital Baby* describes the transfusion of blood from a doctor to a young girl, who will later save him from a near-death experience and marry him. The film focuses on the blood relation between a woman and a man after a transfusion of blood.
90. Stoker, *Dracula*, p.139.
91. Ibid., p.138.
92. Ibid., p.187.
93. Christopher Craft, ' "Kiss Me with Those Red Lips": Gender and Inversion in Bram Stoker's *Dracula*', p.105.
94. Ibid., p.106.
95. Stacey Abbott explains that in this scene 'science is presented to be as Gothic and ritualized as vampire folklore and religious mysticism' (*Celluloid Vampires: Life after Death in the Modern World*, Austin, TX, The University of Texas Press, 2007, p.65). It is transformed into a religious practice through the reading of a Latin text and thus becomes the 'religion of the modern man' (p.65).
96. While Stacey Abbott argues that 'the supernatural and the fantastic win out in the end as Dracula's blood proves more powerful than Eidleman's cure' (Abbott, *Celluloid Vampires*, p.68), the film seems to suggest something different.
97. Nicola Nixon, 'When Hollywood Sucks, or, Hungry Girls, Lost Boys, and Vampirism in the Age of Reagan', in Joan Gordon and Veronica Hollinger (eds.), *Blood Read: The Vampire as Metaphor in Contemporary Culture*, Philadelphia, PA, University of Pennsylvania Press, 1997, p.115.
98. Waldby and Mitchell, *Tissue Economies*, p.41.
99. Ibid.
100. Ronald Bayer and Eric Feldman, *Blood Feuds: AIDS, Blood, and the Politics of Medical Disaster*, Oxford and New York, Oxford University Press, 1999, p.8.
101. Waldby and Mitchell, *Tissue Economies*, p.56.
102. Ibid., p.45.
103. Vanessa Martlew, 'Transfusion Medicine towards the Millennium', in A. Oakley and J. Ashton (eds.), *Richard Titmuss, The Gift Relationship: From Human Blood to Social Policy*, London, LSE, 1997, pp.41–54.
104. See Jacob Copeman, *Veins of Devotion: Blood Donation and Religious Experience in North India*, New Brunswick, NJ, and London, Rutgers University Press, 2009, p.40.
105. Copeman, *Veins*, p.43.
106. Waldby and Mitchell, *Tissue Economies*, p.32.

107. 'The organic becomes the living and the living is that which produces, grows, and reproduces' (Foucault, *The Order of Things*, p.232).
108. Robert A. Freitas Jr., 'Respirocytes: A Mechanical Artificial Red Cell: Exploratory Design in Medical Nanotechnology', *Foresight Institute*, p.4, <http://www.foresight. org/Nanomedicine/Respirocytes.html>
109. Ibid., p.3.
110. Ibid., p.4.
111. Ibid.
112. Ibid.
113. Eugene Thacker, *Biomedia*, Minneapolis, MN, University of Minnesota Press, 2004, p.129.
114. Ibid., p.137.
115. Ibid.
116. Ibid., n. pag.
117. Wilhelm Worringer, *Form Problems of the Gothic*, New York, G.E. Stechert & Co., 1920, p.48.
118. Ibid., p.47.
119. Ibid.
120. Ibid., p.69.
121. Luciana Parisi and Tiziana Terranova, 'Heat-Death: Emergence and Control in Genetic Engineering and Artificial Life', *CTheory: Theory, Technology and Culture*, 23. 1–2, 2000, n. pag, <http://www.ctheory.net/ articles.aspx? id=127>.
122. Franco Moretti, 'Dracula and Capitalism', in Glennis Byron (ed.), *Dracula*, New York, St. Martin's Press, 1999, pp.43–54.
123. Melinda Cooper, *Life as Surplus: Biotechnology and Capitalism in the Neoliberal Era*, Seattle, WA, University of Washington Press, pp.6–7.
124. Foucault, *The Order of Things*, p.227.
125. Ibid., p.232.
126. There are various reports on futurist blogs that suggest that the Temple of the Vampire sells cryonics contracts to its higher members, and advocates, although not publicly, ideas about cryonics (London Futurists). For example, the Temple used to refer to a vampire apocalypse and a final harvest of humanity, where the undead gods will become rulers of the world. Such fictional beliefs have been substituted recently by a more scientific approach to the idea of physical immortality based on the work of the English gerontologist Aubrey de Grey.
127. World Transhumanist Association, Humanity+, <http://humanityplus.org/ learn/ transhumanist-faq/#answer_19>.
128. Eugene Thacker, 'Data Made Flesh: Biotechnology and the Discourse of the Posthuman', *Cultural Critique*, 53, 2003, pp.72–97.
129. Elaine L. Graham, *Representations of the Post/human: Monsters, Aliens, and Others in Popular Culture*, Manchester, University of Manchester Press, 2002, p.160.
130. http://www.extropy.org/About.htm
131. Robert C.W. Ettinger, *The Prospect of Immortality*, New York, Doubleday, 1964, p.164.
132. Ibid., p.16.
133. Ibid., p.84.

134. Unlike the Temple of the Vampire, which relies on scientific beliefs, other self-identified vampires follow holistic health practices and believe in blood as a carrier of the vital principle. This vitalism is closer to the occult and theological vitalism of eighteenth- and nineteenth-century physicians.
135. See Doyle, *Wetwares*, p.79.
136. Ettinger, *The Prospect of Immortality*, p.11.
137. Doyle, *Wetwares*, p.74.
138. Ibid., p.69.
139. See Carlos Novas and Nikolas Rose, 'Genetic Risk and the Birth of the Somatic Individual', *Economy and Society* 29.4, 2000, pp.485–513.
140. Waldby and Mitchell, *Tissue Economies*, pp.125–9.
141. Ibid., p.129.
142. Nixon points out that a year before the film was released John Doolittle 'sponsored a Senate bill that "legalized the creation of designated-donor pools to keep donated blood *within families* so as to prevent transmission" of certain blood diseases passed from anonymous donors to "the general population." It passed, in 1986, without a murmur of opposition' (Nixon, 'When Hollywood Sucks', p.126).
143. Temple of the Vampire, <www.vampiretemple.com/index.html>.
144. Ibid.
145. Doyle, *Wetwares*, p.85.

2   The Biopolitics of the Vampire Narrative: Vampire Epidemics, AIDS and Bioterrorism

1. Morley Roberts, *Warfare in the Human Body: Essays on the Method, Malignity, Repair, and Allied Subjects*, New York, E.P. Dutton Company, 1921.
2. Morley Roberts, *Bio-Politics: An Essay in the Physiology, Pathology and Politics of the Social and Somatic Organism*, London, Dent, 1938, pp.200–1.
3. Ibid., p.166.
4. Ibid., p.99.
5. Ibid.
6. Ibid.
7. For example, Francisco Varela and Mark Anspach in 'Immu-Knowledge: The Process of Somatic Individuation' (in William Irwin Thompson (ed.), *Gaia 2, Emergence, The New Science of Becoming*, Hudson, NY, Lindisfarne Press, 1991) have pointed out that the standard discourse of immunity is characterised by militaristic language that describes the protection of the 'self' from the 'assault of foreign infections' or 'non-self' and the production of 'defences against invaders' in metaphors of defence, invasion and combat.
8. See Michael Hardt and Antonio Negri, *Empire*, Cambridge, MA and London, England, Harvard University Press, 2000, p.136; Roberto Esposito, *Terms of the Political: Community, Immunity, Biopolitics*, New York, Fordham University Press, 2013, p.60.
9. See Mary Douglas, *Purity and Danger* [1966], London and New York, Routledge, 2002, and René Girard, *Violence and the Sacred* [1979], London and New York, Continuum, 2005.
10. Morley Roberts, *Warfare in the Human Body*, p.137.

11. Roberto Esposito, *Bios: Biopolitics and Philosophy*, trans. Timothy Campbell, Minneapolis, MN, University of Minnesota Press, 2008, p.183.
12. Ibid., pp.182–3.
13. Girard, *Violence*, p.37.
14. Nikolas Rose, *The Politics of Life Itself: Biomedicine, Power and Subjectivity in the Twenty-First Century*, Princeton, NJ and Oxford, Princeton University Press, 2007, p.13.
15. Esposito, *Terms of the Political*, p.59.
16. Esposito, *Bíos*, p.46.
17. Esposito, *Terms of the Political*, p.61.
18. Ibid., pp.61–2.
19. Nükhet Varlik, 'Contagion Theory of Disease, Premodern', in Joseph Patrick Byrne (ed.), *Encyclopedia of Pestilence, Pandemics, and Plagues*, Westport, CT, Greenwood Press, 2008, pp.133–6.
20. Christopher Frayling, 'Lord Byron to Count Dracula', in Christopher Frayling (ed.), *Vampyres: Lord Byron to Count Dracula*, London and Boston, Faber and Faber, 1992, pp.3–84.
21. Rabies was later another alteration of the theme of epidemic to explain vampirism.
22. Frayling, 'Lord Byron to Count Dracula', p.25.
23. Ibid., p.26.
24. Ibid., p.27.
25. Gabriel Tarde, *The Laws of Imitation*, New York, Henry Holt and Company, 1903.
26. Le Fanu, 'Carmilla', p.94.
27. Ibid., p.101.
28. Ibid., p.84.
29. Ibid.
30. Le Fanu, 'Carmilla', p.83.
31. Ibid., p.88.
32. Ibid., p.130.
33. Ibid., p.102.
34. Ibid., p.93.
35. Ibid., p.136.
36. Ibid., p.106.
37. Thomas Herbert Barker, *On Malaria and Miasmata and their Influence in the Production of Typhus and Typhoid Fevers, Cholera, and the Exanthemata*, London, John W. Davies, 1863, p.1.
38. Le Fanu, 'Carmilla', p.93.
39. Ibid., p.104.
40. Ibid.
41. Ibid., p.95.
42. Ibid.
43. Barker, *On Malaria*, p.10.
44. Ibid., pp.41–2.
45. Ibid., p.42.
46. Ernest Jones, *On the Nightmare*, New York, Liverlight, 1951, p.122.
47. Le Fanu, 'Carmilla', p.133.
48. Ibid., p.99.

49. Ibid., p.94.
50. Ibid., p.101.
51. Esposito, *Bíos*, p.126.
52. Le Fanu, 'Carmilla', p.104.
53. Ibid., p.116.
54. Ibid., p.127.
55. Ibid., p.134.
56. Ibid.
57. Bram Stoker, *Dracula*, London, Penguin, [1897],1993, p.265.
58. The connection between rats and disease is strikingly emphasised in the 1992 film *Bram Stoker's Dracula* when Dracula dissolves into a form that is composed of rats.
59. It is the bacterial disease plague, an infection caused by the bite of an infected flea found in rodents such as rats and mice.
60. See Stephen Arata's essay 'The Occidental Tourist: *Dracula* and the Anxiety of Reverse Colonisation', in Glennis Byron (ed.), *Dracula*, New York, St. Martin's Press, 1999, pp.119–44, and David Glover's 'Travels in Romania: Myths of Origins, Myths of Blood', in Glennis Byron (ed.), pp.197–217.
61. See Maria Tatar's reading of *Nosferatu* in *Lustmord: Sexual Murder in Weimar Germany*, Princeton, NJ, Princeton University Press, 1995, pp.57–8.
62. The motif of the wandering Jew has appeared in such gothic texts as Matthew Lewis' *The Monk* (1796) and Charles Robert Maturin's *Melmoth the Wanderer* (1820).
63. Richard Matheson, *I Am Legend*, London, Gollancz, [1954], 2001, p.80.
64. Robert Koch, 'The Etiology of Anthrax, Founded on the Course of Development of the Bacillus Anthracis' [1876], in K. Codell Carter (ed.), *Essays of Robert Koch*, New York, Greenwood Press, 1987, p.2.
65. Ibid.
66. See Michel Foucault, *'Society Must Be Defended': Lectures at the Collège de France, 1975–76*, trans. David Masey, Mauro Bertani and Alessandro Fontana (eds.), New York, Picador, 2003, pp.242, 249.
67. Matheson, *I Am Legend*, p.136.
68. Ibid.
69. Ibid.
70. Ibid., p.145.
71. Ibid., p.157.
72. Foucault, *Society*, pp.82, 83.
73. Ibid., p.61.
74. Matheson, *I Am Legend*, p.11.
75. Ibid., p.16.
76. Ibid., p.111.
77. Ibid., p.12.
78. Ibid., p.17.
79. Ibid., p.30.
80. Ibid., p.34.
81. Ibid.
82. In the 1959 film *Curse of the Undead*, released by Universal Studios, vampirism is related to disease and specifically the McCarthyist disease of communism. In the 1958 film *The Return of Dracula*, Dracula is portrayed as

a communist threat to America. For a detailed analysis on vampirism and films in the 1950s see 'Vampires in Cold War Film', in Cyndy Hendershot's *I Was a Cold War Monster: Horror films, Eroticism, and the Cold War Imagination*, Bowling Green, OH, Bowling Green State University Popular Press, 2001, pp.43–54.

83. George Kennan, 'Moscow Embassy Telegram #511, The Long Telegram', [1946], in Thomas Etzold and John Lewis Gaddis (eds.), *Containment: Documents on American Policy and Strategy 1945–50*, New York, Columbia University Press, 1978, pp.50–63.

84. HUAC: House Un-American Activities Committee.

85. Quoted in Ellen Schrecker, *The Age of McCarthyism: A Brief History with Documents*, New York, St. Martin's Press, 2002, p.133.

86. Matheson, *I Am Legend*, p.149.

87. Ibid., p.150.

88. Ibid., p.157.

89. Keith Ansell Pearson, *Viroid Life: Perspectives on Nietzsche and the Transhuman Condition*, London and New York, Routledge, 1997, p.134.

90. Lynn Margulis and Dorion Sagan, *What is Life*, Berkeley and Los Angeles, CA, University of California Press, 2000, p.141.

91. Ibid., p.144.

92. According to the Oxford English Dictionary, AIDS (Acquired Immune Deficiency Syndrome) is 'an illness (often if not always fatal) in which opportunistic infections or malignant tumours develop as a result of a severe loss of cellular immunity, which is itself caused by earlier infection with a retrovirus, HIV, transmitted in sexual fluids and blood. Freq. *attrib.* Cf. *acquired immune deficiency syndrome.*'

93. Gay Related Immunodeficiency Disease.

94. Douglas Starr, *Blood: An Epic History of Medicine and Commerce*, London, Little, Brown, and Company, 1998, pp.262–3.

95. See Paul Reed, 'Early AIDS Fiction', in Judith Laurence Pastore (ed.), *Confronting AIDS Through Literature: The Responsibilities of Representation*, Illinois, Chicago, University of Illinois, 1993, pp.91–4.

96. The novel is concerned with a mother's fear about her gay son's disease in a San Francisco neighbourhood.

97. Priscilla L. Walton regards *The Hunger* as one of the first post-AIDS vampire films (*Our Cannibals, Ourselves*, Illinois, University of Illinois, 2004, p.78).

98. Nicola Nixon, 'When Hollywood Sucks, or, Hungry Girls, Lost Boys, and Vampirism in the Age of Reagan', in Joan Gordon and Veronica Hollinger (eds.), *Blood Read: The Vampire as Metaphor in Contemporary Culture*, Philadelphia, PA, University of Pennsylvania Press, 1997, pp.115–28.

99. Jesse Kohn, 'Believing in the Disease: Virologies and Memetics as Models of Power Relations in Contemporary Science Fiction', Culture Machine 3, 2001, <http://www.culturemachine.net/index.php/cm/article/viewArticle/289/274>.

100. David P. Clark and Nanette J. Pazdernik, *Molecular Biology*, Oxford, Academic Press, 2013, p.30.

101. Stableford, *The Empire of Fear*, p.477.

102. Ibid., p.485.

103. Simon Watney, 'Missionary Positions: AIDS, "Africa," and Race', *Differences*, 1.1, 1989, pp.83–101.
104. Stableford, *The Empire of Fear*, p.477.
105. Starr, *Blood*, p.292.
106. Nina Auerbach views the normalisation of vampirism as the imprisonment of subjects in an eternal state that is stagnant and non-productive (*Our Vampires, Ourselves*, London and Chicago, The University of Chicago Press, 1995, p.170).
107. Micheal Romkey, *The Vampire Virus*, New York, Fawcett Gold Metal, 1997, p.93.
108. Ibid., p.135.
109. Ibid., p.115.
110. Haraway, *Modest Witness*, London, Routledge, 1997, p.251.
111. Ibid., p.253.
112. Ibid., p.252.
113. Eugene Thacker, *The Global Genome: Biotechnology, Politics, and Culture*, Cambridge, MA, London, MIT Press, 2005, p.163.
114. Romkey, *The Vampire Virus*, p.54.
115. Starr, *Blood*, p.158.
116. Romkey, *The Vampire Virus*, p.240.
117. Guillermo del Toro and Chuck Hogan, *The Night Eternal*, London, HarperCollins, 2011, p.179.
118. Slavoj Žižek's *Welcome to the Desert of the Real: Five Essays on September 11 and related Dates*, London and New York, Verso, 2002, and Jean Baudrillard's *The Spirit of Terrorism and Other Essays*, London and New York, Verso, 2002, argue that Americans cannot integrate September 11 into reality because the event is experienced and devoured constantly as a Hollywood spectacle. Justin Cronin echoes this when he describes the terrorist attacks as the 'money shot of the new millennium, the ultimate reality show broadcast 24–7' (Justin Cronin, *The Passage*, London, Orion Books, 2010, p.84).
119. Slavoj Žižek, 'Welcome to the Desert of the Real (Reflections on WTC)', in *Lacan.com*, 7 October 2001, <http://www.lacan.com/reflections.htm>.
120. The FBI gave the name Amerithrax to the anthrax letters.
121. Gregory D. Koblentz in *Living Weapons: Biological Warfare and International Security*, Ithaca, NY, Cornell University Press, 2009, explains that 'Third-generation biological terrorism capabilities require the ability to disseminate pathogens or toxins in an aerosol of particles in the 1–10 micron range' (p.205). Although no spray device was used, the anthrax letters, because of the high quality of the powder, were a 'potent aerosolization hazard in their own right' (p.205).
122. Ibid.
123. Ibid.
124. Ibid., p.207.
125. Melinda Cooper, *Life as Surplus: Biotechnology and Capitalism in the Neoliberal Era*, Seattle and London, University of Washington Press, 2008, p.74.
126. Ibid.
127. Ibid., p.75.
128. Ibid., p.98.
129. Ibid.

130. Ibid.
131. Cronin, *The Passage*, p.19.
132. Ibid., p.43.
133. Ibid., p.87.
134. The derogatory word 'smokes' was first used to describe freed black slaves as 'smoked Yankees', and was later shortened to 'smokes' or 'mokes' (Leon Rappoport, *Punchlines: The Case for Racial, Ethnic, and Gender Humor*, Westport, CT, Greenwood Publishing Group, 2005, p.47).
135. Paul Virilio, *Crepuscular Dawn*, introd. Sylvère Lotringer, Los Angeles, CA and New York, Semiotext(e), 2002, p.173.
136. Cronin, *The Passage*, p.85.
137. Ibid., p.84.
138. For Giorgio Agamben, asylum seekers, refugees and the brain dead are examples of 'bare life', people without rights or state, whose existence is reduced to biological functions (*Homo Sacer: Sovereign Power and Bare Life*, trans. Daniel Heller-Roazen, Stanford, CA, Stanford University Press, 1998).
139. See Ernest Lee Tuveson, *Redeemer Nation: The Idea of America's Millennial Role*, Chicago and London, The University of Chicago Press, 1968.
140. Thomas Jefferson, *Notes on the State of Virginia*, [1785], London, John Stockdale, 1787, p.274.
141. John Greville Agard Pocock, *The Machiavellian Moment: Florentine Political Thought and the Atlantic Republican Tradition*, Princeton, NJ, Princeton University Press, 1975, p.543.
142. Guillermo del Toro and Chuck Hogan, *The Strain*, [2009], London, Harper, 2010, p.338.
143. Guillermo del Toro and Chuck Hogan, *The Fall*, London, Harper Collins, 2010, p.52.
144. Del Toro and Hogan, *Strain*, p.423.
145. Ibid., p.424.
146. Ibid., p.425.
147. Ibid., p.221.
148. Ibid., p.220.
149. Ibid., p.221.
150. Ibid.
151. Del Toro and Hogan, *The Night Eternal*, p.5.
152. Ibid., p.85.
153. Ibid., p.5.
154. Ibid., p.172.
155. Del Toro and Hogan, *Fall*, p.286.
156. Quoted in Michael Dillon and Julian Reid, 'Global Liberal Governance: Biopolitics, Security and War', *Millennium: Journal of International Studies*, 30.1, 2001, pp.41–66, p.41. See Michel Foucault's 'La Naissance de la Medicine Sociale', *Dits et Ecrits*, Paris, Gallimard, 1994, p.36.
157. Del Toro and Hogan, *Fall*, p.154.
158. Del Toro and Hogan, *The Night Eternal*, p.178.
159. Ibid., p.85.
160. Ibid., p.6.
161. Ibid., p.11.
162. Del Toro and Hogan, *Strain*, p.343.

163. Ibid., p.284.
164. Del Toro and Hogan, *Fall*, p.240. The stinger is a tumorous growth underneath the tongue which injects with a paralysing agent (Del Toro and Hogan, *Strain*, pp.223, 284). It can be expelled from the chest cavity of the vampire, 'shooting out well over four and up to even six feet (Del Toro and Hogan, *Strain*, p.284).
165. Michel Foucault in *Power/Knowledge* (New York, Pantheon Books, 1980) writes: 'But in thinking of the mechanisms of power, I am thinking rather of its capillary form of existing, the point where power reaches into the very grain of individuals, touches their bodies and inserts itself into their actions and attitudes, their discourses, learning processes and everyday lives' (p.39).
166. According to Jean-Luc Nancy, essentialist or immanent communities are based on the idea of a common language, belief or custom. As he writes, there is a fusional unity of common being where what connects singular beings is not their individuality or interests but a common fundament, a common identity: community 'is made up principally of the sharing, diffusion, or impregnation of an identity by a plurality wherein each member identifies himself only through the supplementary mediation of his identification with the living body of the community' (Jean-Luc Nancy, *The Inoperative Community*, Minneapolis, MN, University of Minnesota Press, 1991, p.9).

3 ' 'Tis My Heart, Be Sure, She Eats for Her Food': Female Consumptives and Female Consumers

' 'Tis my heart, be sure, she eats for her food; / And it makes one's whole flesh creep / To think that she drinks and drains my blood / Unawares, when I am asleep' (Robert Lord Lytton, 'The Vampire', [1882], *The Poetical Works of Owen Meredith*, New York, Thomas Y. Crowell and Co., 1884–95, p.203).

1. Ambrose Bierce, 'The Damned Thing', [1893], in Joyce Carol Oates (ed.), *American Gothic Tales*, New York, Plume, 1996, pp.121–8.
2. Rob Latham, *Consuming Youth: Vampires, Cyborgs, and the Culture of Consumption*, Chicago and London, The University of Chicago Press, 2002, p.1.
3. See Anna Sonser's *A Passion for Consumption: The Gothic Novel in America*, Bowling Green, Bowling Green State University Popular Press, 2001, and Fred Botting's *Gothic Romanced: Consumption, Gender and Technology in Contemporary Fictions*, London and New York, Routledge, 2008.
4. Bram Dijkstra, *Idols of Perversity: Fantasies of Feminine Evil in Fin-de-Siècle Culture*, New York and Oxford, Oxford University Press, 1986, p.355.
5. Susan Sontag, *Illness as Metaphor and AIDS and Its Metaphors*, [1978] London, Penguin Books, 1991, p.63.
6. ' "Eating Well", or The Calculation of the Subject: Interview with Jacques Derrida' is an interview by Jean-Luc Nancy initially published in the journal *Topoi* in English translation in October 1988 (vol. 7, no. 2). The issue was reprinted in book form as Eduardo Cadava, Peter Connor and Jean-Luc Nancy (eds.), *Who Comes after the Subject?*, New York, Routledge, 1991. The interview was also published in *Cahiers Confrontation* 20 (Winter

1989). My references to the interview are taken from Elisabeth Weber (ed.), *Points...: Interviews, 1974–1994*, trans. Peggy Kamuf and others, Stanford, CA, Stanford University Press, 1995, pp.255–87.

7. Derrida, 'Eating Well', p.282.

8. Ibid.

9. Caroline Walker Bynum writes that nutrition in Patristic writings, particularly cannibalism, 'is the basic image of positive change and the basic threat to identity' (*The Resurrection of the Body in Western Christianity, 200–1336*, New York, Columbia University Press, 1995, p.27).

10. See Caroline Walker Bynum, *The Resurrection of the Body*, pp.35–41.

11. For example, in Paul Solet's film *Grace* (2009) maternity is covered in slime and the stench of the grave as a vampire baby is resurrected and lives on by feeding literally on the breast and blood of the mother. While the mouth feeds the reanimated corpse of the child, it also consumes the living mother. The mouth destabilises the domesticated appetite for proper food, and threatens to devour its subject as food, and thus, as mere thing.

12. Susan Bordo, *Unbearable Weight: Feminism, Western Culture, and the Body*, Berkeley and Los Angeles, CA, University of California Press, 2003, p.171.

13. Rosi Braidotti, *Metamorphoses: Towards a Materialist Theory of Becoming*, Cambridge and Malden, MA, Polity, 2002, p.200.

14. Braidotti, *Metamorphoses*, p.12.

15. Ibid., p.11.

16. See Sigmund Freud's *Three Essays on the Theory of Sexuality* [1915], James Strachey (ed.), New York, Perseus Books, 2000; *Beyond the Pleasure Principle* [1920], trans. James Strachey (ed.), London, Hogarth Press and the Institute of Psycho-Analysis, 1961; *Totem and Taboo* [1912–13], trans. James Strachey, London, Routledge and Kegan Paul Ltd., 1950; *Civilization and Its Discontents* [1930], trans. Joan Riviere, New York, Jonathan Cape and Harrison Smith, 1930; Karl Abraham's *Selected Papers on Psycho-Analysis* [1927], trans. Douglas Bryan and Alix Strachey, New York, Brunner/Mazel, 1927; Melanie Klein's *The Psychoanalysis of Children* [1932], trans. Alix Strachey, London, Hogarth, 1932; and Julia Kristeva's *Powers of Horror: An Essay on Abjection*, New York, Columbia University Press, 1982.

17. Jacques Derrida, *On Touching: Jean-Luc Nancy*, Stanford, California, Stanford University Press, 2005.

18. Luce Irigaray, 'And the One Doesn't Stir without the Other', *Signs*, 7.1, 1981, pp.60–7.

19. Ibid.

20. Ibid.

21. Kristeva, *Powers*, p.41.

22. Ibid.

23. Jacques Lacan, *The Four Fundamental Concepts of Psychoanalysis*, Jacques-Alain Miller (ed.), trans. Alan Sheridan, New York, Norton, 1978, p.168.

24. Joan Copjec, 'Vampires, Breast-Feeding, and Anxiety', *October*, 58, 1991, pp.24–43.

25. Ibid., p.34.

26. Ibid., p.36.

27. Ken Gelder, *Reading the Vampire*, London and New York, Routledge, 1994, p.57.

28. Anna Krugovoy Silver, *Victorian Literature and the Anorexic Body*, Cambridge and New York, Cambridge University Press, 2002, p.135.
29. Ibid., p.125.
30. See Sarah Sceats' *Food Consumption and the Body in Contemporary Women's Fiction*, Cambridge, University of Cambridge, 2000; Susanne Skubal's *Word of Mouth: Food and Fiction after Freud*, New York and London, Routledge, 2002, and Andrea Adolph's *Food and Femininity in Twentieth-Century British Women's Fiction*, Surrey, England and VT, Ashgate Publishing, 2009.
31. Jacques Lacan, 'The Direction of the Treatment and the Principles of Its Treatment', *Ecrits: A Selection*, trans. Alan Sheridan, London, Routledge, 2001, pp.173–214.
32. Kim Chernin, *The Hungry Self: Women, Eating, and Identity*, New York, Times Books, 1985, p.xi.
33. Ibid., p.98.
34. Ibid., p.119.
35. Ibid., p.139.
36. Ibid.
37. Gilles Deleuze and Claire Parnet, 'Dead Psychoanalysis: Analyse', *Dialogues II*, New York and Chichester, West Sussex, Columbia University Press, 2007, pp.77–123.
38. Dorothée Legrand, 'Ex-Nihilo: Forming a Body Out of Nothing', in Robin Mackay and Reza Negarestani (eds.), *Collapse Vol. VII: Culinary Materialism*, 2011, pp.499–558.
39. Braidotti, Metamorphoses, p.210.
40. Ibid., p.62.
41. Ibid., p.116.
42. Legrand, 'Ex-Nihilo', p.550.
43. Consumption of the lungs or pulmonary tuberculosis was also known as *Phthisis pulmonalis*, white plague or white death because the victim developed anaemia and a pallid countenance.
44. Katherine Ott, *Fevered Lives: Tuberculosis in American Culture Since 1870*, Harvard: Harvard University Press, 1996, p.13.
45. Ibid.
46. Ibid., p.9.
47. Ott, *Fevered Lives*, p.10.
48. Dijkstra, *Idols of Perversity*, p.334.
49. Ott, *Fevered Lives*, p.16.
50. Ibid., p.6.
51. Faye Ringel, *New England's Gothic Literature: History and Folklore of the Supernatural from the Seventeenth through the Twentieth Centuries*, New York, Edwin Mellen Press, 1995, p.138.
52. Ringel, *New England's Gothic*, p.141.
53. Ibid.
54. Ibid.
55. Bob Curran, *The Encyclopedia of the Undead: A Field Guide to Creatures that Cannot Rest in Peace*, Franklin Lakes, NJ, Career Press, 2006, p.55.
56. Ibid., p.56.
57. Ibid., p.57.

58. George R. Stetson, 'The Animistic Vampire', *American Anthropologist*, 1896, pp.1–13.
59. 'Bewitched' appeared in *Pictorial Review* on 26 March 1925 and later in 1926 in *Here and Beyond*.
60. Gloria C. Elrich, 'The Female Conscience in Edith Wharton's Shorter Fiction: Domestic Angel or Inner Demon?', in Millicent Bell (ed.), *The Cambridge Companion to Edith Wharton*, Cambridge, Cambridge University Press, 1995, pp.98–116.
61. Edith Wharton, 'Bewitched' [1927], in David J. Skal (ed.), *Vampires: Encounters with the Undead*, New York, Black Dog & Leventhal, 2006, pp.335–51.
62. Ibid., p.336.
63. Ibid., p.337.
64. Ibid.
65. Ibid., p.350.
66. Ibid., p.344.
67. Ibid., p.350.
68. Ibid., p.351.
69. Ibid.
70. Samuel Warren, 'Passages from the Diary of a Late Physician, Ch. IV, "Consumption"', in *Blackwood's Edinburgh Magazine* 28, 1830, p.770.
71. James Clark, *A Treatise on Pulmonary Consumption: Comprehending an Inquiry into the Causes, Nature, Prevention and Treatment of Tuberculous and Scrofulous Diseases in General*, Philadelphia, Carey, Lea, and Blanchard, 1835, p.18.
72. Robert Douglas Hamilton, *The Principles of Medicine: On the Plan of the Beconian [sic] Philosophy*, London, Thomas and George Underwood, 1821, p.123.
73. Ibid., pp.123–4.
74. John Murray, *A Treatise on Pulmonary Consumption: Its Prevention and Remedy*, London, Whittaker, Treacher, and Arnot, 1830, p.3.
75. See a detailed discussion of medicine, consumption and Edgar Allan Poe's female vampires in my article 'Lovely Apparitions and Spiritualized Corpses: Consumption, Medical Discourse and Edgar Allan Poe's Female Vampire', *The Edgar Allan Poe Review*, 14.1, 2013, pp.36–54, <http://muse.jhu.edu/login?auth=0&type=summary& url=/journals/the_edgar_allan_poe_review/v014/14.1.stephanou.html>.
76. E.T.A. Hoffmann, 'Aurelia' [1819–20], in Christopher Frayling (ed.), *Vampyres: Lord Byron to Count Dracula*, London and Boston, Faber and Faber, 1992, pp.190–207.
77. According to the OED, asafoetida is 'a concreted resinous gum, with a strong alliaceous odour, procured in central Asia from the *Narthex asafoetida* and allied umbelliferous plants; used in medicine as antispasmodic, and as a flavouring in made dishes'.
78. Hoffmann, 'Aurelia', p.206.
79. Ibid., p.207.
80. Ibid., p.204.
81. Ambrose Bierce, 'The Damned Thing', [1893], in Joyce Carol Oates (ed.), *American Gothic Tales*, New York, Plume, 1996, pp.121–8.
82. Hoffmann, 'Aurelia', p.205.

83. This resonates with Gilles Deleuze and Claire Parnet's anorexic model in 'Dead Psychoanalysis: Analyse' in which anorexia enables one to escape from the norms of consumption, mechanical family meals and domestic feminine oppression (p.110). For Deleuze, anorexia is a way to escape organic lack.

84. Elizabeth Báthory (1560–1614) was considered very beautiful and became infamous because of her vampiric activities. She is thought to have murdered over 600 maidens, extracted their blood with an iron maiden (this element appears in Leopold von Sacher-Masoch's story 'Eternal Youth', 1886) and bathed in it. Raymond McNally in *Dracula Was a Woman: In Search of the Blood Countess of Transylvania* (New York, McGraw-Hill, 1983) argues that Stoker's *Dracula* is based on the legend of Báthory and not on the historical Prince Vlad III Dracula (1431–76).

85. William Seabrook, *Witchcraft: Its Power in the World Today*, [1940], San Diego, California, Harcourt, Brace and Company, 1945, p.114.

86. According to Kord, the Habsburgs 'had excellent reasons to get rid of her' (Susannne Kord, *Murderesses in German Writing, 1720–1860: Heroines of Horror*, Cambridge, Cambridge University Press, 2009, p.59). The debt they owed her would immediately disappear if she were found guilty.

87. Kord, *Murderesses*, p.60.

88. Ibid., p.61.

89. Ibid., p.62.

90. Ibid., p.63.

91. Ibid., p.66.

92. It was published in German around 1800 and translated into English in 1823. The story is similar to Poe's 'Ligeia'. Both stories present a dark lady who returns from the dead, after the male protagonist's marriage to a fair lady. Also see Paul Lewis' 'The Intellectual Functions of Gothic Fiction: Poe's "Ligeia" and Tieck's "Wake Not the Dead"', in *Comparative Literature Studies*, 16.3, 1979, pp.207–21.

93. The motif of the 'vampire-as-bride' is a German tradition and appears in Johan Wolfgang von Goethe's 'The Bride of Corinth' (1844), E.T.A. Hoffmann's 'Aurelia' (1820) and 'Wake Not the Dead' (1823).

94. Johann Ludwig Tieck, 'Wake Not the Dead' [1823], in Christopher Frayling (ed.), *Vampyres: Lord Byron to Count Dracula*, London and Boston, Faber and Faber, 1992, pp.165–89.

95. Ibid., p.177.

96. Ibid., p.181.

97. Arabella Kenealy, 'A Beautiful Vampire' [1896], in Peter Haining (ed.), *The Vampire Hunter's Casebook*, London, Warner Books, 1996, pp.11–32.

98. Like Eliza Lynn Linton, Kenealy was an antifeminist. In *Feminism and Sex-Extinction* (London, T. Fisher Unwin, 1920), Kenealy expresses the view that the new women and feminists were 'freaks of Nature' or 'Frankensteins of abnormal culture' (p.107).

99. Kenealy, 'A Beautiful Vampire', p.28.

100. Quoted in Dijkstra, *Idols*, p.334.

101. Elinor Glyn's *Three Weeks* ([1907], Middlesex, Echo Library, 2006), presents a Russian aristocrat and sexually aggressive female vampire who desires the semen of the white English man in order to produce an offspring that will

be 'English and beautiful...not black and white like me' (p.105). Here the sexual vampire turns into a maternal, loving figure, colonised by English spirit. The book reads like a textbook for the woman Arabella Kenealy envisioned: maternal and ruled by English manliness.

102. As will be mentioned in Chapter 6, self-identified vampires consider semen as a substitute for blood.

103. Otto Augustus Wall, *Sex and Sex Worship (Phallic Worship): A Scientific Treatise on Sex, Its Nature and Function*, St. Louis, C.V. Mosby Co., 1919, p.363.

104. Bram Dijkstra, *Evil Sisters: The Threat of Female Sexuality and the Cult of Manhood*, New York, Alfred A. Knopf, 1996, p.210.

105. Arabella Kenealy, *Feminism and Sex Extinction*, London, T. Fisher Unwin, 1920, p.33.

106. See <vampirefacelift.com>.

107. Margaret Atwood, *The Robber Bride*, Toronto, Ontario, McClelland & Stewart, 1993, p.154.

108. Ibid., p.345.

109. Ibid., p.456.

110. See Rosi Braidotti's explanation of this as a syndrome of neoliberal post-feminism that fosters isolation among women and new forms of vulnerability, in *Transpositions: On Nomadic Ethics*, Cambridge and Malden, MA, Polity Press, 2006, p.45.

111. Rosi Braidotti, 'A Critical Cartography of Feminist Post-Postmodernism', *Australian Feminist Studies*, 20.47, 2005, pp.1–15.

112. Braidotti, *Transpositions*, p.46.

113. Ibid.

114. For a discussion on the soucouyant and feminism see Giselle Liza Anatol's 'Transforming the Skin-Shedding Soucouyant: Using Folklore to Reclaim Female Agency in Caribbean Literature', *Small Axe*, 4.7, 2000, pp.44–59, and Meredith M. Gadsby's *Sucking Salt: Caribbean Women Writers, Migration and Survival*, Columbia, MO, University of Missouri Press, 2006.

115. Pica is an appetite for unusual, improper and indigestible substances.

116. Helen Oyeyemi, *White is for Witching*, London, Picador, 2009, p.24.

117. Braidotti, *Metamorphoses*, p.262.

4   'Race as Biology Is Fiction': The Bad Blood of the Vampire

1. See Franz Fanon, *Black Skin, White Masks*, New York, Grove Press, 1967.

2. Cherene Sherrard-Johnson, *Portraits of the New Negro Woman: Visual and Literary Culture in the Harlem*, Renaissance, NJ, Rutgers University Press, 2007, p.44.

3. See Nikolas Rose, *The Politics of Life Itself: Biomedicine, Power, and Subjectivity in The Twenty-First Century*, Princeton and Oxford, Princeton University Press, 2007, p.11.

4. John Allen Stevenson, 'A Vampire in the Mirror: The Sexuality of *Dracula*', *PMLA*, 103.2, 1988, pp.139–49.

5. See Audrey Smedley and Brian Smedley, 'Race as Biology is Fiction, Racism as a Social Problem is Real: Anthropological and Historical Perspectives on

the Social Construction of Race', *American Psychologist*, 60.1, 2005, pp.16–26; Luigi Luca Cavalli-Sforza and Francesco Cavalli-Sforza, *The Great Human Diasporas: The History of Diversity and Evolution*, New York, Perseus Books, 1995; Joseph L. Graves, Jr., *The Race Myth: Why we Pretend Race Exists in America*, New York, Plume, 2004.

6. Smedley and Smedley, 'Race as Biology is Fiction', p.16.
7. Dorothy Roberts, *Fatal Invention: How Science, Politics, and Big Business Re-create Race in the Twenty-First Century*, New York and London, The New Press, 2011, p.x.
8. Ibid., p.4.
9. Ibid.
10. Donna J. Haraway, *Modest_Witness@Second_Millenium*, London, Routledge, 1997.
11. Roberts, *Fatal Invention*, p.286.
12. Ibid., p.292.
13. Ibid., p.82–5.
14. Jean-Paul Gaudillière and Ilana Löwy, *Heredity and Infection: The History of Disease Transmission*, 'Horizontal and Vertical Transmission of Diseases: The Impossible Separation?', in Jean-Paul Gaudillière and Ilana Löwy (eds.), *Heredity and Infection: The History of Disease Transmission*, London and New York, Routledge, 2001, pp.1–18.
15. Katherine Ott, *Fevered Lives: Tuberculosis in American Culture Since 1870*, Harvard, Harvard University Press, 1996, p.18.
16. Samuel Kelton Jr. Roberts, *Infectious Fear: Politics, Disease, and the Health Effects of Segregation*, North Carolina, The University of North Carolina Press, 2009, p.88.
17. Roberts, *Fatal Invention*, p.91.
18. Celeste M. Condit, 'How Culture and Science Make Race "Genetic": Motives and Strategies for Discrete Categorization of the Continuous and Heterogeneous', *Literature and Medicine*, 26.1, 2007, pp.240–68.
19. Keith Wailoo, *Dying in the City of the Blues: Sickle Cell Anemia and the Politics of Race and Health*, Chapel Hill, NC, The University of North Carolina Press, 2001, p.78.
20. Roberts, *Fatal Invention*, p.120.
21. Ibid., p.129.
22. Ibid., p.146.
23. Richard Lewontin, *It Ain't Necessarily So: The Dream of the Human Genome and Other Illusions*, New York, New York Review Books, 2001, pp.162–3.
24. Roberts, *Fatal Invention*, p.167.
25. Ibid., p.168.
26. Ibid., p.181.
27. Ibid., p.184.
28. Ibid., p.198.
29. Ibid., p.202.
30. Rose, *The Politics of Life Itself*, p.167.
31. Ibid., p.185.
32. Ibid., p.161.
33. Ibid.
34. Ibid.

35. Ibid., p.157.
36. Ibid.
37. Ibid., p.161.
38. Ibid., p.160.
39. Ibid., p.176.
40. Ibid., pp.185–6.
41. Ibid., p.167.
42. Roberts, *Fatal Invention*, pp.209–10.
43. Ibid., p.225.
44. Ibid., pp.225, 257.
45. Condit, 'How Culture and Science Make Race "Genetic" ', pp.244–5.
46. Ibid., p.262.
47. Roberts, *Fatal Invention*, p.308.
48. The Creole Bertha Mason in *Jane Eyre* (1840) is described as a vampire.
49. Harriet Elizabeth Prescott Spofford (1835–1921) was born in Calais, Maine, and moved in Massachusetts. In 1871 she wrote a historical account of New England entitled *New England Legends*.
50. The story appeared in the *Atlantic* in January and February 1860.
51. Harriet Elizabeth Prescott Spofford, 'The Amber Gods' [1860] in Charles L. Crow (ed.), *American Gothic: An Anthology 1787–1916*, Malden, MA and Oxford, Blackwell Publishers, 1999, pp.197–226.
52. Ibid., p.202.
53. Ronald T. Takaki, *Strangers from a Different Shore: A History of Asian Americans*, Boston and New York, Little, Brown and Company, 1998, p.101.
54. Ibid.
55. Spofford, 'The Amber Gods', p.201.
56. Ibid., p.202.
57. Ibid., p.223.
58. Ibid., p.222.
59. Ibid., p.223.
60. Joan Dayan, 'Amorous Bondage: Poe, Ladies, and Slaves', *American Literature: A Journal of Literary History, Criticism, and Bibliography*, 66.2, 1994, pp.239–73.
61. Teresa A. Goddu, *Gothic America: Narrative, History, and Nation*, New York and Chichester, West Sussex, Columbia University Press, 1997, p.76.
62. Ibid., p.80.
63. Leland S. Person, 'Poe's Philosophy of Amalgamation: Reading Racism in the Tales', in Harold Bloom (ed.), *Edgar Allan Poe*, New York, Chelsea House, 2006, pp.129–48.
64. Sheridan J. Le Fanu, 'Carmilla' [1872], in Alan Ryan (ed.), *The Penguin Book of Vampire Stories*, London, Claremont Books, 1995, pp.71–137.
65. Ibid., p.84.
66. Florence Marryat, *The Blood of the Vampire* [1897], Kansas, Missouri, Valancourt Press, 2009, p.93.
67. Ibid., p.83.
68. Ibid., p.21.
69. Ibid., p.4.
70. Ibid., p.45.
71. Ibid., p.52.
72. Ibid., p.108.

73. Ibid., p.109.
74. Ibid., p.155.
75. Stevenson, 'A Vampire in the Mirror', p.144.
76. Howard L. Malchow, *Gothic Images of Race in Nineteenth-Century Britain*, Stanford, CA, Stanford University Press, 1996, p.171.
77. Sigmund Feud, 'The Unconscious' [1915], *The Standard Edition of the Complete Psychological Works of Sigmund Freud*, vol. XIV, London, Vintage, 2001, pp.159–95.
78. Rose, *The Politics of Life Itself*, p.20.
79. David S. Goyer, *Blade Trinity*, 2004.
80. Ibid.
81. In 'Dracula and Taboo' David Punter writes: 'At the heart of *Dracula* (if the pun may be forgiven) is blood' (in Glennis Byron (ed.), *Dracula*, New York, St. Martin's Press, 1999, pp.22–9).
82. Stephen Norrington, *Blade*, 1998.
83. Guillermo del Toro, *Blade II*, 2002.
84. Norrington, *Blade*.
85. Ibid.
86. Ibid.
87. Del Toro, *Blade II*.
88. Ibid.
89. Butler's fiction is informed by technology and genetic engineering. In her trilogy *Xenogenesis* (*Dawn*; *Adulthood Rites*; *Imago*) she focuses on genetic technologies and the dangers concerned with subjectivity in order to demonstrate the ways subjects interact and the choices they make in a techno-scientific environment. Haraway has praised Butler's science fiction because it resists the fetishisation of sameness and offers alternatives for the other to express his/her differences, whether they are related to gender, race or species (*Simians, Cyborgs, and Women: The Reinvention of Nature*, London, Free Association Books, 1991, p.226). Ethnicity and race are therefore two of the main concerns of Butler's fiction, and *Fledgling* is not an exception.
90. Octavia Butler, *Fledgling*, Boston and New York, Grand Central Publishing, 2005, p.66.
91. Ibid., p.272.
92. In *How we Became Posthuman: Virtual Bodies in Cybernetics, Literature and Informatics* (London and Chicago, University of Chicago Press, 1999) Katherine Hayles argues that the posthuman view privileges 'informational pattern over material instantiation' (p.2), and sees consciousness as an epiphenomenon, and the body as the 'original prosthesis we all learn to manipulate, so that extending or replacing the body with other prostheses becomes a continuation of a process that began before we were born' (p.3). The posthuman cannot be separated from computer simulation, or cybernetic organism; both the biological and the cybernetic are a continuation of one another, without any differences. The posthuman is an informational-material entity (p.11).
93. Rose, *The Politics of Life Itself*, p.80.
94. Ibid., p.27.
95. Butler, *Fledgling*, pp.187, 188.

96. Tananarive Due, *Blood Colony*, New York and London, Atria Books, 2008, p.156.
97. Ibid., p.74.
98. Ibid., p.75.

5 'The Sunset of Humankind Is the Dawn of the Blood Harvest': Blood Banks, Synthetic Blood and Haemocommerce

Guillermo del Toro and Chuck Hogan, *The Fall*, London, Harper Collins, 2010, p.291.

1. Michael Hardt and Antonio Negri, *Empire*, Cambridge, MA and London, Harvard University Press, 2000, p.326.
2. Matt Taibbi, 'The Great American Bubble Machine' (*Rolling Stone*, 9–23 July 2009) writes: 'The world's most powerful investment bank is a great vampire squid wrapped around the face of humanity, relentlessly jamming its blood funnel into anything that smells like money.'
3. Mark Fisher, *Capitalist Realism: Is There No Alternative?*, Winchester and Washington, Zero Books, 2009, pp.68, 15.
4. Michael Hardt and Antonio Negri, *Commonwealth*, Cambridge, MA and London, The Belknap Press of Harvard University Press, 2009, p.266.
5. David Harvey, *A Brief History of Neoliberalism*, Oxford, Oxford University Press, 2005, p.19.
6. Fisher, *Capitalist Realism*, p.34.
7. Hardt and Negri, *Commonwealth*, p.142.
8. Ibid., p.x.
9. Jason Read, 'A Genealogy of Homo-Economicus: Neoliberalism and the Production of Subjectivity', *Foucault Studies*, 6, 2009, pp.25–36.
10. Ibid., p.28.
11. Ibid.
12. Fisher, *Capitalist Realism*, p.22; and Hardt and Negri, *Commonwealth*, p.7.
13. Maurizio Lazzarato, 'Neoliberalism in Action: Inequality, Insecurity and the Reconstitution of the Social', *Theory, Culture & Society*, 26. 6, 2009, pp.109–33.
14. Franco 'Bifo' Berardi, *After the Future*, Gary Genosko and Nicholas Thoburn (eds.), Stirling, Scotland and Oakland, CA, AK Press, 2011, p.115.
15. Maurizio Lazzarato, *The Making of the Indebted Man: An Essay on the Neoliberal Condition*, Los Angeles, CA, Semiotext(e), 2012, p.165.
16. Ibid., p.32.
17. Ibid., p.59.
18. Ibid., p.60.
19. Ibid.
20. Ibid.
21. Sylvanus Urban, 'Political Vampyres', in Sylvanus Urban (ed.), *The Gentleman's Magazine, or, Monthly Intelligencer*, London: F. Jefferies, May 1732, pp.750–2.

22. Hernri A. Giroux, Zombie *Politics and Culture in the Age of Casino Capitalism*, New York, Peter Lang, 2011, p.12.
23. Adam Smith, *The Wealth of Nations: Books I–III* [1775], Andrew Skinner (ed.), London, Penguin, 1999, p.388.
24. Quoted in Susan E. Lederer, *Flesh and Blood: Organ Transplantation and Blood Transfusion in Twentieth-Century America*, Oxford, Oxford University Press, 2008, p.89.
25. Ibid., p.107.
26. Stephen Norrington, *Blade*, 1998.
27. Len Wiseman, *Underworld*, 2003.
28. Michael and Peter Spierig, *Daybreakers*, 2009. In a similar way, *Blade Trinity* alludes to the mass production and storing of blood as the final solution of vampires, in the form of an industrial human farm in which bodies are kept inside cellophane screens resembling human blood bags. The body is reduced to a factory of blood production, and machines are designed to control and extract the necessary blood from the bodies.
29. Following the success of blood banking in 1937, breast milk was also collected and supplied in order to decrease infant mortality. The paediatrician Henry Dwight Chapin used the term 'dairy' instead of 'bank', but later human breast milk dairies were described as 'milk banks' (Lederer, *Flesh and Blood*, p.92). Milk was also one of the first substitutes for blood. In 1854 Edward Hodder used milk to treat Asiatic cholera and believed that milk could regenerate white blood cells.
30. Rod Hardy, *Thirst*, 1979.
31. Ibid.
32. Robert M. Winslow, 'Historical Background', in Robert M. Winslow (ed.), *Blood Substitutes*, London and Burlington, MA, Academic Press, 2006, pp.5–16.
33. Chemical compound that can carry and release oxygen.
34. Iron-containing oxygen-transport metalloprotein in red blood cells.
35. Steve Connor, 'British Scientists to Create "Synthetic Blood"', in *Independent on Sunday*, <http://www.independent.co.uk/ news/science/british-scientists-to-create-synthetic-blood-1651715.html>.
36. George R.R. Martin, *Fevre Dream*, London and Sydney, Sphere Books Ltd., 1984, p.321.
37. Joe Ahearne, *Ultraviolet*, Channel 4, UK, 13 October 1998.
38. Joe Ahearne, 'Terra Incognita', *Ultraviolet*, Channel 4, UK, 13 October 1998.
39. Joe Ahearne 'Persona non Grata', *Ultraviolet*, Channel 4, UK, 20 October 1998.
40. Champagne-flavoured synthetic blood.
41. See the Tru Blood carbonated drink inspired by the show's synthetic blood drank by the vampires at the HBO shop, <http://store.hbouk.com/detail.php? p=256240&v= hbo-uk_best-sellers#tabs>.
42. Giorgio Agamben, *Profanations*, trans. Jeff Fort, New York, Zone Books, 2007, p.82.
43. Guillermo del Toro, *Blade II*, New Line Cinema, 2002.
44. Thomas Hobbes, *Leviathan* [1651], Project Gutenberg, 2010, Chapter xxiv, paragraph entitled 'Mony the Bloud of a Common-wealth', <http://www.gutenberg.org/ebooks/ 3207>.

45. New York physician A.L. Soresi, discussing the value of blood, said: 'If bills were presented in a land where people did not appreciate their value, a person could not buy a loaf of bread with even a thousand dollars. Unless the value of the blood of the donor is "appreciated" by the new organism, it will not only not be of any help to it, but become an element of danger' (Quoted in Lederer, *Flesh and Blood*, p.91).
46. Lederer, *Flesh and Blood*, p.xii.
47. Ibid., p.89.
48. Ibid., p.71.
49. Ibid., pp.71–2.
50. Karl Marx, *Capital*, vol. 1 [1867], trans. Ben Fowkes, Harmondsworth, Penguin, 1976, p.342.
51. Franco Moretti, 'Dracula and Capitalism', in Glennis Byron (ed.), *Dracula*, New York, St. Martin's Press, pp.43–54.
52. Ibid., p.48.
53. Bram Stoker, *Dracula* [1897], London, Penguin, 1993, p.326.
54. Guy Maddin, *Dracula: Pages from a Virgin's Diary*, Vonnie Von Helmolt Film, 2002.
55. Moretti, 'Dracula and Capitalism', p.47.
56. Ibid., p.48.
57. Moretti explains that 'just as the capitalist is "capital personified" and must subordinate his private existence to the abstract and incessant movement of accumulation, so Dracula is not impelled by the *desire* for power but by the *curse* of power, by an obligation he cannot escape' ('Dracula and Capitalism', p.46).
58. Mary Elizabeth Braddon, 'Good Lady Ducayne' [1896], in David J. Skal (ed.), *Vampires: Encounters with the Undead*, New York, Black Dog & Leventhal Publishers, 2006, pp.179–99.
59. Ibid., p.179.
60. Richard M. Titmuss, *The Gift Relationship: From Human Blood to Social Policy*, London, George Allen & Unwin Ltd., 1970, p.13.
61. Marcel Mauss, *The Gift: Forms and Functions of Exchange in Archaic Societies* [1925], trans. Ian Cunnison, Oxford and New York, Routledge, 1969, p.10.
62. Ibid.
63. Titmuss, *The Gift Relationship*, p.73.
64. Ibid., p.158.
65. Ibid.
66. See Catherine Waldby and Robert Mitchell, *Tissue Economies: Blood, Organs, and Cell Lines in Late Capitalism*, Durham and London, Duke University Press, 2006. Although Titmuss' argument is significant in discussing notions of commodified blood, it is necessary to point out that the contemporary conditions of transfusing blood are different and the commodification of blood is inescapable. Waldby and Mitchell offer an in-depth analysis of the issues involved in trading human tissues and blood.
67. An American writer born in Paris (1852–1925). This story appears under the pseudonym 'X.L.'.
68. The story was published in the Pall Mall magazine with Aubrey Beardsley's illustration entitled 'The Kiss of Judas', and was reprinted in his collection of stories *Aut Diabolus Aut Nihil* in 1894.

69. Moretti, 'Dracula and Capitalism', p.45.
70. Mary Ann Pharr, 'Vampiric Appetite in *I Am Legend*, *'Salem's Lot*, and *The Hunger*', in Leonard G. Heldreth and Mary Pharr (eds.), *The Blood is the Life: Vampires in Literature*, Bowling Green, OH, Bowling Green State University Popular Press, 1999, pp.93–103.
71. Fred Botting, *Gothic Romanced: Consumption, Gender and Technology in Contemporary Fictions*, London and New York, Routledge, 2008, p.74.
72. Ibid., pp.74–5.
73. Matt Haig, *The Radleys*, London, Canongate Books, 2010, p.3.
74. Ibid., p.87.
75. Jean Baudrillard, *The Illusion of the End*, trans. Chris Turner, Stanford, CA, Stanford University Press, 1994, p.109.
76. Haig, *The Radleys*, p.22.
77. Ibid., p.187.
78. Ibid., p.188.
79. Eugene Holland, 'Schizoanalysis: The Postmodern Contextualization of Psychoanalysis', in Cary Nelson and Lawrence Grossberg (eds.), *Marxism and the Interpretation of Culture*, Urbana, University of Illinois Press, 1988, pp.405–16.
80. Ibid., p.407.
81. Ibid.
82. Ibid.
83. Ibid.
84. Ibid., p.408.
85. Brian Stableford, *The Empire of Fear* [1988], London, Pan Books, 1991, p.478.
86. Del Toro and Hogan, *The Fall*, p.30.
87. Late capitalism, as defined by Ernest Mandel, refers to capital after the Second World War, and is characterised by transnational corporations, growth of the services sector, state expenditure and economic instability, mass consumption and environmental destruction.
88. David S. Goyer, *Blade Trinity*, 2004.
89. Nick Land, 'Cybergothic', in Joan Broadhurst Dixon and Eric J. Cassidy (eds.), *Virtual Futures*, New York, Routledge, 1998, pp.79–87.
90. Guillermo Del Toro and Chuck Hogan, *The Strain*, London, Harper Collins, 2009.
91. Franco Moretti, 'The Dialectic of Fear', *New Left Review*, 136, 1982, pp.67–85.
92. Majia Holmer Nadesan, *Governmentality, Biopower, and Everyday Life*, Oxford and New York, Routledge, 2008, p.135.
93. Fisher, *Capitalist Realism*, p.15.
94. Ibid., pp.5, 6.
95. Guillermo del Toro and Chuck Hogan, *The Night Eternal*, London, HarperCollins, 2011, p.213.
96. Del Toro and Hogan, *The Night Eternal*, p.5.
97. Ibid., p.6.
98. Ibid., p.232.
99. *Daybreakers* presents a modern-day vampire world where vampires can get blood and coffee from Starbucks-like shops.
100. Spierig, *Daybreakers*.

101. Ibid.
102. Evan Calder Williams, *Combined and Uneven Apocalypse*, Winchester and Washington, Zero Books, 2011, p.111.

6 'Many People Have Vampires *in* Their Blood': 'Real' Vampire Communities

Martin V. Riccardo, *Liquid Dreams of Vampires*, St. Paul, MN, Llewellyn, 1996, p.223.

1. Avery Gordon, *Ghostly Matters: Haunting and the Sociological Imagination*, Minneapolis and London, University of Minnesota Press, 2008.
2. Noémi Szécsi, *The Finno-Ugrian Vampire*, trans. Peter Sherwood, London, Stork Press, 2012, p.4.
3. The Temple of the Vampire, *The Vampire Bible*, Lacey, WA, Temple of the Vampire, 1989, n. pag.
4. See Temple of the Vampire, <http://www.vampiretemple.com/index.html>.
5. I will not continually use quotation marks but it should be understood that 'real' remains a problematic word here. The phrase 'real vampire' is an oxymoron, given that I argue the vampire is a fictional figure imitated by the self-identified vampires who are producing endless simulations of the same.
6. See EveryJoe, 'The Mystery of the Red Seal Letters', 2008, <http://everyjoe.com/entertainment/the-mystery-of-the-red-seal-letters/> and 'What is "TB" and Who are the Revenant Ones?', <http://everyjoe.com/entertainment/what-is-tb-and-who-are-the-revenant-ones/>.
7. BloodCopy, MySpace.com, <http://www.myspace.com/bloodcopy>.
8. BloodCopy, BloodCopy.com, <http://www.archive.bloodcopy.com/>.
9. Tru Blood, HBO Shop, <http://store.hbouk.com/detail.php?p=256240&v=hbo-uk_best-sellers#tabs>.
10. Michelle Belanger is one of the most famous representatives of the vampire community, the founder of the vampire House Kheperu, and a writer of various books and articles on vampirism.
11. Jean Baudrillard, *Simulacra and Simulation*, trans. Sheila Faria Glaser, Michigan, The University of Michigan Press, 1994, pp.5, 6.
12. Ibid., p.14.
13. Other names include sanguine, sangs or blood-drinking vampires.
14. Joseph Laycock, *Vampires Today: The Truth about Modern Vampirism*, Santa Barbara, CA, Praeger, 2009, p.71.
15. Arlene Russo is the editor of *Bite Me*, a magazine dedicated to vampires.
16. Arlene Russo, *Vampire Nation*, London, John Blake, 2005, p.27.
17. Ibid., p.28.
18. Laycock, *Vampires*, p.viii.
19. Joseph Laycock, 'Real Vampires as an Identity Group: Analyzing Causes and Effects of an Introspective Survey by the Vampire Community', *Nova Religio: The Journal of Alternative and Emergent Religions*, 14.1, 2010, pp.4–23, p.6.

20. Vampire allies or those who are friendly to the vampire community, including donors, are called black swans. White swans are antagonistic to vampires, whereas mundanes are people who have no affiliation to the vampire community. These terms have been invented as part of the Sanguinarium lexicon. The Sanguinarium is a vampire network of houses, organisations and clubs created by Father Sebastiaan.
21. Michelle Belanger, *The Vampire Ritual Book*, Internet Sacred Text Archive, Evinity Publishing Inc., 2011, n. pag., <http://www.sacred-texts.com/goth/vrb/index.htm>.
22. Ibid., n. pag.
23. Slavoj Žižek, *The Ticklish Subject: The Absent Centre of Political Ontology*, London and New York, Verso, 1999, p.315.
24. Michel Foucault, *The History of Sexuality, Volume 1: The Will to Knowledge*, [1978], trans. Robert Hurley, London, Penguin Books, 1998, p.148.
25. Christopher Hugh Partridge, *The Re-Enchantment of the West*, vol. II, New York and London, T&T Clark, 2005, p.232.
26. Fred Botting, *Limits of Horror: Technology, Bodies, Gothic*, Manchester, Manchester University Press, 2008, p.6.
27. See Mark Fisher, *Capitalist Realism: Is There No Alternative?*, Winchester and Washington, Zero Books, 2009, p.4.
28. Atlanta Vampire Alliance, *AVA*, 'Educational', <http://www.atlantavampire-alliance.com/educational.html>.
29. Ibid.
30. Suscitatio Enterprises, <http://www.suscitatio.com>.
31. Laycock, *Vampires*, p.10.
32. Unlike Dracula, who dissolves into mist or transforms into a bat, real-life vampires, on the other hand, cannot. Instead of believing in the supernatural, they ground their beliefs on the body, trying to find something stable and real in blood.
33. Christopher Lasch, *The Culture of Narcissism: American Life in the Age of Diminishing Expectations* [1979], New York and London, W.W. Norton & Company, 1991, p.5.
34. Ibid., p.4.
35. Ibid., p.6.
36. Laycock, *Vampires*, p.33.
37. Anne Rice, 'Essay on Earlier Works', *AnneRice.com*, n. pag., <http://www.annerice.com/Bookshelf-EarlierWorks.html>.
38. David Harvey, *A Brief History of Neoliberalism*, Oxford, Oxford University Press, 2005, p.42.
39. Quoted in Russo, *Vampire Nation*, p.44.
40. Harvey, *A Brief History of Neoliberalism*, p.166.
41. Pauline Rosenau, *Post-Modernism and the Social Sciences: Insights, Inroads, and Intrusions*, Princeton, NJ, Princeton University Press, 1992, p.54.
42. Jean Baudrillard, *The Illusion of the End*, trans. Chris Turner, Stanford, CA, Stanford University Press, 1994, p.106.
43. Baudrillard, *Illusion*, p.107.
44. Ibid., p.108.
45. Ibid.
46. Lady Nightdancer has been involved in the vampire community for many years. She has her own vampire house called House Arcadia Bloodmoon.

She is also the Executive Officer of the US Chapter of the Vampire Nation (VN for Vampiresnest), and a member of Dark Nations as an Ambassador for the Temple of Lost Souls. She helped co-found the GraveYard Press and she is the founder of Midnight Magica.

47. Nightdancer, 'Membership Directory', *Voices of the Vampire Community*, <http://www.veritasvosliberabit.com/ memberdirectory.html>.

48. Mike Future has been active in the online vampire community since 2002 and has been a member of several vampire communities. He is the administrator at the Vampire Community Message Board (VCMB). (See 'Member Directory').

49. Future, 'Membership Directory', *Voices of the Vampire Community*, <http://www.veritasvosliberabit.com/memberdirectory.html>.

50. This echoes the fictional universes of Umberto Eco and Dan Brown. Like Jane Austen's Catherine Morland, Future imagines a fictionalised reality.

51. Lady Onyx Ravyn is the Matriarch of House RavenShadow. She has been a sanguinarian for 17 years (Ravyn, 'Membership Directory').

52. The choice of words such as 'the ability to *heal*' is significant in terms of holistic healing beliefs.

53. Lady Onyx Ravyn, 'Membership Directory.'

54. Baudrillard, *The Illusion of the End*, p.101.

55. Robert G. Dunn, 'Identity, Commodification, and Consumer Culture', in Joseph E. Davis (ed.), *Identity and Social Change*, New Brunswick, New Jersey, Transaction Publishers, 2000, pp.109–34.

56. Axel Honneth, 'Pluralization and Recognition: On the Self-Misunderstanding of Postmodern Social Theories', in Charles W. Wright (ed.), *The Fragmented World of the Social: Essays in Social and Political Philosophy*, Albany, NY, State University of New York Press, 1995, pp.220–30.

57. Honneth, 'Pluralization and Recognition', p.223.

58. In *Seminar IV* Lacan refers to fetishism as the 'perversion of perversions' because it intensifies the subject's identification with the maternal phallus (quoted in Sarah Kay, *Žižek: A Critical Introduction*, Oxford and Malden, MA, Polity Press, 2003, p.60).

59. Russo, *Vampire Nation*, p.16.

60. Jeff Guinn and Andy Grieser, *Something in the Blood: The Underground World of Today's Vampires*, Arlington, Texas, The Summit Publishing Group, 1996, p.84.

61. Russo, *Vampire Nation*, pp.115–16.

62. Richard M. Titmuss, *The Gift Relationship: From Human Blood to Social Policy*, London: George Allen & Unwin Ltd., 1970, p.198.

63. Russo, *Vampire Nation*, p.16.

64. Lady CG, *Practical Vampyrism for Modern Vampyres*, Lulu.com, 2005, p.84.

65. Slavoj Žižek, *The Fragile Absolute: Or, Why is the Christian Legacy Worth Fighting For?*, London and New York, Verso, 2000, p.22.

66. Ibid.

67. Ibid.

68. Ibid., p.23.

69. Ibid., p.24.

70. Tru Blood, *HBO Shop*, <http://store.hbouk.com/detail.php?p=256240&v= hbo-uk_best-sellers#tabs>.

71. 'Vampire and Energy Work Research Survey', p.4, <http://www.suscitatio .com/>.
72. Another recommended substitute for blood is semen (also mentioned in Lady CG's *Practical Vampyrism*), which has been associated with blood in vampire literature and film, as well as in nineteenth-century treatises which describe women as femmes fatales absorbing the vital energy of men. See also the discussion on blood-semen analogy in the third chapter.
73. See Suscitatio Enterprises' VEWRS and 'Advanced Vampirism and Energy Work Research Survey' (AVEWRS), <http://www.suscitatio.com/>.
74. The Temple of the Vampire used to refer on its website to the different and unique individuals attracted to the vampire religion as 'born to the Blood' (quoted in Partridge, *The Re-Enchantment of the West*, p.237).
75. Temple of the Vampire, *The Vampire Bible*, n. pag.
76. The Temple of the Vampire has five grades of accomplishment. First, in order to become a member, one needs to purchase *The Vampire Bible*, and later, in order to be initiated into the higher levels in the temple, the member is given permission to purchase the other four bibles: *The Vampire Predator Bible*, *The Vampire Priesthood Bible*, *The Vampire Sorcery Bible* and *The Vampire Adept Bible*. Active memberships are also granted for a certain amount of money.
77. See 'What is the Temple', <http://www.vampiretemple.com/whatis.html>.
78. 'Becoming a Member', <http://www.vampiretemple.com/member.html>.
79. See Christoph Deutschmann, 'The Promise of Absolute Wealth: Capitalism as a Religion?, *Thesis Eleven*, 66, 2001, pp.32–56.
80. Slavoj Žižek, *The Sublime Object of Ideology*, London and New York, Verso, 1989, pp.33, 34.
81. Ibid., p.34.
82. Father Sebastiaan, *Vampyre Sanguinomicon: The Lexicon of the Living Vampire*, San Franscisco, CA, Red Wheel, 2010, p.72.
83. Laycock, *Vampires*, p.87. For Laycock, the existence of mentors who influenced vampire leaders is also highly questionable, as can be seen by Father Sebastiaan's references to Dimitri and the underground vampire scene of New York in the 1990s (*Vampires* pp.96–7).
84. Foucault, *The History of Sexuality*, p.147.
85. Ibid.
86. Eric Hobsbawm, 'Introduction: Inventing Traditions', in Eric Hobsbawm and Terence Ranger (eds), *The Invention of Tradition* [1983], Cambridge, Cambridge University Press, 2003, pp.1–14.
87. Hobsbawm, 'Introduction', p.1.
88. Ibid., p.2.
89. Ibid.
90. Ibid., p.4.
91. Ibid., p.6.
92. Ibid., p.14.
93. Quoted. in Laycock, *Vampires*, p.117.
94. House Quinotaur, 'Hierarchy', <http://www.house-quinotaur.org/hierarchy .html>.
95. Ibid.

96. House Quinotaur, 'Description', <http://www.house-quinotaur.org/description.html>.

97. House Quinotaur, 'Identity Quinotauri', <http://www.house-quinotaur.org/ identityquinotauri.html>.

98. Viola M. Johnson, *Dhampir: Child of the Blood.* Fairfield, Connecticut, Mystic Rose Books, 1996, p.68.

99. Whitley Strieber's trilogy consists of *The Hunger* (1981), *The Last Vampire* (2001) and *Lilith's Dream: A Tale of the Vampire Life* (2002).

100. Temple of the Vampire, *The Vampire Priesthood Bible* 1, <http://www.suscitatio.com/MediaArchive/TempleOfTheVampireTheVampirePriesthood-Bible-1989.pdf>.

101. Philipp Vandenberg, *Mysteries of the Oracles: The Last Secrets of Antiquity*, London and New York, Tauris Parke, 2007, pp.15–16. I am using the 2007 edition of *Mysteries of the Oracles: The Last Secrets of Antiquity* by Tauris Parke, which is based on George Unwin's translation from the German, first published in 1982 as *The Mystery of the Oracles* by Macmillan.

102. Homer, *The Odyssey*, trans. George Herbert Palmer, ed. Robert Squillace, New York, Barnes and Noble, 2003, p.131.

103. Temple of the Vampire, *The Vampire Priesthood Bible*, p.2.

104. Temple of the Vampire, *The Vampire Bible*, n. pag.

105. *The Vampire Priesthood Bible*, p.3.

106. Similarly, the Third Reich turned to ancient Greece in order to connect the 'New Germany' to the great civilisation of Greece and legitimise its ideology.

107. The Temple's carefully written history is relevant to Laycock's point that initiatory groups create more detailed traditions and family lines than awakened vampires, who perceive every vampire to be the same as them (*Vampires*, p.88). Initiatory groups, like the Temple of the Vampire, are organisations with hierarchical systems that want to attract pilgrims and initiates, and their ideas and traditions need to be meticulous and appealing. On the other hand, awakened vampires pay less attention to tradition because their condition is not based on a system, tradition, belief or choice, but is something they are born with and does not need external justifications.

108. Temple of the Vampire, *Vampire Priesthood Bible*, n. pag.

109. Sanguinarius, 'Vampire Lifestyle and Culture', in Michelle Belanger (ed.), *Vampires in Their Own Words: An Anthology of Vampire Voices*, Woodbury, Minnesota, Llewellyn Publications, 2007, pp.125–27.

110. Ibid., p.125.

111. Ibid., p.126.

112. Ibid., p.125.

113. See House MacPhee, <http://www.freewebs.com/housemacphee/o.html>, <http://www.freewebs.com/ housemacphee/shaolin.html>.

114. Ibid.

115. For example, Michelle Belanger's *The Vampire Ritual Book* (2003) includes rites of passage (seasonal and initiation rituals), or celebrations of holidays that function to reaffirm the bonds of the vampire community (Chapter 1 n. pag). Gods and goddesses with chthonic associations are sometimes invoked, such as Lilith, Set and Lucifer (Chapter 1 n. pag.).

116. For Father Sebastiaan, the Kheprian castes can correspond to the old guild system of the Sanguinarium. In the Sanguinarium guild system, Mradu, the guild of sanguine scholars, designates the caste of Warriors. Ramkht, the guild of vampire artists, is similar to the Priests, and Kitra describes the Concubine caste (Belanger, *Vampire Ritual*, Chapter 2). While the Sanguinarium's guilds are an imitation of the clans and families in the role-playing game *Vampire: The Masquerade*, they nonetheless serve as a system of organisation during rituals and vampiric feeding. House Eclipse has introduced a new caste, the 'nomaj' or 'sangomancer', and divided each caste into four paths: guardian, avenger, wolfwalker and deathspeaker.
117. Belanger, *Vampire Ritual*, Chapter 2.
118. Nicholas B. Dirks, *Castes of Mind: Colonialism and the Making of Modern India* Princeton, NJ and Oxford, Princeton University Press, 2001, pp.5, 8.
119. Father Sebastiaan, *Vampyre Sanguinomicon: The Lexicon of the Living Vampire*, San Franscisco, CA, Red Wheel, 2010, pp.29, 216.
120. The bladed ankh that Ordo Strigoi Vii use is inspired by the ankh Miriam wears in Tony Scott's film *The Hunger* (Sebastiaan, *Vampyre Sanguinomicon*, p.43).
121. Belanger, *Vampire Ritual*, Chapter 7. The exchange of energy between people is referred to symbolically as a 'blood bond' (Belanger, *Vampire Ritual*, Chapter 6).
122. During wedding ceremonies the couple mixes their blood with wine (Belanger, *Vampire Ritual*, Chapter 8). Ordo Sekhemu, associated with House Kheperu, follows similar blood rituals, where blood drinking is part of ceremonies and it is mixed with wine, or used during relations, not necessarily sexual, with donors or lovers. Sekhrians explain that drinking or offering one's blood 'is a most special and intimate act that requires trust as the sharing of one's blood has a tendency to bond people' (<www.ordo-sekhemu .org/LucemSekh/faq.shtml>).
123. In *The Queen of the Damned* (1988) Rice uses blood and Christian metaphors to convey a vampiric family connected through blood.
124. Hobsbawm, 'Introduction', p.10.
125. Lady CG, 'Re: A Sanguinarian Treatise: An Argument for Partition From the Vampire Community by CJ', *Smokes and Mirrors Forum*, Yuku.com.
126. According to Jean-Luc Nancy, the idea of community as work, as the result of planning and labour, opposes his inoperative or un-working community, a community that is incomplete.
127. Jean-Luc Nancy, *The Inoperative Community*, Minneapolis and Oxford, University of Minnesota Press, 1991), p.25.
128. Jean-Joseph Goux, 'General Economics and Postmodern Capitalism', *Yale French Studies*, 78, 1990, pp.206–24.

Conclusion: The Blood of the Vampire: Globalisation, Resistance and the Sacred

1. Robin Wood, *Mosaic*, XVI/1–2, 1983, pp.175–87, p.186.
2. Michael Hardt and Antonio Negri, *Empire*, Cambridge, MA and London, Harvard University Press, 2000, p.194.

3. Maurizio Lazzarato, 'Neoliberalism in Action: Inequality, Insecurity and the Reconstitution of the Social', *Theory, Culture & Society*, 26. 6, 2009, pp.109–33.

4. Franco Bifo Berardi, *After the Future*, Gary Genosko and Nicholas Thoburn (eds.), Edinburgh, Oakland, Baltimore, AK Press, 2011, p.18.

5. Lacey, WA: Temple of the Vampire, 1989.

6. See Costas Douzinas' discussion on new forms of resistance in *Philosophy and Resistance in the Crisis: Greece and the Future of Europe*, Cambridge and Malden, MA, Polity Press, 2013.

7. Jean Comaroff and John L. Comaroff, 'Occult Economies and the Violence of Abstraction: Notes from the South African Postcolony', *American Ethnologist*, 26.2, 1999, pp.297–303.

8. Ibid., p.284.

9. Ibid., p.282.

10. Michael Hardt and Antonio Negri, *Multitude: War and Democracy in the Age of Empire*, New York, The Penguin Press, 2004, p.127.

11. See Matthew Gibson, 'Jane Cranstoun, Countess Purgstall: A Possible Inspiration for Le Fanu's "Carmilla" ', *Le Fanu Studies*, 2.2, 2007.

12. Dom Augustine Calmet, *The Phantom World: The History and Philosophy of Spirits, Apparitions, & c.*, Philadelphia, A. Hart, Late Carey & Hart, 1850, pp.78–9.

13. See Eugene Thacker, 'The Shadows of Atheology: Epidemics, Power and Life after Foucault', *Theory, Culture & Society*, 26.6, 2009, pp.134–52, and Roberto Esposito's *Bíos* and *Terms of the Political: Community, Immunity, Biopolitics*, New York, Fordham University Press, 2013.

14. Gilles Deleuze, *Pure Immanence: Essays on A Life*, New York, Zone Books, 2001, p.29.

Bibliography

Primary Texts

Literature

Atwood, Margaret (1993) *The Robber Bride*, Toronto, Ontario: McClelland & Stewart.

Bierce, Ambrose (1996) 'The Damned Thing', 1893, in Joyce Carol Oates (ed.), *American Gothic Tales*, New York: Plume, pp.121–8.

Braddon, Mary Elizabeth (2006) 'Good Lady Ducayne', 1896, in David J. Skal (ed.), *Vampires: Encounters with the Undead*, New York: Black Dog & Leventhal Publishers, pp.179–99.

Butler, Octavia (2005) *Fledgling*, Boston and New York: Grand Central Publishing.

Cronin, Justin (2010) *The Passage*, London: Orion Books.

Del Toro, Guillermo and Hogan, Chuck (2010) *The Fall*, London: Harper Collins.

Del Toro, Guillermo and Hogan, Chuck (2010) *The Strain*, 2009, London: Harper Collins.

Del Toro, Guillermo and Hogan, Chuck (2011) *The Night Eternal*, London: Harper Collins.

Due, Tananarive (1997) *My Soul to Keep*, London: Piatkus.

Due, Tananarive (2001) *The Living Blood*, New York and London: Washington Square Press.

Due, Tananarive (2008) *Blood Colony*, New York and London: Atria Books.

Due, Tananarive (2011) *My Soul to Take*, New York and London: Washington Square Press.

Glyn, Elinor (2006) *Three Weeks*, 1907, Middlesex: Echo Library.

Haig, Matt (2010) *The Radleys*, London: Canongate Books.

Harris, Charlaine (2009) *Dead until Dark*, London: Gollanz.

Hoffmann, E.T.A. (1992) 'Aurelia', 1819–20, in Christopher Frayling (ed.), *Vampyres: Lord Byron to Count Dracula*, London and Boston: Faber and Faber, pp.190–207.

Homer (2003) *The Odyssey*, trans. George Herbert Palmer, Robert Squillace (ed.), New York: Barnes and Noble.

Kenealy, Arabella (1996) 'A Beautiful Vampire', 1896, in Peter Haining (ed.), *The Vampire Hunter's Casebook*, London: Warner Books, pp.11–32.

Le Fanu, Sheridan J. (1997) 'Carmilla', 1872, in Alan Ryan (ed.), *The Penguin Book of Vampire Stories*, London: Claremont Books, pp.71–137.

Lord Lytton, Robert (1882) 'The Vampire', *The Poetical Works of Owen Meredith*, New York: Thomas Y. Crowell and Co.

Marryat, Florence (2009) *The Blood of the Vampire*, 1897, Kansas, Missouri: Valancourt Press.

Martin, George R.R. (1984) *Fevre Dream*, London and Sydney: Sphere Books Ltd.

Matheson, Richard (2001) *I Am Legend*, 1954, London: Gollancz.

Oyeyemi, Helen (2009) *White is for Witching*, London: Picador.

Romkey, Micheal (1997) *The Vampire Virus*, New York: Fawcett Gold Metal.

Spofford, Harriet Elizabeth Prescott (1999) 'The Amber Gods', 1860, in Charles L. Crow (ed.), *American Gothic: An Anthology 1787–1916*, Malden, MA and Oxford: Blackwell Publishers, pp.197–226.

Stableford, Brian (1991) *The Empire of Fear*, 1988, London: Pan Books.

Stoker, Bram (1993) *Dracula*, 1897, London: Penguin.

Tieck, Johann Ludwig (1992) 'Wake Not the Dead', 1823, in Christopher Frayling (ed.), *Vampyres: Lord Byron to Count Dracula*, London and Boston: Faber and Faber, pp.165–89.

Wharton, Edith (2006) 'Bewitched', 1927, in David J. Skal (ed.), *Vampires: Encounters with the Undead*, New York: Black Dog & Leventhal, pp.335–51.

Films

Blade, dir. Stephen Norrington, 1998.

Blade II, dir. Guillermo del Toro, 2002.

Blade Trinity, dir. David S. Goyer, 2004.

Daybreakers, dirs. Michael and Peter Spierig, 2009.

Dracula, dir. Tod Browning, 1931.

Dracula: Pages from a Virgin's Diary, dir. Guy Maddin, 2002.

Grace, dir. Paul Solet, 2009.

House of Dracula, dir. Erle C. Kenton, 1945.

Near Dark, dir. Kathryn Bigelow, 1987.

Nosferatu, dir. Friedrich Wilhelm Murnau, 1922.

Thirst, dir. Rod Hardy, 1979.

Ultraviolet, dir. Joe Ahearne, Channel 4, UK,1998.

Ultraviolet, 'Persona non Grata', dir. Joe Ahearne, 20 October 1998.

Ultraviolet, 'Terra Incognita', dir. Joe Ahearne, 13 October 1998.

Underworld, dir. Len Wiseman, 2003.

Secondary Texts

Abbott, Stacey (2007) *Celluloid Vampires: Life after Death in the Modern World*, Austin, TX: The University of Texas Press.

Abraham, Karl (1927) *Selected Papers on Psycho-Analysis*, trans. Douglas Bryan and Alix Strachey, New York: Brunner/Mazel.

Adolph, Andrea (2009) *Food and Femininity in Twentieth-Century British Women's Fiction*, Surrey, England and VT: Ashgate Publishing.

Agamben, Giorgio (1998) *Homo Sacer: Sovereign Power and Bare Life*, trans. Daniel Heller-Roazen, Stanford, CA: Stanford University Press.

Agamben, Giorgio (2007) *Profanations*, trans. Jeff Fort, New York: Zone Books.

Anatol, Giselle Liza (2000) 'Transforming the Skin-Shedding Soucouyant: Using Folklore to Reclaim Female Agency in Caribbean Literature', *Small Axe*, 4.7, pp.44–59.

Arata, Stephen (1999) 'The Occidental Tourist: *Dracula* and the Anxiety of Reverse Colonisation', in Glennis Byron (ed.), *Dracula*, New York: St. Martin's Press, pp.119–44.

Atlanta Vampire Alliance, *AVA*, 'Educational', <http://www.atlantavampire-alliance.com/educational.html>.

Auerbach, Nina (1995) *Our Vampires, Ourselves*, London and Chicago: The University of Chicago Press.

Barker, Thomas Herbert (1863) *On Malaria and Miasmata and their Influence in the Production of Typhus and Typhoid Fevers, Cholera, and the Exanthemata*, London: John W. Davies.

Baudrillard, Jean (1994) *Simulacra and Simulation*, trans. Sheila Faria Glaser, Michigan: The University of Michigan Press.

Baudrillard, Jean (1994) *The Illusion of the End*, trans. Chris Turner, Stanford, CA: Stanford University Press.

Baudrillard, Jean (2002) *The Spirit of Terrorism and Other Essays*, London and New York: Verso.

Bayer, Ronald and Feldman, Eric (1999) *Blood Feuds: AIDS, Blood, and the Politics of Medical Disaster*, Oxford and New York: Oxford University Press.

Belanger, Michelle (2011) *The Vampire Ritual Book, Internet Sacred Text Archive*, Evinity Publishing Inc., <http://www.sacred-texts.com/goth/vrb/index.htm>.

Berardi, Franco 'Bifo' (2011) *After the Future*, Gary Genosko and Nicholas Thoburn (eds.), Stirling, Scotland and Oakland, CA: AK Press.

Bichat, Xavier (1815) *Physiological Researches on Life and Death*, trans. F. Gold, London: Longman, Hurst, Rees, Orme and Browne.

Bildhauer, Bettina (2006) *Medieval Blood*, Cardiff: University of Wales Press.

BloodCopy, MySpace.com, <http://www.myspace.com/bloodcopy> and *BloodCopy*, BloodCopy.com, <http://www.archive.bloodcopy.com/>.

Blundell, James (1818) 'Experiments on the Transfusion of Blood by the Syringe', *Medico- Chrurgical Transactions*, 9, pp.56–92.

Blundell, James (1828) 'Lectures on the Theory and Practice of Midwifery', Lecture XVI, 'Management of the more Copious Floodings', *Lancet*, 1, pp.609–14.

Blundell, James (1828–9) 'Observations on Transfusion of Blood by Dr. Blundell, with a Description of his Gravitator', *The Lancet*, 2, pp.321–4.

Bordo, Susan (2003) *Unbearable Weight: Feminism, Western Culture, and the Body*, Berkeley and Los Angeles, CA: University of California Press.

Botting, Fred (2003) 'Metaphors and Monsters', *Journal for Cultural Research*, 7.4, pp.339–65.

Botting, Fred (2005) ' "Monsters of the Imagination": Gothic, Science, Fiction', in David Seed (ed.), *A Companion to Science Fiction*, Malden, MA and Oxford: Blackwell, pp.111–26.

Botting, Fred (2008) *Gothic Romanced: Consumption, Gender and Technology in Contemporary Fictions*, London and New York: Routledge.

Botting, Fred (2008) *Limits of Horror: Technology, Bodies, Gothic*, Manchester: Manchester University Press.

Braidotti, Rosi (2002) *Metamorphoses: Towards a Materialist Theory of Becoming*, Cambridge and Malden, MA: Polity.

Braidotti, Rosi (2005) 'A Critical Cartography of Feminist Post-Postmodernism', *Australian Feminist Studies*, 20.47, pp.1–15.

Braidotti, Rosi (2006) *Transpositions: On Nomadic Ethics*, Cambridge and Malden, MA: Polity Press.

Bynum, Caroline Walker (1986) 'The Body of Christ in the Later Middle Ages: A Reply to Leo Steinberg', *Renaissance Quarterly*, 39.3, pp.399–439.

Bynum, Caroline Walker (1995) *The Resurrection of the Body in Western Christianity, 200–1336*, New York: Columbia University Press.

Bynum, Caroline Walker (2007) *Wonderful Blood: Theology and Practice in Late Medieval Northern Germany and Beyond*, Philadelphia: University of Pennsylvania Press.

Byron, Glennis (ed.) (1999) *Dracula*, New York: St. Martin's Press.

Callaway, Mr. (1829) 'London Medical Society', *The Lancet*, 2, p.120.

Calmet, Dom Augustine (1850) *The Phantom World: The History and Philosophy of Spirits, Apparitions, & c.*, Philadelphia: A. Hart, Late Carey & Hart.

Carpenter, Mary Wilson (2010) *Health, Medicine and Society in Victorian England*, Santa Barbara, CA: Praeger.

Cartwright, Samuel (1852) 'The Haematokinetic or Blood-Moving Power of Inspired Air, Proved by Further Experiments on the Crocodile', *Boston Medical and Surgical Journal*, 46–7, pp.392–8.

Cavalli-Sforza, Luigi Luca and Cavalli-Sforza, Francesco (1995) *The Great Human Diasporas: The History of Diversity and Evolution*, New York: Perseus Books.

Černý, Jaroslav (1955) 'Reference to Blood Brotherhood Among Semites in an Egyptian Text of the Ramesside Period', *Journal of Near Eastern Studies*, 14.3, pp.161–3.

Chernin, Kim (1985) *The Hungry Self: Women, Eating, and Identity*, New York: Times Books.

Clark, David P. and Pazdernik, Nanette J. (2013) *Molecular Biology*, Oxford: Academic Press.

Clark, James (1835) *A Treatise on Pulmonary Consumption: Comprehending an Inquiry into the Causes, Nature, Prevention and Treatment of Tuberculous and Scrofulous Diseases in General*, Philadelphia: Carey, Lea, and Blanchard.

Comaroff, Jean and Comaroff, John L. (1999) 'Occult Economies and the Violence of Abstraction: Notes from the South African Postcolony', *American Ethnologist*, 26.2, pp.297–303.

Condit, Celeste M. (2007) 'How Culture and Science Make Race "Genetic": Motives and Strategies for Discrete Categorization of the Continuous and Heterogeneous', *Literature and Medicine*, 26.1, pp.240–68.

Connor, Steve (2009) 'British Scientists to Create "Synthetic Blood"', in *Independent on Sunday*, <http://www.independent.co.uk/news/science/british-scientists-to-create-synthetic-blood-1651715.html>, 23 March.

Conticelli, Valentina (2002) 'Sanguis Suavis: Blood between Microcosm and Macrocosm', in James Bradburne (ed.), *Blood: Art, Power, Politics and Pathology*, London: Prestel, pp.55–63.

Cooper, Melinda (2008) *Life as Surplus: Biotechnology and Capitalism in the Neoliberal Era*, Seattle, WA: University of Washington Press.

Copeman, Jacob (2009) *Veins of Devotion: Blood Donation and Religious Experience in North India*, New Brunswick, NJ, and London: Rutgers University Press.

Copjec, Joan (1991) 'Vampires, Breast-Feeding, and Anxiety', *October*, 58, pp. 24–43.

Craft, Christopher (1999) '"Kiss me with Those Red Lips": Gender and Inversion in Bram Stoker's *Dracula*', in Glennis Byron (ed.), *Dracula*, New York: St. Martin's Press, pp.93–118.

Curran, Bob (2006) *The Encyclopedia of the Undead: A Field Guide to Creatures that Cannot Rest in Peace*, Franklin Lakes, NJ: Career Press.

Dayan, Joan (1994) 'Amorous Bondage: Poe, Ladies, and Slaves', *American Literature: A Journal of Literary History, Criticism, and Bibliography*, 66.2, pp.239–73.

Deleuze, Gilles (2001) *Pure Immanence: Essays on A Life*, New York: Zone Books.

Deleuze, Gilles and Guattari, Felix (2004) *A Thousand Plateaus: Capitalism and Schizophrenia*, trans. Brian Massumi, London and New York: Continuum.

Deleuze, Gilles and Parnet, Claire (eds.), (2007) 'Dead Psychoanalysis: Analyse', *Dialogues II*, New York and Chichester, West Sussex: Columbia University Press, pp.77–123.

De Man, Paul (1996) 'The Epistemology of Metaphor,' in Andrej Warminski (ed.), *Aesthetic Ideology*, Minneapolis, MN: University of Minnesota Press, pp.34–50.

Derrida, Jacques (1995) ' "Eating Well", or The Calculation of the Subject: Interview with Jacques Derrida', in Elisabeth Weber (ed.), *Points... : Interviews, 1974–1994*, trans. Peggy Kamuf and others, Stanford, CA: Stanford University Press, pp.255–87.

Derrida, Jacques (2005) *On Touching: Jean-Luc Nancy*, Stanford, CA: Stanford University Press.

Deutschmann, Christoph (2001) 'The Promise of Absolute Wealth: Capitalism as a Religion?, *Thesis Eleven*, 66, pp.32–56.

Dijkstra, Bram (1986) *Idols of Perversity: Fantasies of Feminine Evil in Fin-de-Siècle Culture*, New York and Oxford: Oxford University Press.

Dijkstra, Bram (1996) *Evil Sisters: The Threat of Female Sexuality and the Cult of Manhood*, New York: Alfred A. Knopf.

Dillon, Michael and Reid, Julian (2001) 'Global Liberal Governance: Biopolitics, Security and War', *Millenium*, 30.1, pp.41–66.

Dirks, Nicholas B. (2001) *Castes of Mind: Colonialism and the Making of Modern India* Princeton, NJ and Oxford: Princeton University Press.

Douglas, Mary (2002) *Purity and Danger*, [1966], London and New York: Routledge.

Douzinas, Costas (2013) *Philosophy and Resistance in the Crisis: Greece and the Future of Europe*, Cambridge and Malden, MA: Polity Press.

Doyle, Richard (2003) *Wetwares: Experiments in Postvital Living*, Minneapolis, MN: University of Minnesota Press.

Dunn, Robert G. (2000) 'Identity, Commodification, and Consumer Culture', in Joseph E. Davis (ed.), *Identity and Social Change*, New Brunswick, NJ: Transaction Publishers, pp.109–34.

Edwards, Henri Milne (1835-6) 'Blood', in Robert Bentley Todd (ed.), *The Cyclopaedia of Anatomy and Physiology*, vol. 1, London: Longman, Brown, Green, Longmans, & Roberts, pp.404–15.

Elrich, Gloria C. (1995) 'The Female Conscience in Edith Wharton's Shorter Fiction: Domestic Angel or Inner Demon?', in Millicent Bell (ed.), *The Cambridge Companion to Edith Wharton*, Cambridge: Cambridge University Press.

Esposito, Roberto (2008) *Bios: Biopolitics and Philosophy*, trans. Timothy Campbell, Minneapolis, MN: University of Minnesota Press.

Esposito, Roberto (2013) *Terms of the Political: Community, Immunity, Biopolitics*, New York: Fordham University Press.

Ettinger, Robert C.W. (1964) *The Prospect of Immortality*, New York: Doubleday.

EveryJoe (2008) 'The Mystery of the Red Seal Letters', <http://everyjoe.com/entertainment/the-mystery-of-the-red-seal-letters/> and 'What is 'TB' and

Who are the Revenant Ones?', <http://everyjoe.com/entertainment/what-is -tb-and-who-are-the-revenant-ones/>.

Fanon, Franz (1967) *Black Skin, White Masks*, New York: Grove Press.

Father Sebastiaan (2010) *Vampyre Sanguinomicon: The Lexicon of the Living Vampire*, San Franscisco, CA: Red Wheel.

Fisher, Mark (2009) *Capitalist Realism: Is there no Alternative?*, Hampshire, Winchester: Zero Books.

Foucault, Michel (1973) *The Order of Things: An Archaeology of the Human Sciences*, New York: Vintage Books.

Foucault, Michel (1977) *Discipline and Punish: The Birth of the Prison*, trans. Alan Sheridan, New York: Pantheon Books.

Foucault, Michel (1977) 'Nietzsche, Genealogy, History', in Donald F. Bouchard (ed.), *Language, Counter-Memory, Practice: Selected Essays and Interviews*, Ithaca: Cornell University Press.

Foucault, Michel (1980) *Power/ Knowledge: Selected Interviews & Other Writings 1972–1977*, Colin Gordon (ed.), New York: Pantheon Books.

Foucault, Michel (1994) 'La Naissance de la Medicine Sociale', in Daniel Defert and François Ewald (eds.), *Dits et Ecrits* Tome III: 1976–1979, Paris: Gallimard.

Foucault, Michel (1998) *The History of Sexuality, Vol. 1: The Will to Knowledge*, trans. Robert Hurley, London: Penguin.

Foucault, Michel (2002) 'The Politics of Health in the Eighteenth Century', in James D. Faubion (ed.), *Power: Essential Works of Foucault, 1957–1984*, vol. 3, London: Penguin, pp.90–105.

Foucault, Michel (2003) *Society Must Be Defended: Lectures at the Collège de France, 1975–76*, trans. David Masey, Mauro Bertani and Alessandro Fontana (eds.), New York: Picador.

Franklin, Sarah and Lock, Margaret (eds.) (2003) *Remaking Life and Death: Toward an Anthropology of the Biosciences*, Santa Fe, NM: School of American Research Press.

Frayling, Christopher (1992) 'Lord Byron to Count Dracula', in Christopher Frayling (ed.), *Vampyres: Lord Byron to Count Dracula*, London and Boston: Faber and Faber, pp.3–84.

Freitas Jr., Robert A. (1996–9) 'Respirocytes: A Mechanical Artificial Red Cell: Exploratory Design in Medical Nanotechnology', *Foresight Institute*, <http:// www.foresight.org/Nanomedicine/Respirocytes.html>.

Freud, Sigmund (1930) *Civilization and Its Discontents*, trans. Joan Riviere, New York: Jonathan Cape and Harrison Smith.

Freud, Sigmund (1950) *Totem and Taboo* [1912–13], trans. James Strachey, London: Routledge and Kegan Paul Ltd.

Freud, Sigmund (1961) *Beyond the Pleasure Principle* [1920], trans. James Strachey (ed.), London: Hogarth Press and the Institute of Psycho-Analysis.

Freud, Sigmund (2000) *Three Essays on the Theory of Sexuality* [1915], James Strachey (ed.), New York: Perseus Books.

Freud, Sigmund ([1915] 2001) 'The Unconscious', in James Strachey (ed.) *The Standard Edition of the Complete Psychological Works of Sigmund Freud*, vol. XIV, London: Vintage, pp.159–95.

Future, Mike 'Membership Directory', *Voices of the Vampire Community*, <http:// www.veritasvosliberabit.com/memberdirectory.html>.

Gadsby, Meredith M. (2006) *Sucking Salt: Caribbean Women Writers, Migration and Survival*, Columbia, MO: University of Missouri Press.

Gaudillière, Jean-Paul and Löwy, Ilana (2001) 'Horizontal and Vertical Transmission of Diseases: The Impossible Separation?', in Jean-Paul Gaudillière and Ilana Löwy (eds.), *Heredity and Infection: The History of Disease Transmission*, London and New York: Routledge, pp.1–18.

Gelder, Ken (1994) *Reading the Vampire*, London and New York: Routledge.

Gibson, Matthew (2007) 'Jane Cranstoun, Countess Purgstall: A Possible Inspiration for Le Fanu's "Carmilla" ', *Le Fanu Studies*, 2.2, <http://www.lefanustudies.com/cranstoun.html>.

Gilders, William K. (2004) *Blood Ritual in the Hebrew Bible: Meaning and Power*, Baltimore: The John Hopkins University Press.

Girard, René (2005) *Violence and the Sacred*, London and New York: Continuum.

Giroux, Hernri A. (2011) *Zombie Politics and Culture in the Age of Casino Capitalism*, New York: Peter Lang.

Glover, David (1999) 'Travels in Romania: Myths of Origins, Myths of Blood', in Glennis Byron (ed.), *Dracula*, New York: St. Martin's Press, pp.197–217.

Goddu, Teresa A. (1997) *Gothic America: Narrative, History, and Nation*, New York and Chichester, West Sussex: Columbia University Press.

Gordon, Avery (2008) *Ghostly Matters: Haunting and the Sociological Imagination*, Minneapolis and London: University of Minnesota Press.

Goux, Jean-Joseph (1990) 'General Economics and Postmodern Capitalism', *Yale French Studies*, 78, pp.206–24.

Graham, Elaine L. (2002) *Representations of the Post/human: Monsters, Aliens, and Others in Popular Culture*, Manchester: University of Manchester Press.

Graves, Jr., Joseph L. (2004) *The Race Myth: Why We Pretend Race Exists in America*, New York: Plume.

Grosz, Elizabeth (1994) *Volatile Bodies: Toward a Corporeal Feminism*, Bloomington, IN: Indiana University Press.

Guinn, Jeff and Grieser, Andy (1996) *Something in the Blood: The Underground World of Today's Vampires*, Arlington, TX: The Summit Publishing Group.

Guthrie, William Keith Chambers (1965) *History of Greek Philosophy: The Presocratic Tradition from Parmenides to Demokritus*, vol. 2, Cambridge: Cambridge University Press.

Hamilton, Robert Douglas (1821) *The Principles of Medicine: On the Plan of the Beconian [sic] Philosophy*, London: Thomas and George Underwood.

Hanson, Kenneth C. (1993) 'Blood and Purity in Leviticus and Revelation', *Listening: Journal of Religion and Culture*, 28, pp.215–30.

Haraway, Donna J. (1991) *Simians, Cyborgs, and Women: The Reinvention of Nature*, London: Free Association Books.

Haraway, Donna J. (1997) *Modest_Witness@Second_Millenium*, London: Routledge.

Hardt, Michael and Negri, Antonio (2000) *Empire*, Cambridge, MA and London, England: Harvard University Press.

Hardt, Michael and Negri, Antonio (2004) *Multitude: War and Democracy in the Age of Empire*, New York: The Penguin Press.

Hardt, Michael and Negri, Antonio (2009) *Commonwealth*, Cambridge, MA and London: The Belknap Press of Harvard University Press.

Harvey, David (2005) *A Brief History of Neoliberalism*, Oxford: Oxford University Press.

Hayles, Katherine (1999) *How We Became Posthuman: Virtual Bodies in Cybernetics, Literature and Informatics*, London and Chicago: University of Chicago Press.

Hendershot, Cyndy (2001) *I Was a Cold War Monster: Horror films, Eroticism, and the Cold War Imagination*, Bowling Green, OH: Bowling Green State University Popular Press.

Hobbes, Thomas (2010) *Leviathan* [1651], Project Gutenberg, Chapter xxiv, paragraph entitled 'Mony the Bloud of a Common-wealth', <http://www.guten berg.org/ebooks/ 3207>.

Hobsbawm, Eric (2003) 'Introduction: Inventing Traditions', in Eric Hobsbawm and Terence Ranger (eds.), *The Invention of Tradition* [1983], Cambridge: Cambridge University Press, pp.1–14.

Holland, Eugene (1988) 'Schizoanalysis: The Postmodern Contextualization of Psychoanalysis', in Cary Nelson and Lawrence Grossberg (eds.), *Marxism and the Interpretation of Culture*, Urbana: University of Illinois Press, pp.405–16.

Honneth, Axel (1995) 'Pluralization and Recognition: On the Self-Misunderstanding of Postmodern Social Theories', in Charles W. Wright (ed.), *The Fragmented World of the Social: Essays in Social and Political Philosophy*, Albany, NY: State University of New York Press, pp.220–30.

House MacPhee, <http://www.freewebs.com/housemacphee/o.html>.

House Quinotaur, <http://www.house-quinotaur.org>.

Hunter, John (1828) *A Treatise on the Blood, Inflammation, and Gun-Shot Wounds*, London: Sherwood, Gilbert, and Piper.

Irigaray, Luce (1981) 'And the One Doesn't Stir without the Other', *Signs*, 7.1, pp.60–7.

Jefferson, Thomas (1787) *Notes on the State of Virginia*, 1785, London: John Stockdale.

Johnson, Viola M. (1996) *Dhampir: Child of the Blood*, Fairfield, CT: Mystic Rose Books.

Jones, Ernest (1951) *On the Nightmare*, New York: Liveright.

Jones, John (1825) 'Pathology of Fever, & c. Founded on the Blood's Vitality', *The London Medical and Physical Journal*, January 1825–June 1825, LIII, pp.108–15, cont. pp.289–93.

Jordan, John J. (1999) 'Vampire Cyborgs and Scientific Imperialism: A Reading of the Science-Mysticism Polemic in Blade', *Journal of Popular Film and Television*, 27.2, pp.4–15.

J.S.C. (1829) 'Vitality of the Blood', *Lancet*, 2, pp.139–40.

Kay, Sarah (2003) *Žižek: A Critical Introduction*, Oxford and Malden, MA: Polity Press.

Keller, Catherine (2002) 'Process and Chaosmos: The Whiteheadian Fold in the Discourse of Difference', in Catherine Keller and Anne Daniell (eds.), *Process and Difference: Between Cosmological and Poststructuralist Postmodernisms*, Albany: State University of New York Press, pp.55–72.

Kember, Sarah, Fraser, Mariam and Lury, Celia (2006) *Inventive Life: Approaches to the New Vitalism*, London, California and New Delhi: Sage Publications.

Kenealy, Arabella (1920) *Feminism and Sex Extinction*, London: T. Fisher Unwin.

Kennan, George (1978) 'Moscow Embassy Telegram #511, The Long Telegram', 1946, in Thomas Etzold and John Lewis Gaddis (eds.), *Containment: Documents on American Policy and Strategy 1945–1950*, New York: Columbia University Press, pp.50–63.

Klein, Harvey G. and Anstee, David J. (2005) *Mollison's Blood Transfusion in Clinical Medicine*, 11th ed, Malden, MA and Oxford: Blackwell.

Klein, Melanie (1932) *The Psychoanalysis of Children*, trans. Alix Strachey, London: Hogarth.

Koblentz, Gregory D. (2009) *Living Weapons: Biological Warfare and International Security*, Ithaca, NY: Cornell University Press.

Koch, Robert (1987) 'The Etiology of Anthrax, Founded on the Course of Development of the Bacillus Anthracis', 1876, in K. Codell Carter (ed.), *Essays of Robert Koch*, New York: Greenwood Press.

Kohn, Jesse (2001) 'Believing in the Disease: Virologies and Memetics as Models of Power Relations in Contemporary Science Fiction', *Culture Machine*, 3, <http://www.culturemachine.net/index.php/cm/article/viewArticle/289/274>.

Kord, Susannne (2009) *Murderesses in German Writing, 1720–1860: Heroines of Horror*, Cambridge: Cambridge University Press.

Kristeva, Julia (1982) *Powers of Horror: An Essay on Abjection*, New York: Columbia University Press.

Lacan, Jacques (1978) *The Four Fundamental Concepts of Psychoanalysis*, Jacques-Alain Miller (ed.), trans. Alan Sheridan, New York: Norton.

Lacan, Jacques (2001) 'The Direction of the Treatment and the Principles of its Treatment', *Ecrits: A Selection*, London: Routledge, pp.173–214.

Lady, C.G. 'Re: A Sanguinarian Treatise: An Argument for Partition From the Vampire Community by CJ', *Smokes and Mirrors Forum*, Yuku.com.

Lady, C.G. (2005) *Practical Vampyrism for Modern Vampyres*, Lulu.com.

Lady Nightdancer 'Membership Directory', *Voices of the Vampire Community*, <http://www.veritasvosliberabit.com/memberdirectory.html>.

Lady Onyx Ravyn, 'Membership Directory', *Voices of the Vampire Community*, <http://www.veritasvosliberabit.com/memberdirectory.html>.

Land, Nick (1998) 'Cybergothic', in Joan Broadhurst Dixon and Eric J. Cassidy (eds.), *Virtual Futures*, New York: Routledge, pp.79–87.

Langton, Christopher (1989) 'Artificial Life', in Christopher Langton (ed.), *Artificial Life*, Redwood City, CA: Addison-Wesley, pp.1–47.

Lasch, Christopher (1991) *The Culture of Narcissism: American Life in the Age of Diminishing Expectations*, 1979, New York and London: W.W. Norton & Company.

Latham, Rob (2002) *Consuming Youth: Vampires, Cyborgs, and the Culture of Consumption*, Chicago and London: The University of Chicago Press.

Law, Jules (2010) *The Social Life of Fluids: Blood, Milk, and Water in the Victorian Novel*, Ithaca, NY: Cornell University Press.

Laycock, Joseph (2009) *Vampires Today: The Truth about Modern Vampirism*, Santa Barbara, CA: Praeger.

Laycock, Joseph (2010) 'Real Vampires as an Identity Group: Analyzing Causes and Effects of an Introspective Survey by the Vampire Community', *Nova Religio: The Journal of Alternative and Emergent Religions*, 14.1, pp.4–23.

Lazzarato, Maurizio (2009) 'Neoliberalism in Action: Inequality, Insecurity, and the Reconstitution of the Social', *Theory, Culture and Society*, 26.6, pp.109–33.

Lazzarato, Maurizio (2012) *The Making of the Indebted Man: An Essay on the Neoliberal Condition*, Los Angeles, CA: Semiotext(e).

Lederer, Susan E. (2008) *Flesh and Blood: Organ Transplantation and Blood Transfusion in Twentieth-Century America*, Oxford: Oxford University Press.

Legrand, Dorothée (2011) 'Ex-Nihilo: Forming a Body Out of Nothing', in Robin Mackay and Reza Negarestani (eds.), *Collapse Vol. VII: Culinary Materialism*, pp.499–558.

Lemattre, Gustave (1873) 'On the Transfusion of Blood', *Popular Science*, 2.41, pp.679–95, April.

Leviticus 17:11, 'Atonement by the Life in the Blood', *The Holy Bible: New International Version*, <http://www.biblegateway.com/passage/?search=Leviticus%2017:11& version=NIV>.

Lewes, George Henry ([1859], 1860) *The Physiology of Common Life, Vol. 1* New York: D. Appleton and Company.

Lewis, Paul (1979) 'The Intellectual Functions of Gothic Fiction: Poe's "Ligeia" and Tieck's "Wake Not the Dead"', *Comparative Literature Studies*, 16.3, pp.207–21.

Lewontin, Richard (2001) *It Ain't Necessarily So: The Dream of the Human Genome and Other Illusions*, New York: New York Review Books.

Malchow, Howard L. (1996) *Gothic Images of Race in Nineteenth-Century Britain*, Stanford, CA: Stanford University Press.

Margulis, Lynn and Sagan, Dorion (2000) *What is Life*, Berkeley and Los Angeles, CA: University of California Press.

Martlew, Vanessa (1997) 'Transfusion Medicine towards the Millennium', in A. Oakley and J. Ashton (eds.), *Richard Titmuss, The Gift Relationship: From Human Blood to Social Policy*, London: LSE, pp.41–54.

Marx, Karl (1976) *Capital*, vol. 1 [1867], trans. Ben Fowkes, Harmondsworth: Penguin.

Mauss, Marcel (1969) *The Gift: Forms and Functions of Exchange in Archaic Societies*, [1925], trans. Ian Cunnison, Oxford and New York: Routledge.

McCarthy, Dennis J. (1973) 'Further Notes on the Symbolism of Blood and Sacrifice', *Journal of Biblical Literature*, 92.2, pp.205–10.

McNally, Raymond (1983) *Dracula was a Woman: In Search of the Blood Countess of Transylvania*, New York: McGraw-Hill.

Meyer, Melissa (2005) *Thicker than Water: The Origins of Blood as Symbol and Ritual*, London: Routledge.

Milburn, Colin (2008) *Nanovision: Engineering the Future*, Durham and London: Duke University Press.

Moretti, Franco (1982) 'The Dialectic of Fear', *New Left Review*, 136, pp.67–85.

Moretti, Franco (1999) 'Dracula and Capitalism', in Glennis Byron (ed.), *Dracula*, New York: St. Martin's Press, pp.43–54.

Murray, John (1830) *A Treatise on Pulmonary Consumption: Its Prevention and Remedy*, London: Whittaker, Treacher, and Arnot.

Murray, John (1838) *Considerations on the Vital Principle*, London: Relfe and Fletcher Cornhill.

Nadesan, Majia Holmer (2008) *Governmentality, Biopower, and Everyday Life*, Oxford and New York: Routledge.

Nancy, Jean-Luc (1991) *The Inoperative Community*, Minneapolis, MN: University of Minnesota Press.

Nixon, Nicola (1997) 'When Hollywood Sucks, or, Hungry Girls, Lost Boys, and Vampirism in the Age of Reagan', in Joan Gordon and Veronica

Hollinger (eds.), *Blood Read: The Vampire as Metaphor in Contemporary Culture*, Philadelphia, PA: University of Pennsylvania Press, pp.115–28.

Novas, Carlos and Rose, Nikolas (2000) 'Genetic Risk and the Birth of the Somatic Individual', *Economy and* Society, 29.4, pp.485–513.

Ordo Sekhemu, <http://www.ordo-sekhemu.org/Lucem Sekh/faq.shtml>.

Ott, Katherine (1996) *Fevered Lives: Tuberculosis in American Culture Since 1870*, Harvard: Harvard University Press.

Parisi, Luciana and Terranova, Tiziana (2000) 'Heat-Death: Emergence and Control in Genetic Engineering and Artificial Life', *CTheory: Theory, Technology and Culture*, 23, pp. 1–2, <http://www.ctheory.net/ articles.aspx?id=127>.

Partridge, Christopher Hugh (2005) *The Re-Enchantment of the West*, vol. 2, New York and London: T&T Clark.

Pearson, Keith Ansell (1997) *Viroid Life: Perspectives on Nietzsche and the Transhuman Condition*, London and New York: Routledge.

Pelis, Kim (1997) 'Blood Clots: The Nineteenth-Century Debate over the Substance and Means of Transfusion in Britain', *Annals of Science Fiction*, 54, pp.331–60.

Pelis, Kim (2002) 'Transfusion with Teeth', in James M. Bradburne (ed.), *Blood: Art, Power, Politics, and Pathology*, Munich: Prestel, pp.175–91.

Person, Leland S. (2006) 'Poe's Philosophy of Amalgamation: Reading Racism in the Tales', in Harold Bloom (ed.), *Edgar Allan Poe*, New York: Chelsea House, pp.129–48.

Pharr, Mary Ann (1999) 'Vampiric Appetite in *I Am Legend, Salem's Lot*, and *The Hunger*', in Leonard G. Heldreth and Mary Pharr (eds.), *The Blood is the Life: Vampires in Literature*, Bowling Green, OH: Bowling Green State University Popular Press, pp.93–103.

Pocock, John Greville Agard (1975) *The Machiavellian Moment: Florentine Political Thought and the Atlantic Republican Tradition*, Princeton, NJ: Princeton University Press.

Pope, Rebecca E. (1999) 'Writing and Biting in *Dracula*', in Glennis Byron (ed.), *Dracula*, New York: St. Martin's Press, pp.68–92.

Punter, David (1999) 'Dracula and Taboo', in Glennis Byron (ed.), *Dracula*, New York: St. Martin's Press, pp.22–9.

Rappoport, Leon (2005) *Punchlines: The Case for Racial, Ethnic, and Gender Humor*, Westport, CT: Greenwood Publishing Group.

Read, Jason (2009) 'A Genealogy of Homo-Economicus: Neoliberalism and the Production of Subjectivity', *Foucault Studies*, 6, pp.25–36.

Reed, Paul (1993) 'Early AIDS Fiction', in Judith Laurence Pastore (ed.), *Confronting AIDS Through Literature: The Responsibilities of Representation*, Chicago, IL: University of Illinois, pp.91–4.

Riccardo, Martin V. (1996) *Liquid Dreams of Vampires*, St. Paul, MN: Llewellyn.

Rice, Anne 'Essay on Earlier Works', *AnneRice.com*, n. pag., <http://www.annerice.com/Bookshelf-EarlierWorks.html>.

Ringel, Faye (1995) *New England's Gothic Literature: History and Folklore of the Supernatural from the Seventeenth through the Twentieth Centuries*, New York: Edwin Mellen Press.

Roberts, Dorothy (2011) *Fatal Invention: How Science, Politics, and Big Business Re-create Race in the Twenty-First Century*, New York and London: The New Press.

Roberts, Morley (1921) *Warfare in the Human Body: Essays on the Method, Malignity, Repair, and Allied Subjects*, New York: E.P. Dutton Company.

Roberts, Morley (1938) *Bio-Politics: An Essay in the Physiology, Pathology and Politics of the Social and Somatic Organism*, London: Dent.

Roberts, Samuel Kelton Jr. (2009) *Infectious Fear: Politics, Disease, and the Health Effects of Segregation*, North Carolina: The University of North Carolina Press.

Rose, Nikolas (2007) *Politics of Life Itself: Biomedicine, Power, and Subjectivity in the Twenty-First Century*, Princeton and Oxford: Princeton University Press.

Rosenau, Pauline (1992) *Post-Modernism and the Social Sciences: Insights, Inroads, and Intrusions*, Princeton, NJ: Princeton University Press.

Roth, Phyllis A. (1999) 'Suddenly Sexual Women in Bram Stoker's *Dracula*', in Glennis Byron (ed.), *Dracula*, New York: St. Martin's Press, pp.30–42.

Runels, Charles <vampirefacelift.com>.

Russo, Arlene (2005) *Vampire Nation*, London: John Blake.

Sanguinarius (2007) 'Vampire Lifestyle and Culture', in Michelle Belanger (ed.), *Vampires in Their Own Words: An Anthology of Vampire Voices*, Woodbury, MN: Llewellyn Publications, pp.125–7.

Sceats, Sarah (2000) *Food Consumption and the Body in Contemporary Women's Fiction*, Cambridge: University of Cambridge.

Schrecker, Ellen (2002) *The Age of McCarthyism: A Brief History with Documents*, New York: St. Martin's Press.

Seabrook, William (1945) *Witchcraft: Its Power in the World Today*, 1940, San Diego, CA: Harcourt, Brace and Company.

Sherrard-Johnson, Cherene (2007) *Portraits of the New Negro Woman: Visual and Literary Culture in the Harlem Renaissance*, New Jersey: Rutgers University Press.

Silver, Anna Krugovoy (2002) *Victorian Literature and the Anorexic Body*, Cambridge and New York: Cambridge University Press.

Skubal, Susanne (2002) *Word of Mouth: Food and Fiction after Freud*, New York and London: Routledge.

Smedley, Audrey and Smedley, Brian (2005) 'Race as Biology is Fiction, Racism as a Social Problem is Real: Anthropological and Historical Perspectives on the Social Construction of Race', *American Psychologist*, 60.1, pp.16–26.

Smith, Adam (1999) *The Wealth of Nations: Books I–III*, 1775, Andrew Skinner (ed.), London: Penguin.

Sonser, Anna (2001) *A Passion for Consumption: The Gothic Novel in America*, Bowling Green: Bowling Green State University Popular Press.

Sontag, Sontag (1991) *Illness as Metaphor and AIDS and its Metaphors*, 1978, London: Penguin Books.

Starr, Douglas (1998) *Blood: An Epic History of Medicine and Commerce*, London: Little, Brown, and Company.

Stephanou, Aspasia (2013) 'Lovely Apparitions and Spiritualized Corpses: Consumption, Medical Discourse and Edgar Allan Poe's Female Vampire', *The Edgar Allan Poe Review*, 14.1, pp.36–54.

Stetson, George R. (1896) 'The Animistic Vampire', *American Anthropologist*, 9, pp.1–13.

Stevenson, John Allen (1988) 'A Vampire in the Mirror: The Sexuality of *Dracula*', *PMLA*, 103.2, pp.139–49.

Suscitatio Enterprises, <http://www.suscitatio.com>.

Suscitatio Enterprises 'Advanced Vampirism and Energy Work Research Survey' (AVEWRS), <http://www.suscitatio.com/>.

Suscitatio Enterprises 'Vampire and Energy Work Research Survey', <http://www.suscitatio.com/>.

Szécsi, Noémi (2012) *The Finno-Ugrian Vampire*, trans. Peter Sherwood, London: Stork Press.

Taibbi, Matt (2009) 'The Great American Bubble Machine', *Rolling Stone*, 1082–3, 9–23 July.

Takaki, Ronald T. (1998) *Strangers from a Different Shore: A History of Asian Americans*, Boston and New York: Little, Brown and Company.

Tarde, Gabriel (1903) *The Laws of Imitation*, New York: Henry Holt and Company.

Tatar, Maria (1995) *Lustmord: Sexual Murder in Weimar Germany*, Princeton, NJ: Princeton University Press.

Temple of the Vampire, <http://www.vampiretemple.com/index.html>.

Temple of the Vampire (1989) *The Vampire Bible*, Lacey, WA: Temple of the Vampire.

Temple of the Vampire (1989) *The Vampire Priesthood Bible* 1, <http://www.suscitatio.com/MediaArchive/TempleOfTheVampireTheVampirePriesthood Bible-1989.pdf>.

Thacker, Eugene (2003) 'Data Made Flesh: Biotechnology and the Discourse of the Posthuman', *Cultural Critique*, 53, pp.72–97.

Thacker, Eugene (2004) *Biomedia*, Minneapolis, MN: University of Minnesota Press.

Thacker, Eugene (2005) 'Biophilosophy for the Twenty-First Century', *CTheory .net*, <http://www.ctheory.net/articles.aspx?id=472>.

Thacker, Eugene (2005) *The Global Genome: Biotechnology, Politics, and Culture*, Cambridge, MA, London: MIT Press.

Thacker, Eugene (2009) 'The Shadows of Atheology: Epidemics, Power and Life after Foucault', *Theory Culture Society*, 26.6, pp.134–52.

Thacker, Eugene (2011) 'Darklife: Negation, Nothingness, and the Will-to-Life in Schopenhauer', *Parrhesia*, 12, pp.12–27.

Titmuss, Richard M. (1970) *The Gift Relationship: From Human Blood to Social Policy*, London: George Allen & Unwin Ltd.

Tru Blood, HBO Shop, <http://store.hbouk.com/detail.php?p=256240&v=hbo -uk_best -sellers#tabs>.

Tuveson, Ernest Lee (1968) *Redeemer Nation: The Idea of America's Millennial Role*, Chicago and London: The University of Chicago Press.

Urban, Sylvanus (1732) 'Political Vampyres', in Sylvanus Urban (ed.), *The Gentleman's Magazine, or, Monthly Intelligencer*, London: F. Jefferies, pp.750–2, May.

Vandenberg, Philipp (2007) *Mysteries of the Oracles: The Last Secrets of Antiquity*, London and New York: Tauris Parke.

Vardaxis, Nicholas J. (1995) *Immunology for the Health Sciences*, South Melbourne: Macmillan.

Varela, Francisco and Anspach, Mark (1991) 'Immu-Knowledge: The Process of Somatic Individuation', in William Irwin Thompson (ed.), *Gaia 2, Emergence, The New Science of Becoming*, Hudson, NY: Lindisfarne Press, pp. 70–83.

Varlik, Nükhet (2008) 'Contagion Theory of Disease, Premodern', in Joseph Patrick Byrne (ed.), *Encyclopedia of Pestilence, Pandemics, and Plagues*, Westport, CT: Greenwood Press, pp.133–6.

Virilio, Paul (2002) *Crepuscular Dawn*, introd. Sylvère Lotringer, Los Angeles, CA and New York: Semiotext(e).

Wailoo, Keith (2001) *Dying in the City of the Blues: Sickle Cell Anemia and the Politics of Race and Health*, Chapel Hill, NC: The University of North Carolina Press.

Waldby, Catherine and Mitchell, Robert (2006) *Tissue Economies: Blood, Organs, and Cell Lines in Late Capitalism*, Durham and London: Duke University Press.

Wall, Otto Augustus (1919) *Sex and Sex Worship (Phallic Worship): A Scientific Treatise on Sex, Its Nature and Function*, St. Louis: C.V. Mosby Co.

Walton, Priscilla L. (2004) *Our Cannibals, Ourselves*, Illinois: University of Illinois.

Warren, Samuel (1830) 'Passages from the Diary of a Late Physician, Ch. IV, "Consumption"', *Blackwood's Edinburgh Magazine*, 28, pp.770–86.

Watney, Simon (1989) 'Missionary Positions: AIDS, "Africa," and Race', *Differences*, 1.1, pp.83–101.

Williams, Evan Calder (2011) *Combined and Uneven Apocalypse*, Winchester and Washington: Zero Books.

Winslow, Robert M. (2006) 'Historical Background', in Robert M. Winslow (ed.), *Blood Substitutes*, London and Burlington, MA: Academic Press, pp.5–16.

Wood, Robin (1983) *Mosaic*, XVI/1–2, pp.175–87.

World Transhumanist Association, Humanity+, <http://humanityplus.org/learn/transhumanist-faq/#answer_19>.

Worringer, Wilhelm (1920) *Form Problems of the Gothic*, New York: G.E. Stechert & Co.

Žižek, Slavoj (1989) *The Sublime Object of Ideology*, London and New York: Verso.

Žižek, Slavoj (1999) *The Ticklish Subject: The Absent Centre of Political Ontology*, London and New York: Verso.

Žižek, Slavoj (2000) *The Fragile Absolute: Or, Why is the Christian Legacy Worth Fighting For?*, London and New York: Verso.

Žižek, Slavoj (2001) 'Welcome to the Desert of the Real (Reflections on WTC)', in *Lacan.com*, <http://www.lacan.com/reflections.htm>, October 7.

Žižek, Slavoj (2002) *Welcome to the Desert of the Real: Five Essays on September 11 and Related Dates*, London and New York: Verso.

Index

Note: The letter 'n' following locators refers to notes.

Printed and bound in the United States of America